WELFARE AND VALUES

Wel  ues

Challenging the Culture of Unconcern

Edited by

Peter Askonas
Visiting Lecturer
Heythrop College
University of London

and

Stephen F. Frowen
Honorary Research Fellow
University College, London
and
Senior Research Associate
Von Hügel Institute
St Edmund's College, Cambridge

under the auspices of
Theology and Society
Forum for Interdisciplinary Reflection
in association with
St George's House, Windsor Castle

First published in Great Britain 1997 by
MACMILLAN PRESS LTD
Houndmills, Basingstoke, Hampshire RG21 6XS and London
Companies and representatives throughout the world

A catalogue record for this book is available from the British Library.

ISBN 0–333–67405–7 hardcover
ISBN 0–333–69910–6 paperback

First published in the United States of America 1997 by
ST. MARTIN'S PRESS, INC.,
Scholarly and Reference Division,
175 Fifth Avenue, New York, N.Y. 10010

ISBN 0–312–17256–7

Library of Congress Cataloging-in-Publication Data
Welfare and values : challenging the culture of unconcern / edited
by Peter Askonas and Stephen F. Frowen.
p. cm.
Includes bibliographical references and index.
ISBN 0–312–17256–7 (cloth)
1. Welfare economics. 2. Social justice. 3. Social policy.
I. Askonas, Peter, 1919– II. Frowen, Stephen F.
HB846.W445 1997
361.6'1—dc21   96–46620
                                                             CIP

Selection and editorial matter © Peter Askonas and Stephen F. Frowen 1997
Chapter 12b © Stephen F. Frowen 1997
Chapter 18 © Peter Askonas 1997
Other chapters © Macmillan Press Ltd 1997

All rights reserved. No reproduction, copy or transmission of this publication may be made without written permission.

No paragraph of this publication may be reproduced, copied or transmitted save with written permission or in accordance with the provisions of the Copyright, Designs and Patents Act 1988, or under the terms of any licence permitting limited copying issued by the Copyright Licensing Agency, 90 Tottenham Court Road, London W1P 9HE.

Any person who does any unauthorised act in relation to this publication may be liable to criminal prosecution and civil claims for damages.

The authors have asserted their rights to be identified as the authors of this work in accordance with the Copyright, Designs and Patents Act 1988.

This book is printed on paper suitable for recycling and made from fully managed and sustained forest sources.

10 9 8 7 6 5 4 3 2 1
06 05 04 03 02 01 00 99 98 97

Printed and bound in Great Britain by
Antony Rowe Ltd, Chippenham, Wiltshire

Contents

Acknowledgements	vii
List of Contributors	viii
Setting out Markers by Peter Askonas and Stephen F. Frowen	x

I ECONOMIC REALITIES

1. Crisis in Welfare?
   Andrew Dilnot — 3

2. A Mixed Economy of Care: The Incisive Role of the Voluntary Sector
   Jeremy Kendall and Martin Knapp — 18

3. Transfer through Taxation: Social Policy in Germany – Past, Present and Outlook for the Future
   Dieter Biehl — 30

4. Economic Restraints
   Ian Steedman — 42

II SELF AND COMMUNITY – 'DOING THEOLOGY'

5. A Platform – Moral and Spiritual Values
   Rupert Hoare — 53

6. Jewish Tradition and Ethos of Generosity
   Meir Tamari — 69

7. The Idea of the Public Good: Religious Conviction and the Interdependence of the Individual and Society
   James O'Connell — 77

8. Theology and Sharing the Economic Cake
   Peter Vardy — 90

9. Looking Behind the Scenes: Self-interest, Civic Generosity, Altruism
   Peter Askonas and Cho Ngye Kwan — 103

III GENEROSITY

10 'Enthusiasm'
   Maggie Baxter, Jane Tewson, Michael Walsh — 119

11 After Darkness:
   Flourishing of Generosity in an Evolving Environment
   Martin Šály — 125

IV WHAT CAN BE DONE – BY ECONOMISTS AND POLITICIANS

12a Economic Expansion
   Gavin Davies — 135

12b Need for Economic Expansion
   Stephen F. Frowen — 138

13 Choking on Growth: A Theologian Reflects
   Frank Turner — 144

14 On De-escalating Wants
   Ian Steedman — 157

15 The Welfare Debate:
   Managing Self-interest, Self-improvement, Altruism
   Frank Field — 165

16 Paying for Social Security – an Ever-rising Spiral?
   William Goodhart — 176

17 Contribution by Two Faith Groups towards Education Spending
   Jeremy Kendall — 185

V CULTIVATING CIVIC GENEROSITY

18 Steps towards Maturing – from Compulsion to Consent
   Peter Askonas — 197

19 Civic Virtue, Poverty and Social Justice
   Raymond Plant — 211

A Hopeful Afterthought — 220

Index — 221

Acknowledgements

This book would not have been undertaken were it not for St George's House, Windsor Castle, who were hosts to a preliminary conference in 1991 and sponsored a consultation in December 1994 on the subject. To the Reverend Canon Alan Coldwells we are obliged for generous encouragement and much practical advice and to his staff for making us extremely comfortable. Not least, also to Lucy Gibbons who did a brilliant job of decoding the sometimes near unintelligible tape-recording of the proceedings.

We must express appreciation to Heythrop College, where some of the gestation of the project took place in an atmosphere entirely conducive to that undertaking, and where numerous colleagues made themselves available for comment and supplementary input.

To Michael Nevin, trusted councillor of many years, we owe an immense amount of important advice and unceasing stimulation. We are indebted also to Professor Frank Cowell of the London School of Economics for giving us the benefit of his expertise on tax governance and for access to valuable material. Grateful thanks to Victoria Harrison and Edwina Vardey who helped with judicious editing, and with translating some dense texts into a readable idiom. Thanks also to Clare Ewins who worked at all hours and missed the Euro 96 match between England and Spain, to collate and tidy up the text.

This book advocates community. A practical illustration is provided by our community of contributors. They have given most generously of thought and time, in spite of other pressures and overloaded schedules. The editors are particularly grateful for their patience in the face of unexpected requests and of constant reminders that in view of our subject's topicality 'our time is at hand'.

PETER ASKONAS
STEPHEN F. FROWEN

List of Contributors

Peter Askonas, Visiting Lecturer, Heythrop College; Hon. Vice President, Christian Association of Business Executives

Maggie Baxter, Grants Director, Charity Projects – Comic Relief

Professor Dieter Biehl, Department of Economics, University of Frankfurt

Revd Cho, Ngye Kwan, Kings College, London

Gavin Davies, Chief International Economist, Goldman Sachs

Andrew Dilnot, Director, Institute of Fiscal Studies

Frank Field, MP

Professor Stephen F. Frowen, Honorary Research Fellow, Department of Economics, University College, London; Senior Research Associate, Von Hügel Institute, St Edmund's College, Cambridge

Sir William Goodhart, QC

The Rt. Revd Dr Bishop Rupert Hoare, Bishop of Dudley

Jeremy Kendall, Research Fellow, PSSRU (Personal Social Services Research Unit)

Professor Martin Knapp, London School of Economics; Director, PSSRU (Personal Social Services Research Unit)

Professor James O'Connell, Department of Peace Studies, University of Bradford

Lord Plant of Highfield, Master of St Catherine's College, Oxford; Labour Member, House of Lords

Contributors

Martin Šály, Managing Director, TH'*final* Ltd, Czech Republic

Professor Ian Steedman, Manchester Metropolitan University

Dr Meir Tamari, Director, Jewish Business Ethics Institute, Jerusalem

Jane Tewson, Chief Executive, Comic Relief

Dr Frank Turner, SJ, Lecturer, Political Theology, Heythrop College, University of London

Dr Peter Vardy, Lecturer, Philosophy of Religion, Heythrop College

Michael Walsh, Librarian, Heythrop College

Setting out Markers
Peter Askonas and Stephen F. Frowen

> ... the importance in life of 'reality checks'. They save us from an unreal spirituality which can only cope with the messiness of human existence by pretending it does not exist.
>
> G. M. Hughes[1]

We citizens in today's sophisticated society expect all manner of services for ourselves and perhaps even for others. Yet almost all of us are reluctant, even unwilling, to pay enough to meet the bill.

How to fill the gap between the escalating costs of social needs and revenues from statutory and voluntary sources has become a major preoccupation of politicians, academics and the public at large. This is the case not only in respect of 'welfare' payments, health care, education, but of the entire range of communal services and institutions, including culture, administration of justice, national and civic security. The requirements and the bill are truly formidable, and so is therefore the gap. Almost all advanced economies, irrespective of their government's political shade, experience this phenomenon. Pick up a newspaper in London, Frankfurt, Stockholm or Marseilles, you will encounter similar preoccupations almost daily.

CONFRONTING THE GAP

In response, there exists now a plethora of studies and publications by research units, think tanks, political groupings and individuals, offering analysis and not a few original proposals. Some entertain the possibility of a gradual narrowing of the gap by structural and economic reordering. Others put forward prescriptions for cutting back services, in terms of quantity and quality as the inevitable route; though many of them refuse to consider, or simply do not mind how economizing on social costs enfeebles the ethical foundations necessary for social cohesion. Most dominant are proposals to *privatize* payments for social costs. For the foreseeable future two facts stand out. The first: the lion's share of incomings still will have to be derived from statutory revenues; and at present these incomings are inadequate to pay for equitable services. Yet: to revert to past policies of increased taxation is considered to be politically impracticable and economically counter-productive. Nowadays politicians on both sides of the spectrum worldwide share the aversion to electorally risky tax measures. Our book will devote considerable space to analysing this particular dilemma. Similarly, another way to fund social expenditure by swelling public indebtedness is seen widely as undesirable. It is yet another addition to social costs for which, in a roundabout way, we all have to pay.

Have we then reached an impasse? This may turn out to be the case, if our only guidelines are merely prescriptions provided by this or that economic theory. Neither will changes in the methods of levying fiscal revenues go to the heart of the problem. There is indeed a proper place for economic and political fiscal adjustments, and also a need for their constant refinement. But that is not enough. The gap and its narrowing or widening is an expression of human aspirations and desires with all that this implies in terms of creative or destructive drives, emotions, and human irrationality. We must therefore address the problem at the level of the human condition in its totality. This means coming to grips with its moral and spiritual constituents.

A consultation to explore this challenge took place in 1994 at St George's House, Windsor Castle. It brought together personalities in the field of economics, politics and welfare organizations, as well as prominent representatives of several faith groups. The present publication was initiated by their deliberations. At its core is the question: are there ways of modifying the tension between egocentric self-interest in economic behaviour and civic generosity, in favour of the latter? Using a different formulation: how can we balance the imperatives of economic pressures with the promptings within us to reach out towards those values which make human existence less confrontational, more humane and increasingly meaningful? And to get down to practicalities: what can be done to counteract the deep-seated aversion to parting with a slice of our incomings – let alone with capital – when it is a matter of paying this into the public purse for the benefit of others or for our own future needs?

Our team of contributors have been conscious of different temptations. One is to respond by devising an intellectual construct, good debating matter for the curious enquirer. This can be enjoyable, but is sterile. Another is to proffer strongly held political convictions without being open to the possibility that there could be truth in alternative propositions. Yet another one is to say simply 'human nature is flawed and cannot be changed; let us therefore muddle along with an insolvable puzzle – let the economic future take care of itself as it unfolds'. And still a further option, the most dangerous one, is to revert to past ideologies. By now we have ample evidence of the social traumas which previously have resulted from all these positions. None of them is in tune with the unique needs of post-modernity. Today's experience confirms that the patterning of social interaction is in a state of perennial flux. It is a patterning which mirrors the complex reality of our humanity and interaction between generosity and grasping, commitment and betrayal, creativity and destructiveness. Our present social and political structures make too little allowance for the potential which inhabits that reality. Instead there persists the inclination to reduce what really is a blend of different motives and conditioning influences, into simple and bland categories. Moreover, social analysis inclines to concentrate on a single component, the dark, apparently irredeemably selfish side of the human make-up.

Here is the taking-off point for dealing with the 'gap'. Public policy, and the institutions with an impact on civic behaviour will have to take human complexity and human potential much more seriously. That means restraining the cynicism now in fashion and ceasing to underrate the human capacity for mutual concern. It also means resisting a facile optimism. Not least, it means accepting discipline: resist proclaiming grand and populist proposals and promising simplistic solutions. Thus, to offer responsible proposals means that all cannot be perfectly well the day after these are enacted. We have had enough over-reliance on any one economic or political formula to know better. A more realistic route is to be found by cultivating in different spheres of civic life, and over an extended time-span, a multiplicity of initiatives with the specific objective to enhance a sense of personal responsibility and civic generosity.

Sober realism tells us that in the present climate a high rating is not given to moral dispositions of this kind. Playing on human inclinations toward down-grading responsibility, especially for the sake of party political advantage is the rule of the game. Moreover, that same sober realism reminds us of the economic constraints which tend to inhibit generosity, and which limit the scope for radical departures. It is clear that there is no recipe for disposing of the gap definitively. But it is also clear in the light of our present impasse that pragmatic proposals on their own are inadequate, unless they are set in the framework of moral and spiritual values. Our book aims to look for the right balance between these and economic values.

THE SPECIFICITY OF THIS BOOK

Social economics, politics, theology, down-to-earth spontaneity must interact. A multi-disciplinary approach is essential. This book is not a compendium of economic analysis for the cognoscenti, though the pros and cons of several economic approaches are debated. It is not a book about behaviourism or about theories provided by the social sciences, though human behaviour is one of its main concerns. It is not a collection of papers on social morality and related philosophical issues, though ideas like virtue and the common good are recurring implicitly. It is not a 'religious book', though faith and its dynamics are a significant component of what we have to say (which means that the theologians amongst us are not *writing* theology but *doing* theology).[2] But we are attempting to generate interaction of a broad range of different insights to do justice to the many-sidedness of contemporary experience.

Such an enterprise has to contend with serious obstacles. First, the vastness of any one discipline and the huge volume of literature for each. We may be accused of being facile; of not taking sufficient account of what various disciplines have to tell, the latter being the very accusation which one might level at some specialists and their prescriptions.

For that reason, we felt it to be essential to get away from compartmentalization – morality/spirituality here, social sciences/economics there – which will set any issue, and not least complex phenomena like that of the 'gap', in a vacuum of abstraction and diminishes the possibility of making progress towards solutions. In fact there is ample evidence nowadays that pure economic models developed without reference to human destiny – destiny fraught with paradox and intangibles – are running out of steam. And similarly, many pronouncements originating from ethicist and from institutional religion regarding economic and civic patterning are unimpressive. 'Doing theology' is not the same as formulating rigorous abstract propositions, but the application of the practical context of here-and-now, of economics and politics to the search for meaningfulness – and vice versa.

We had to impose strictures on our contributors regarding length and scholarly detail which would normally be part of their professional practice; and it should be no suprise that this caused frustrations. We had to guess: what can be assumed to be general knowledge? What ought to be explained, even if only with broad pen strokes? What might put off some readers? (Any of them may be excused if they read selectively.) Then there is the problem of language: one word meaning different things in different disciplines. A veritable tower of Babel.[3] And correspondingly there are profound differences of mindsets. Only very few economists will think in a theological perspective – and vice versa. Specialists often do not appreciate the relevance of other thought-worlds.[4] The most serious obstacle goes by the name 'pluralism'. Pluralism of insights concerning the nature of existence. Pluralism of theories about how to develop human dispositions, and whether a fundamental development is at all possible; or about the approach to tension between economic necessity, political feasibility and hope for a less self-seeking world. Pluralism of political convictions; or economic theories. Pluralism of faiths, of belief and disbelief within particular groups. Pluralism of norms for what is just and unjust. The very proposition at the heart of the present exercise, that there exist transcendent values and that these can have an impact on economic activity, is subject to a plurality of perceptions throughout society, and even amongst our small group of contributors.[5]

We are aware of yet another challenge, one rather down to earth. At the present juncture of economic life all over the globe, an enquiry such as the present one ought to be driven by urgency. But by its very nature our approach will tend towards producing long-term answers. 'So,' it will be asked, 'what use are these when we are confronted by pressing necessities? Bills for the costs of social needs have to be paid today, not tomorrow.' Today and tomorrow do not exclude one another. Our proposals are indeed part of a long-term project, a project extending from a past, a *history*, into a future. But part of that future is actualized, even though only fragmentarily, in what can be achieved in the present.

A PATTERN FOR OUR STORY

So there are many obstacles to blending the thoughts of our contributors into a continuous 'story'. That may be all to the good. It prevents us from aiming at neatly coherent conclusions, satisfying for the scholar but inadequate to depict an untidy reality. But we do have a unifying theme: the impact of moral and spiritual values – potential and actual – on political and economic patterning.

The opening group of chapters in Part I is designed to provide an economic context for the story. The writers keep well clear of moralizing, but even so the need to add an ethical dimension to what they describe is implicit. We have included a chapter (Chapter 3) which describes a very different tradition and four decades of very effective social funding, namely that of Germany. Today this country finds itself faced by the gap like everyone else.

A narrative of what this ethical dimension might be, is intended to emerge from Part II. Each chapter asks the same question but in different ways: 'what social responsibility do persons in advanced societies have to bear, especially those who experience faith, however diverse and remote?' Then follows a complementary question: 'do we have the capacity to bear that responsibility more effectively?'.[6] It is significant that the writers of Chapters 7, 8 and 9 start from antinomous philosophical or political positions, yet share a crucial conviction. It focuses on the essential call for relationship, *'You and me, I and Thou'*. Here, for all these contributors, is the ground for the flourishing of civic responsibility and generosity, the unifying factor within diversity of opinions.

Next: from analysis to experience. We have inserted two vignettes, Chapters 10 and 11, as a reminder of what enthusiasm and human generosity can achieve. This is the good news, sadly not commercial news and therefore not given much showing. We should add: these stories are *not* placed here to make some political point, for example that social care is best left to the private sector, but to emphasize the dynamics of civic generosity and its potential to inspire.

We then proceed in Part IV to macro-economic and micro-proposals, some pragmatic, some visionary. Without vision, without risk-taking, even without recurring failure, there can be no movement forward. The latter is an electorally unpalatable fact. Wish that politicians had the courage – and the honesty – to face up to that challenge.

And the conclusions? It might be tempting to quip that there are no easy ones – but that would need to be understood correctly. The book does have a simple message: we all, and foremost those who enjoy abundance, must pay more; or else a majority has to make do with less. Of course simple messages addressed to inconsistent, unreasonable and delightfully complex creatures with their even more complex works usually fail to bite. A supplementary message is therefore required: exhortations (except by the evil of demagogy and with correspondingly evil outcomes) get nowhere, the plunge into a culture resting on greater confidence of one for the other, can get somewhere. The process will be, of course, gradual and often paradoxical.

To narrow the gap presents a tall order when we consider 'the messiness of existence'. *Enhancement of Civic Generosity* is a critical step in that process. Without it any other initiative will not get very far. We must proceed at two levels. At the pragmatic level:

- by a combination of communal pressures, incentives and appeal to beneficent and creative self-interest. This will tend to release more of the generosity latent in a large section of society;
- by reordering some fiscal measures;
- by communicating insistently and convincingly the economic facts of the gap, and cultivating a sense that each person's role matters. By every means, and by all who are aware of what is at stake, a climate of personal concern must be fostered to counterbalance the current 'culture of unconcern'.

At the level of hope:

- by bridging the other gap, that between a utilitarian rationality and awareness of ultimate values, and therefore of more complete possibilities for ourselves.

We conclude with an appeal to anyone, anyone; and especially to anyone who experiences the reality of faith, to rise to this challenge.

NOTES AND REFERENCES

1. G. M. Hughes, *God of Surprises*, Darton, Longman & Todd, 1982.
2. N. Lash, 'Who is a theologian?' in *Theology on the way to Emmaus*, SCM, 1986, ch.1, pp.6–7, Lash suggests that all of us are theologians when we do what we do with a sense of it being part of a transcendent purpose.
3. Gillian Rose, 'Architecture to Philosophy – The Postmodern Complicity' in *Theory, Culture and Society*, Sage, 1988. Rose provides an exposition of the tower as symbol of destructive power and ensuing punishment.
4. This dilemma is central to much of contemporary philosophy and its preoccupation with incommunicability of meaning.
5. The nigh impossibility of formulating in the post-modern world common moral norms on a common rational basis is expounded by Alastair MacIntyre in his seminal book, *After Virtue*, Duckworth, 1981, 1985.
6. N. Lash, in a paper presented at a consultation on Personal Responsibility, St George's House, March 1991.

Part I
Economic Realities

1 Crisis in Welfare?
Andrew Dilnot

1. INTRODUCTION

This chapter sets out some of the economic background to the debate about welfare. In Section 2 we describe current government spending, and trends in the post-war period, and look briefly at revenues. In Section 3 we examine the arguments for the existence of welfare provision. In Section 4 we consider the cost and other pressures on modern welfare states, and examine possible responses. Section 5 concludes.

2. WHAT DOES GOVERNMENT SPEND?[1]

Government activity in modern developed economies is vast. In the UK in 1995–6 total government spending will be a little over £300 billion, or around £15,000 per household, or some 42 per cent of GDP. Figure 1.1 shows a breakdown of this spending into its various parts.

Perhaps the most striking feature of Figure 1.1 is the very large share of social security spending in the overall total, £93.3 billion, almost £4500 for every household in the UK, and over 30 per cent of government spending. The next two largest elements in government spending are also part of what we have traditionally thought of as the welfare state, being health and personal social services at £49 billion and education at £35.9 billion, around £2300 and £1700 per household respectively, and 16 per cent and 12 per cent of total government spending. Added together, three elements of the welfare state, the three largest elements of government spending, absorb £178.2 billion, £8500 per household, almost 60 per cent of total government spending, and 25 per cent of national income. The welfare state is with little doubt the largest activity in the UK.

Before moving on to look at how the welfare state has grown, it is worth describing the UK tax system, to give some sense of where the money to fund UK welfare comes from. Figure 1.2 breaks down total government receipts for 1995–6.

The largest source of revenue is income tax of £68.9 billion, although this only accounts for 25 per cent of revenue. Social security

Figure 1.1   General government spending, 1995–6 (£ billions)

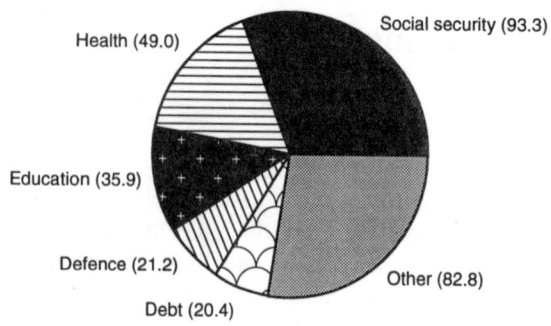

contributions, both employer and employee, raise £44.4 billion, rather more than half of which comes from employers' contributions. VAT raises around £44.8 billion, and corporation tax £24.7 billion. The total revenue from all these taxes in 1995–6 was £182 billion compared with the cost of the welfare state at £178.2 billion. The commonly held view that employees' national insurance contributions, raising around £20 billion, cover the health and social security systems, can be seen to be a huge misunderstanding. In reality, the welfare state absorbs all the revenue raised by our four largest taxes.

In the long sweep of history, such extensive government action is a very recent development. 'Modern' welfare states are largely the invention of the last hundred years or so. The first steps towards social insurance for old age were taken in Bismarck's Germany in the early 1880s, while Denmark had such a system from 1891, and New Zealand from 1898 (see Kohler and Zacher, 1982).[2] Action on pensions in the UK was slower, but began in 1908, with social insurance against sickness and unemployment introduced for some in the 1911 National Insurance Act, but with voluntary and mutual provision still common in the pre-war years.

In education, the beginning of state compulsion came slightly earlier in the UK, with the 1870 Forster Elementary Education Act permitting school boards to make education compulsory, although not free. Forster himself argued that free provision would be 'not only unnecessary but mischievous. Why should we relieve the parent from all payments for the education of his child . . . the enormous majority of them are able, and will continue to be able to pay these fees'. (See Timmins, (1995)[3] for further discussion of this and the history of the UK welfare

Figure 1.2 General government revenue, 1995–6 (£ billions)

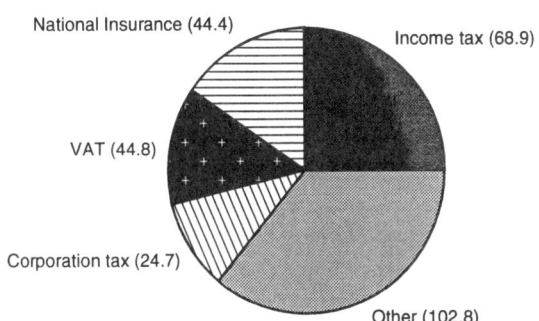

state generally.) In 1880, school was made compulsory for all five- to ten-year-olds, and this age band grew steadily until the Second World War.

In health, the large role of the private sector in the UK continued right up to the Second World War, with much revenue, for hospitals especially, coming from charges to patients, financed by various mutual funds and saving schemes, but by no means providing uniform cover or equality of care. The 1911 National Insurance Act sought to cover family doctor or general practitioner (GP) services, and by 1938 43 per cent of the adult population was covered by a 'panel' doctor.

In Europe at least, the Second World War and its aftermath brought to an end much of the pre-war mix of private, mutual, and state funding and control, substituting more uniform, more generous, and more expensive provision in all three of the main welfare state areas. Diversity remained from one country to another, but within nations much diversity of outcome was removed. In the UK, the Beveridge Report and its subsequent large-scale implementation between 1946 and 1948 created a largely new social security system; the 1944 Butler Act created a new state education system; and in 1948 the National Health Service, a state-run, state-funded health care system, free to all at the point of use, was instituted on 5 July. It was a brave new world, mirrored in different guises throughout the developed nations.

These policy innovations were costly, but during the 50 years that have followed, other factors have added to the growth in costs. First, social security benefits were increased more quickly than necessary to keep up with price inflation, until 1980. Second, the number of elderly people, unemployed people, lone parents, and long-term sick has grown. Third, decisions to improve the quality of health and education provision

Figure 1.3 Welfare state spending as a percentage of GDP 1946-91

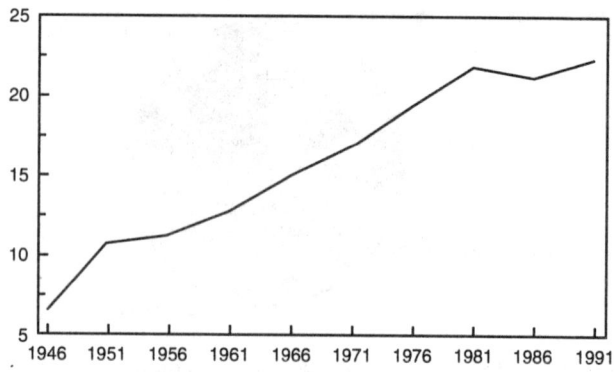

have been taken. Figure 1.3 illustrates this growth, from little more than five per cent of GDP in 1946, to close to 25 per cent in 1991. This substantial increase in costs has largely been financed through increases in the general level of taxation.

3. WHY?

So the welfare state is large, and has grown, and is a relatively recent development. But why does it exist? Two broad kinds of reason are put forward, although the dividing line is not clear, either in practice or principle. First, there are economic efficiency reasons, arguing that some parts of these functions either can only be achieved by the state, or are much more efficiently done by the state. Second, ethical and political principles about just distribution and redistribution, and the relative roles and responsibility of the individual, family, wider community, and state, shape preferences over the nature and extent of welfare provision and are reflected in government policy.

(i) Efficiency Arguments

There are three broad sets of efficiency arguments that relate to 'public goods'[4] and 'externalities',[5] paternalism, and the nature of insurance markets.

Public goods and externalities

It is hard to argue that any of the three main welfare state expenditure programmes are close to being pure public good in the technical sense that a private market will fail to provide them. The provision of social security benefits, health care, and education is to a large extent quite feasible for the private sector. The simple fact that in most parts of the world, for all but recent periods, these activities have often been provided by the private sector where they have been provided at all, reminds us that these are private goods now publicly provided. There are, of course, positive externalities from the consumption of these services which confer an element of public-good status on them, and imply that without public provision at least some individuals would consume less of these services than was optimal for the community as a whole. In the case of education, perhaps the clearest externality is that we all benefit from a better-educated labour force in terms of greater productivity, and from the more civilized and humane society that we expect to flow, *ceteris paribus*, from a more educated population. In health, the traditional argument is about disease control, with vaccination programmes being the most obvious example of an activity where our own behaviour has the potential for substantial spillovers. In social security, ignoring for now the political and ethical preferences we may have related to the distribution of well-being, the economic case is about unrest. The introduction of social insurance in Germany by Bismarck was inspired by a desire to avoid revolutionary impulses by giving the mass of the population a larger stake in what might be lost from violent change: the social security system as an instrument of public order.

Paternalism

But these externalities arguments seem far too weak to explain activities which absorb a quarter of total economic output in the UK, and rather more in many countries. A second potential set of market failures which might be said to call for state activity relates to information and preference failure. Here the suggestion is that individuals will make the wrong decision; that they will consume too little education (or too much) and regret it later; that they will fail to save enough for their retirement; that they will not insure against unemployment, believing it will never happen to them; that they will not know enough to choose an appropriate doctor, and so must be protected by a state-regulated regime.

All these sound plausible, since we do not really believe it likely that we can have all the information we need to make decisions, or that if we did we would also make the 'right' decision. The extent to which we should expect the state to intervene obviously varies from one area to another. Even the most extreme libertarian would be unlikely to expect or allow infants to leave school at the age of seven because they really did not see the point, and few would be happy to see people planning to have zero incomes in retirement, simply because it was a long way off.

But it should be clear that here the question is really one of compulsion and regulation, rather than provision. We do not need to have state-run and/or financed education to have compulsory education up to a certain age; we can make private pension provision compulsory, rather than rely on state pensions for all; and, in principle, we could have a privately run and financed health care regime, funded by compulsory insurance with the state paying for those unable to buy insurance. It might be easier and more effective in some cases to achieve our aims here through state provision, but there is an alternative route that relies more heavily on regulated private provision.

Insurance markets
A final set of efficiency, or market-failure arguments relate to insurance markets. The particular problem that might argue for state intervention regardless of any distributional objectives is that of so-called 'adverse selection'. If insurance is voluntary, only the bad risks will seek insurance, and a private insurance market may fail to thrive or even not exist. But as when we talked of preference or information failure, the response could be either state provision or state compulsory.

None of this is meant to imply that there are not economic efficiency arguments for welfare provision, or that existing welfare provision has no effect on economic efficiency. But it should be clear that the state welfare provision which can be defended on purely economic efficiency grounds would be very limited, and in particular much less substantial than what we see in modern developed economies.

(ii) Ethical and Political Arguments

Tempting as it is for economists to attempt to explain all features of economic life without appealing to ethical and political principles, any such attempt is absurd when we consider the welfare state, which is fundamentally about political and ethical values. Two broad sets of issues arise here. First, who is responsible for certain events, and second, what do just distributions look like?

The question of responsibility is perhaps most clearly seen in the context of unemployment. Those who have advocated private unemployment insurance (such as Minford, 1983)[6] have typically seen unemployment very much as the responsibility of the individual, whereas those who have advocated state-run insurance, with Beveridge the classic example, have seen unemployment as a 'disease of society, not of the individual' (Beveridge, 1924). If unemployment is caused and cured at the level of society as a whole, it seems reasonable to see the provision of income to the unemployed as an appropriate activity of government. If, on the other hand, unemployment is a matter for the individual, perhaps the private sector can be left to cope alone. It is worth noting that no developed country of which I am aware takes this last view to its conclusion.

But far more important than the question of responsibility is the question of what is just and right. Inherent in welfare states is a view of what is required for an acceptable society. We all have views about what a just distribution of income would be like, what a just distribution of education opportunity would be like, and what a just distribution of health care consumption and outcome would be like. And it is these views which have formed and shaped welfare states, and which will determine the nature of the changes we see in the future. As we discuss later, the nature of distributional goals and the redistributive effect of the welfare state cannot be separated from the debate about the 'affordability' of the current system.

4. IS THERE A PROBLEM?

That there is a crisis facing the welfare state, or at the very least a major problem, has become a commonplace in political debate in the UK, as in much of the rest of the developed world. Two broad problems seem to be identified: rising costs and dissatisfaction with the quality of public provision.

(i) Costs

Concern about escalating costs, and the consequences for taxation are not new. The debates which surrounded the beginning of each phase of welfare provision were characterized by heated discussion of cost and taxation; even during the heady days of the 1945–50 government in the UK, which saw the foundations laid for the modern British welfare state, finance was seen to be a crucial element in the viability of any proposals.

But in the last 15 or 20 years the question of cost has become more pressing as resistance to higher taxation has developed and hardened. For the first three decades of the post-war period, taxes in much of the developed world rose quite quickly alongside rapid economic growth and increasingly generous welfare states. In more recent times, more unsettled economic performance, and suggestions that high taxes can damage incentives, have coincided with, and may have helped to create, a climate in which politicians seem loath to offer higher taxes, and voters loath to pay them.

Increasing costs were not a crisis when taxes could rise to pay for them. But if that option is ruled out, higher costs may indeed be a crisis. Restricting our vision to the member states of the European Union (EU) we certainly find concern both at the level of public servants and governments. In its latest report (European Commission, 1995)[7] the EU information system on social protection identified three overlapping crises, one acute, one chronic, and one impending.

> The acute crisis [is] the unemployment crisis, which catches social protection schemes in the classic squeeze of mounting costs and falling income ... The chronic crisis is the ever rising cost of publicly financed health care, as the increase in provision never seems able to meet the public's growing appetite for medical services. The impending crisis is the demographic crisis as the children of the post-war baby boom advance towards retirement in the second decade of the next millennium, ready to claim their matured pension rights from their children and grandchildren whose ranks have been thinned by decades of falling birth rates.

The European Commission report goes on to note that the pressure of these crises has created a real convergence of policies in European social protection ministries:

> pension reform, restrictions of unemployment and other cash benefits, control of medical costs, adjustment of contributions, alternative methods of financing (including privatisation), administrative changes and active employment measures ... Nor is this scheduled to be the final tightening of the belt ... more austerity is promised.

This analysis leaves no doubt that in Europe at least, the belief in a

Table 1.1   A century of population estimates and projections (millions)

	1960	1970	1980	1991	2000	2010	2020	2030	2040	2050	2060
Working age	31.0	31.9	32.5	34.4	35.2	36.0	37.5	35.8	34.4	33.8	32.5
Pension age	7.6	8.7	9.4	10.4	10.5	11.7	11.5	13.5	14.3	13.5	13.2
Support ratio	4.1	3.7	3.5	3.3	3.4	3.1	3.3	2.7	2.4	2.5	2.5

Note: Support ratio is number of working age over number of pensionable age (65 for men and 60 for women until 2010, 65 for both from 2020).

Source: Government Actuary's projections.[8]

crisis is widespread, and similar views are expressed in North America and the Antipodes.

If we look for causes of cost pressures, we see demographic change increasing the numbers in groups which tend to be more dependent on the welfare state, especially the elderly; social change doing the same, with the growth in lone parenthood being the most obvious example; economic change, which has brought higher unemployment; and technological change, which may make the health care we have provided in the past cheaper, but opens up new and expensive forms for new facilities. Taking all these together, there is no doubt that without measures to restrict growth in spending, a more rapid growth than is occurring would result.

As we look to the future there is much talk of crisis, and there is no doubt that the proportion of our national income that we devote to providing income in retirement, and to the unemployed, the sick and the otherwise needy, will grow, as will that spent on health and education. The greatest focus of concern is often the so-called 'demographic time-bomb', but this is much misunderstood, while also being a clear example of the choices we face.

It is true that the number of elderly people in the UK will grow in the future, and it also seems likely that the number of working age will level off and even fall. The support ratio, the ratio of those of working age to those of pension age will therefore decline, as shown in Table 1.1.

If we were to attempt to finance a state old age pension for all, as we broadly do now, at a level which is constant relative to earnings, and financed from taxes on the earnings of those of working age, the tax rate on those earnings would need to rise, although not soon. By 2050, the combined employee and employer National Insurance contribution rate, which is now 20 per cent, would rise to around 25 per cent. This is a substantial increase, but no larger than that we have seen in the last 50 years; in fact it is rather smaller.

But we are *not* holding the pension constant relative to earnings, we are holding it constant relative to prices, which grow more slowly than earnings. If we had done this since the war the single person's pension would not be the roughly £60 p.w. it is now, but around £25 p.w. If we go on simply increasing the pension in line with prices, and earnings continue to grow as they have in the past 50 years, the pension will *fall* from the 20 per cent of average male earnings it was in 1977, to the 15 per cent it is now, to some seven per cent by 2050. And if this is the pattern, the joint National Insurance contribution rate could *fall* from 20 per cent to around 14 per cent. The crisis would not be a tax crisis, but a crisis of exclusion, since a pension of seven per cent of average earnings is clearly inadequate without some supplementary private or state provision.

If we were to attempt to maintain broadly the current level of services relative to general living standards, so that benefit levels keep up with the growth in the net incomes of those in work, and the earnings of staff in health and education grow in line with earnings elsewhere, spending and tax would need to rise by around five per cent of national income over the next 50 years.

By historical standards, five per cent of national income is not an unthinkably large amount, as we have already shown. But even five per cent would not be enough to cope, since we will undoubtedly want to improve healthcare, education, and incomes in retirement and need. To continue with the welfare state as it now is would require very substantial tax increases, although not so substantial that they would necessarily damage the economy.

(ii) Dissatisfaction

Thus far the discussion of costs has all been in terms of providing a broadly constant standard of service. But that has not been the experience of the last hundred years, nor is it likely to be acceptable in the future. Not only are we continuing to see general increases in the standard of living, with which welfare provision needs to keep pace, but the main items of welfare provision are classically superior goods. That is, as income rises, whether for an individual or as a nation, the proportion of income allocated to consumption of these goods rises. As we grow more prosperous, we wish to spend a larger part of our income

Crisis in Welfare? 13

in retirement, on healthcare, on educating our children, and there seems little likelihood that such preferences will soon change.

This increased demand for provision helps to explain the dissatisfaction commonly expressed despite the very dramatically increased public spending we have seen. It is also worth noting that if we see the better off increasing their income more rapidly than the rest, as we have in the UK, the pressures are increased. As the best off increase their incomes, their demands and expectations will tend to grow, increasing the likelihood that they will seek to opt out of consuming the publicly provided services. While this might slightly reduce costs, it would seem likely to reduce their inclination to pay taxes to fund what would become other people's services.

As we look to the future, there is little doubt that without dramatic reform, costs of public provision will continue to rise.

In the UK, such dramatic reform has been introduced, in the form of price rather than earnings indexation of social security benefits. Tight controls on health and education spending are now also in place, but even with all this, the share of GDP absorbed seems resolutely not to fall, as increases in the size of entitled groups, medical progress, and enhanced expectations keep up the pressure on spending. Other countries are now experiencing similar pressures, although, as Hills (1995)[9] shows, many face more challenging demographic developments than the UK.

One choice open to governments would be to opt for increasing spending and taxation so as to maintain the current relative level of services, rather than cut them back to restrain cost growth. Hills shows that to do this in the UK would require an increase in public spending and therefore taxation over the next 50 years to a level some five per cent of GDP higher than at present, the equivalent of an increase in the basic rate of tax from 25 per cent to a little over 40 per cent. Increases in other European countries to maintain the status quo would typically be much larger. And such tax increases would not address increasing expectations which would demand even more money. It is these types of tax increase which it is argued cannot be afforded.

But 'afford' seems the wrong word to use in this context. There are few who would suggest that the proportion of GDP absorbed by the activities we think of as now being covered by the welfare state will do anything other than continue to rise, as it has done throughout the developed world for as long as we know. The component parts of the welfare state are 'superior' goods. Throughout history, as individual and national incomes have grown, a greater proportion of them has

Table 1.2 Tax shares in selected OECD countries, 1993 (%)

UK	36
France	49
Germany	47
Denmark	58

Source: OECD (1994), Table A27, p.30.

been devoted to these goods. When state provision is restrained or reduced the desire to spend more overall is not removed, so private spending will rise. There are two possibilities. Either (1) taxes must rise or (2) private spending must rise. The question then is not can we afford to pay for welfare, but will we pay more tax to provide better services for all through the state, or will we choose a more individualized system, relying more heavily on self-provision? Either way, spending will rise.

Before addressing this question we must briefly tackle the suggestion that higher taxes damage economies. This is not the place to rehearse this argument in detail, but Table 1.2 demonstrates that the burden of taxation as a share of GDP arises hugely across developed nations, and in a way that is *not* systematically related to GDP growth. If the UK chose a tax burden as high as that in Denmark, we could *double* spending on health and education. While such a massive increase in taxation might find little political support, it should be clear that there is no correlation between economic performance and the burden of taxation. Undoubtedly, at the margin, high tax rates and generous social provision can cause problems, but there are genuine choices available in this field.

Despite the fairly continuous and substantial growth in the size of government across the world in the last hundred years, politicians throughout the developed world now seem unprepared to offer higher taxes, whatever the starting point. Politicians certainly perceive that the resistance to tax increases is so great as to mean that tax increases are only possible once in office, and generally in contravention of prior promises. Why?

One answer is a general trend towards individualism with the consequence that people are less and less concerned with others. This possibility goes to the economic heart of the welfare state debate. As Hauser (1995)[10] argues, successful welfare states rely on solidarity:

the extent of solidarity among the members of society must not diminish. The willingness of those who have to bear the burden of high taxes and contributions must be maintained... If solidarity is greatly diminished in the decades to come, then we will see a real crisis of the... welfare state.

This is the crux. We have to confront attitudes to redistribution.

If a welfare state effects little redistribution, or if there is widespread support for the distribution it does effect, political difficulties should be slight. As the amount of redistribution rises, the strength of solidarity required to support the system grows. As Hills shows for the UK, and as is true to a greater or lesser extent across all systems, substantial redistribution is implemented, although the extent of redistribution may be less great if whole lifetimes are considered. The best off ten per cent of UK households in 1994–5, those with household net incomes in excess of £25,000 p.a., paid 25.4 per cent of all tax, and received only 4.8 per cent of government spending, both directly on social security benefits, and indirectly on services like health and education. Problems of support or solidarity are growing because a number of forces are increasing the amount of actual and expected redistribution.

The most obvious factor which has necessitated increased redistribution is the growth in numbers among recipient groups – the elderly, the unemployed, lone parents. But two further factors are at work. First, in the UK, and in many other countries in rather less clear a fashion, underlying inequality of earnings is rising. As the inequality of earnings rises, so the inequality of tax payments will rise if aggregate tax systems are progressive or even proportional. If those in the top half of the income distribution pay a larger share of total taxation, while their share of welfare state consumption is unchanged, redistribution grows. And the second factor is reduction in promised benefits. There is a growing belief, borne out by experience, that welfare states will continue to change, so as to reduce entitlements in the future, especially for the currently younger generation. For this group, as their expectations of what they will receive from the state shrink, their perception of the extent of redistribution grows.

The Shift to Private Provision

The natural response to cost pressures in the face of resistance to tax rises is to attempt to shift responsibilities from the public to the private sector. This shift is happening in many countries. Yet the balance between public and private provision varies from one country to another. In Germany, for example, the better off must already take out private health insurance (see Hauser, 1995). But we must be clear about what can and cannot be done by public and private sectors. The main characteristic of public sector provision is systematic redistribution from better to worse off, which it is very hard to achieve, and impossible to enforce, in the private sector. We can attempt to force private companies to redistribute by compelling certain forms of contract, but such efforts are unlikely to succeed, are unaccountable, and are in the end simply a bad form of taxation. Redistribution is fundamentally the role of communities and, in modern societies, of the state. Shifting responsibility to the private sector is not largely a problem of feasibility, although that may be troublesome. The main problem with a shift to private sector provision is that it may not solve or reduce the underlying pressures. By shifting responsibility to private provision we leave public provision with a role that is ever more redistributive. We may be able to avoid raising taxes by making the better off responsible for their own pensions, but if they get less in return for the tax they still pay, they may be little happier, or even less happy.

CONCLUSIONS

The welfare state is not fundamentally about economics, although economics may constrain it, help to explain its effects, and indeed help us to understand why and when it is popular and/or criticized. But the essential truth is that the welfare state is a reflection of ethical arguments and beliefs. We have ethical views about the extent of low income and inequality that is unacceptable, and why. We have ethical views about the right distribution of healthcare outcomes and educational access.

Over the last century we have seen a massive growth in communal, tax funded state provision in these areas; and in the last two decades or so, we have seen a challenging of this route, with confidence in the state's effectiveness declining, and acceptance of large scale redistribution also being questioned.

It is quite possible to achieve unchanged redistributional goals with changed structures of public and private activity, by targeting government spending more closely on those in need, for example. But the bigger question, so often ignored, is what our redistributional objectives should be. We can *afford* to allocate more or less of our national income to health, education and transfers to the retired, unemployed, sick, or those on low incomes. But we have to make a choice, and in making that choice economics is of second order importance; it can help us achieve goals in the most effective way, yet it cannot and should not be expected to set them.

NOTES AND REFERENCES

1. See H M Treasury, 1996, for further details. H M Treasury (1996), Public Expenditure, Statistical Analyses 1996–7 Cm 3201.
2. Kohler, P. H. And Zacher, H. F. (eds) (1982). *The Evolution of Social Insurance*, London: Frances Pinter.
3. Timmins, N. (1995). *The Five Giants: A Biography of the Welfare State*, London: HarperCollins.
4. A public good is a commodity such that adding extra consumers has little or no cost, and for which excluding individuals from consumption is hard or impossible. National defence and lighthouses are good examples.
5. An externality is a benefit or cost affecting someone other than the purchaser of a commodity.
6. Minford, P. (1983). *Unemployment: Cause and Cure*, Oxford: Martin Robinson.
7. European Commission (1995). *Social Protection in the Member States of the Community*, Brussels.
8. Government Actuary's Department (1995). *National Insurance Fund Long Term Financial Estimates*, London: HMSO.
9. Hills, J. (1993). *The Future of Welfare: A Guide to the Debate*, York: Joseph Rowntree Foundation.
10. Hauser, R. (1995). Social Security in Germany, *Oxford Review of Economic Policy*, Vol. 11, No. 3.

2 A Mixed Economy of Care
The Incisive Role of the Voluntary Sector
Jeremy Kendall and Martin Knapp

1. INTRODUCTION

This chapter deals with one specific component of civic structures for meeting the cost of social needs, the voluntary sector. A framework is essential for an understanding of the position and roles of the voluntary sector in the UK today. The most relevant framework is the *mixed economy of care*, which explicitly recognizes four broad groups of service providers: the public, voluntary and the private (for-profit) sectors, together with the informal or household sector. Along a different dimension, there is a variety of ways in which services are accessed or purchased, from the so-called 'coerced collective demands' – when needs and expectations force the community to provide or purchase things collectively, paid for through taxation – through funding from charitable trusts, businesses and individual purchases, to individual donations of money and time. The provider and purchasing dimensions interact in the form of transactions to define the pattern of the mixed economy. In our increasingly pluralist environment these categories are multiplying.

The voluntary sector is a key component of Britain's mixed economy. Although there is widespread support for the many bodies that constitute the voluntary sector, this is not informed by a clear understanding of precisely what the sector comprises, how it is resourced, how it relates to other sectors and the nature of its social and economic role. In recent years, many government and policy analysts have registered increasing interest in the actual and potential contribution of voluntary organizations. This interest is linked to a number of broad political goals, ranging from reassertion by the right of conservative moral values, to solidaristic empowerment by the left. Moreover, there prevails evident dissatisfaction with exclusive reliance on either the state or for-profit organizations, for reasons of cost, quality and effectiveness; hence the desire to mobilize private action for public purposes.

In response, the 13-country *Comparative Nonprofit Sector Project* was launched in 1990, directed by Lester Salamon and Helmut Anheier of Johns Hopkins University, Baltimore, USA. The Project's aims were to close gaps in knowledge about the voluntary or nonprofit sector, and to do so within an explicitly comparative study design, describing the scope and scale of the sector in each country, and developing an understanding of its evolving roles. The UK component of this international study was undertaken by the Personal Social Services Research Unit. In what follows we draw heavily on the UK findings to identify how the voluntary sector can be defined, and to chart the sector's overall scope and scale.

2. DEFINING AND MAPPING THE VOLUNTARY SECTOR IN THE 1990s

Definition and Classification

A common 'structural operational definition' of the sector was applied in each country, which aimed to include all bodies with a formal structure, self governing and constitutionally independent of the state, not profit distributing, and benefiting from voluntarism (Salamon and Anheier, 1996a).[1] A common classification of organizations within it was then applied to organizations with these features – the *International Classification of Nonprofit Organizations*, or *ICNPO* – as shown in Box 2.1.

It is important to note that the structural operational definition is not without controversy (as is the case with *every* previous definition of the voluntary sector). Significantly, in the UK this definition seems not to correspond with the set of entities implicitly covered in the most common taken-for-granted usage of the term 'voluntary sector' by the general public, practitioners and many government officials.

We therefore developed a second definition for utilization in discussing the project's aggregate findings in the UK. The UK *Broad Voluntary Sector (BVS)* simply corresponds to the structural–operational definition as described above; while the UK *Narrow Voluntary Sector (NVS)* is a subset of this BVS, excluding broad groups of organizations that many UK commentators have, implicitly or explicitly, filtered out of their definition. This is because they are often regarded as too 'exclusive', insufficiently 'altruistic' or not sufficiently 'independent' or 'noncommercial' (despite their constitutional status) to be meaningfully regarded as components of the 'true' voluntary sector. The main categories

Box 2.1 The International Classification of Nonprofit Organizations (ICNPO)

Group 1: Culture and Recreation
1 100 *Culture*
1 200 *Recreation***
1 300 *Service Clubs*

Group 2: Education and Research
2 100 *Primary and Secondary Education***
2 200 *Higher Education***
2 300 *Other Education*
2 400 *Research*

Group 3: Health
3 100 *Hospitals and Rehabilitation*
3 200 *Nursing Homes*
3 300 *Mental Health and Crisis Intervention*
3 400 *Other Health Services*

Group 4: Social Services
4 100 *Social Services*
4 200 *Emergency and Relief*
4 300 *Income Support and Maintenance*

Group 5: Environment
5 100 *Environment*
5 200 *Animals*

Group 6: Development and Housing
6 100 *Economic, Social and Community Development*
6 200 *Housing*
6 300 *Employment and Training*

Group 7: Law, Advocacy, and Politics
7 100 *Civic and Advocacy Organization*
7 200 *Law and Legal Services*
7 300 *Political Organizations**

Group 8: Philanthropic Intermediaries and Voluntarism Promotion
8 100 *Philanthropic Intermediaries and Voluntarism Promotion*

Group 9: International Activities
9 100 *International Activities*

Group 10: Religion*
10 100 *Religious Congregations and Associations*

Group 11: Business, Professions and Unions**
11 100 *Business, Professions and Unions***

Group 12: (Not Elsewhere Classified)*
12 100 *NEC*

* In Broad Voluntary Sector, but not included for statistical mapping purposes
** In Broad Voluntary Sector for all purposes, but excluded from Narrow Voluntary Sector

excluded in describing this narrow voluntary sector are in fact discrete fields of activity in our classificatory system, and are marked in Box 2.1 with two asterisks. The impact of including or excluding these organizations is extremely significant in economic terms, and highlights the need for careful disaggregation. For this reason, after a brief sector-wide survey of our findings under each of the two definitions, our discussion of findings concentrates on identifying how the characteristics of the sector vary in different ICNPO fields of activity.

Overall scale of the voluntary sector

At the heart of the Comparative Nonprofit Sector Project lay the most comprehensive statistical mapping of the voluntary sector undertaken to date in each of the 13 countries. While the basic data collected in each country were the same to ensure full comparability, the strategy adopted to collect it varied considerably by country. In the UK, economic data were collected by mapping each ICNPO field of activity in turn, building up an estimate of the overall scale of the sector under each definition by aggregating these components. To this end, maximum possible use was made of existing data collections, and new data were gathered through our own territorial and field-focused surveys when this was the only way to fill the statistical gaps.

Figure 2.1 illustrates the overall size of the voluntary sector under both our definitions in 1990. Size is measured in terms of total operating income – £29.5 billion overall – and its three major components. Note that in Chapter 1 Andrew Dilnot speaks of a forecast for 1995–6 for spending by government on health, education and social services of approximately £178 billion. We analyse income flows in more detail below. Table 2.1 shows the scale of operating expenditures and full-time equivalent (FTE) paid employment, and the latter compared with employment in the economy as a whole. At four per cent of total UK employment, the UK BVS figure is similar to the proportions in France and Germany, considerably smaller than the US, but significantly larger than Hungary, Italy and Japan (Salamon and Anheier, 1996b).[2] Both the figure and the table highlight the marked impact on the size of the sector of using different definitions.

A common view is that volunteers and private giving dominate the voluntary sector, with other aspects of its resourcing often receiving rather less attention. Volunteering and donations are indeed integral parts of the sector. We are talking about very considerable amounts of

Figure 2.1 UK voluntary sector income, 1990. (a) Broad voluntary sector: total operating income £29.5 billion; (b) Narrow voluntary sector: total operating income £12.3 billion

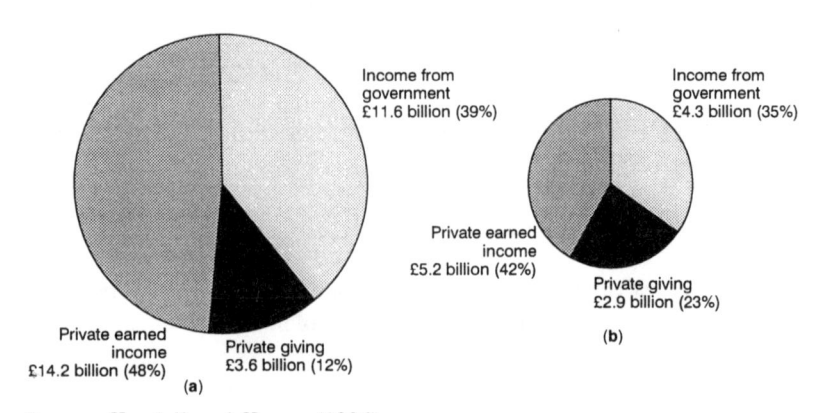

(a) Income from government £11.6 billion (39%); Private earned income £14.2 billion (48%); Private giving £3.6 billion (12%)

(b) Income from government £4.3 billion (35%); Private earned income £5.2 billion (42%); Private giving £2.9 billion (23%)

Source: Kendall and Knapp (1996).

money and activity. At least three out of four people make regular donations (Halfpenny and Lowe, 1994).[3] Significantly, half the UK adult population volunteer; though perhaps not very regularly, maybe half an hour to an hour per week. What counts is that there are many people doing many little activities. Our data also shows the sector is also a significant employer of *paid* labour.

Yet the lion's share of the sector's income is derived from government in a variety of ways, or is earned commercially. The latter resource is the most important one, a feature which the sector shares with its counterparts in the USA, Hungary, Japan and Italy (Salamon and Anheier, 1996b). So, once again, an illustration of our initial framework of 'mixed economy of care'.

As one would expect, the effect of narrowing the definition of the sector (moving from the BVS to the NVS) is to increase the relative share of private giving in total income. In fact, its share is nearly doubled as fields of activity which are heavily reliant on earned income and/or funding from government are excluded. To some analysts, moving to this narrower definition might represent an appropriate homing in on the true 'core' of the voluntary sector (for example, Ware, 1989). But even after narrowing the definition, it is noteworthy that private giving is *still* outweighed by government support and earned income.

Table 2.1 The UK voluntary sector, 1990

Sector	Number of FTE paid employees	FTE paid employees as % of whole economy	Total operating expenditure (£ billion)
UK broad voluntary sector[a]	946,000	4.0	26.4
UK narrow voluntary sector[b]	390,000	1.7	10.0
Seven-country BVS average (%)	n/a	3.4	n/a

Notes: [a] Definition used for international comparative purposes.
[b] Broad voluntary sector *less* ICNPO groups 1200, 2100, 2200 and 11 100.

Sources: UK figures from GUSTO mapping strategy; estimates built up individually for each ICNPO group.
Seven-country averages from Salamon and Anheier (1995).

Paid Employment and Operating Expenditures

Table 2.2 shows the distribution of paid employment by field of activity in 1990. In the broad voluntary sector, the single most important field was education and research. In the higher education subfield, this activity includes both the old and new universities (variously excepted and exempted charities). In the primary and secondary education area, the sector's major economic presence is in part accounted for by the continued contribution of voluntary schools within the 'maintained' system. These are primarily schools of an Anglican or Catholic foundation, whose origins will be traced in Chapter 17. In addition, it is a reflection of the operations of charitable schools funded by private fees outside the maintained system, which accounted for around six per cent of all pupils in 1990. This includes both the socially prominent and well known Anglican and Catholic 'public schools', the Muslim schools which have flourished in recent years, and a whole variety of other institutions with diverse styles of religious and secular orientation (Walford, 1991).

Social services have traditionally been regarded by many people as the centre of gravity of the UK voluntary sector. Table 2.2 shows that organizations in this field were employing just under 150,000 full-time equivalent paid staff, accounting for nearly two-fifths of all paid employment in the Narrow Voluntary Sector. This includes providers of residential or nursing home care for adults or children, as well as domiciliary care, day care, and advice and advocacy services. Finally, the

Table 2.2 Full-time equivalent employment in the voluntary sector

ICNPO group	Broad voluntary sector Number ('000s)	%	Narrow voluntary sector Number ('000s)	%
Culture and recreation	262	27.7	56	14.4[a]
Education and research	330	34.9	16	4.0[b]
Health	43	4.6	43	11.1
Social services	146	15.4	146	37.4
Environment	17	1.8	17	4.3
Development and housing	74	7.8	74	18.8
Civic and advocacy organizations	9	0.9	9	2.3
Philanthropic intermediaries and voluntarism promotion	7	0.8	7	1.8
International activities	23	2.4	23	5.8
Business and professional associations, trade unions	35	3.7	–[c]	–[c]
Totals	946	100	390	100

Notes: [a] Excludes recreation (primarily sports and social clubs) but includes culture and arts, service clubs.
[b] Excludes primary, secondary and higher education (all universities, most independent and maintained voluntary schools) but includes other education and research.
[c] Excluded under narrow definition of the sector.

Source: Kendall and Knapp (1996).

culture and recreation, and development and housing fields are also of particular economic significance. Under the broad definition, organizations of the former type collectively employ more paid workers than social service providers, including the large numbers of part time and temporary staff in nonprofit sports and social clubs (which are included under the NVS).

Volunteers

The contribution of volunteer labour is a major facet of the sector's voluntarism. The Volunteer Centre UK has defined volunteering as 'any activity which involves spending time, unpaid, doing something which aims to benefit someone (individuals or groups), other than or in addition to close relatives, or to benefit the environment'. In our own research, we did not systematically collect data on the numbers of volunteers in voluntary organizations, but the Volunteer Centre UK's own survey research (Lynn and Davis Smith, 1991) provides a large body of evidence on volunteering (across all sectors). This surveyed *individuals* rather than organizations. While the survey did not structure activities or organizations in such a way as to make it possible to project volunteer inputs onto each of the groups of the ICNPO, looking at people who had volunteered at least once in the month preceding the survey, the main areas in which they were active included 28 per cent in (ecclesial) religion, a category not covered in our own research (see Box 2.1). Other areas were:

- sports and exercise (25 per cent)
- children's education/schools (25 per cent)
- youth/children (outside school) (25 per cent)
- health and social welfare (21 per cent)
- hobbies/recreation/arts (21 per cent).

Sources of Revenue

We have already noted that private giving is a smaller source of revenue than commercial income or government funding for the sector as a whole. What are the revenue sources in individual fields?

Commercially earned income is concentrated in two fields: culture and recreation, and education and research, as shown in Figure 2.2. A large proportion of this is accounted for by charges paid for services delivered in these fields, ranging from net income generated by bars attached to sports and social clubs, to private fee payments to charitable independent schools. Fees are also an important source of revenue in other fields, including acute hospitals, nursing and residential care homes, and housing. Another major form of income of this type is the significant concentrations of endowment and investment income in the grant-making foundation sector, reflecting the UK's rich and long tradition of accumulated wealth in this area. Finally membership subscriptions are a primary source of revenue in the fields of culture and recreation, trade unions and business and professional associations.

Figure 2.2 also shows how *funding from the state* is distributed by the main fields of activity. (These figures do not include the value of tax concessions, 'hidden' expenditure by government worth around £1 billion in 1990.) Public sector support includes direct funding of voluntary organizations through grants and contracts, as well as 'user subsidies' channelled through individual clients. Statutory funding of the broad sector in 1990 was in fact dominated by contractual or quasi-contractual

Figure 2.2 Three primary income sources, broad voluntary sector, 1990

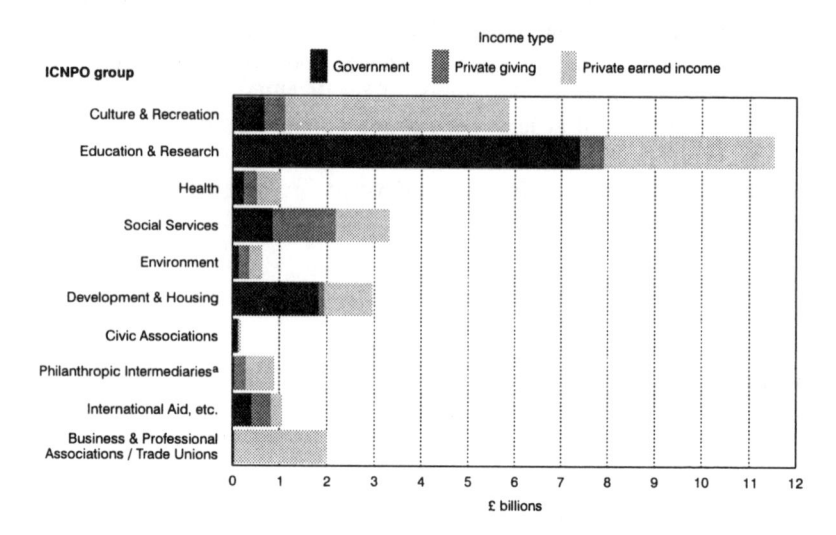

Note: [a] Excludes government funding of arms-length charitable quangos (including Arts Councils etc.) to avoid double counting.

Source: GUSTO mapping strategy: estimates built up individually for each ICNPO group.

funding of education: higher education by central government; primary and secondary education by local government, reflecting state finance for mainly church schools. In fact, payments to these ICNPO subgroups accounted for some 62 per cent of all direct public statutory support for the BVS (and are excluded by definition from the NVS).

State funding is also an extremely important source of revenue in other fields, including development and housing, and social services, which dominate receipts from government under a narrow definition of the sector. In these fields, recent policy initiatives have sought to remix the economy away from direct provision by the state through local authorities. This has provided new opportunities for the sector to grow through accessing public funds, but organizations thus funded face a major challenge in attempting to manage intimate links with the state without losing, or appearing to lose, their autonomy.

Finally, although smaller in aggregate than commercial and government income, it is often argued that *private giving* is fundamental to the well-being and autonomy of many parts of the voluntary sector (for example, see Salamon and Anheier, 1996b). Notwithstanding concerns about the stagnation in contributions in the late 1980s and early 1990s, *individuals* remained the sector's most significant source of private donations in 1990. Social services, health and international nongovernmental organizations receive significant amounts of individual donations, followed closely by philanthropic intermediaries and environmental bodies.

When looking at personal giving, whether in the form of money or volunteering, evidently some people donate in order to relieve guilt, to gain prestige or to comply with peer behaviour. Many people volunteer in order to gain experience, to make social contacts, or to gain intellectual enrichment. Altruism, concern for other people without expecting anything in return, is clearly a very common reason for giving. These motivations cannot easily be expressed statistically. The directions for giving and volunteering are by definition not controlled by society; in the main they are free choices and not necessarily targeted according to priorities of social needs. Yet however elusive all these factors are, we need a greater understanding of motivations if we are to encourage people to become even more committed to giving time and money.

Individual giving is only one form of private donation. Our disaggregated data also show corporate funding and support from grant-making trusts, the former outweighs the latter. With active encouragement from umbrella and promotional bodies, and also from government, corporate giving has expanded rapidly over the past two decades, although, like individual giving, it may now have reached a plateau. Moreover, it should be noted that our figures tend to overstate the extent of corporate 'philanthropy', as they (unavoidably) include considerable amounts of essentially sponsorship income, much of which should probably more appropriately be treated as earned income.

3. CONCLUSIONS

Nearly 50 years ago, William Beveridge abandoned his attempt to map 'voluntary action', and counselled others to do likewise (Beveridge, 1948). As he found, the inherent variability within the voluntary sector – variability of size, governance structures, orientation, goals, resources, constraints, ideologies and many other things – makes any mapping complex. But it is precisely because of this variability that such endeavours are important. The voluntary sector's contributions to the UK economy, polity and society are so many and various that its distinguishing features and its distinctive contributions need to be charted accurately and appreciated widely.

To conclude we offer several suggestions of a more general nature. The voluntary sector in Britain is in danger of becoming handicapped by what in the USA has come to be called the 'paradigm of conflict'. In our country conflict arises, for example, over resources from taxation. Many voluntary bodies see their tax benefits as entitlements, whereas government may consider them as concessionary. Another source of tension is political lobbying by some charitable bodies, who thereby tread very closely to the boundary of political activity not commonly conceived to be within their terms of reference. There is also the issue of government funding and the consequent accountability to government, which can be utilized, not only as a politically expedient way to cut the size of the public sector's share in meeting social costs, but also as a means for public sector bodies to control the (supposedly) independent sector. The voluntary sector needs to think carefully about moving from the role of contract agent to that of partner. The state funds voluntary organizations for numerous reasons: they are innovative, flexible, cost-effective and they are specialists; but a relationship which leaves them too close to government could undermine some of the voluntary sector's advantages. Ways must be found to move the sectors back to the partnership model, if they have strayed, and to reinforce the many important contributions of voluntary bodies to meeting social needs.

REFERENCES

Beveridge, W. (1948). *Voluntary Action*, London: George Allen and Unwin.
Halfpenny, P. and Lowe, D. (1994). *The 1993 Individual Giving Survey*, Tonbridge: Charities Aid Foundation.
Kendall, J. and Knapp, M. (1966). *The Voluntary Sector in the UK*, Manchester: Manchester University Press.
Lynn, P. and Davis Smith, J. (1991). *The National Survey of Voluntary Activity in the UK*, Berkhamsted: Volunteer Centre UK.
Salamon, L. M. and Anheier, H. K. (1995). *The Emerging Sector: An Overview*, Manchester: Manchester University Press.

Salamon, L. M. and Anheier, H. K. (1996a). *Defining the Nonprofit Sector: A Cross-National Analysis*, Manchester: Manchester University Press.
Salamon, L. M. and Anheier, H. K. (1996b). *The Emerging Nonprofit Sector: An Overview*, Manchester: Manchester University Press.
Walford, G. (1991). *Private Schooling: Tradition, Change and Diversity*, London: Paul Chapman.
Ware, A. (ed.) (1989). *Between Profit and State*, Cambridge: Polity Press.

3 Transfer through Taxation
Social Policy in Germany – Past, Present and Outlook for the Future
Dieter Biehl

1. INTRODUCTION

'*Sozialpolitik*' (social policy)[1] in Germany has developed in the main during the last 200 years. One can argue, however, that a complex interaction of numerous factors had been taking place much earlier and had led to the gradual emergence of previously unrecognized social issues and to new perceptions of these. They would range from improvement of sanitary and health conditions with resulting population increase, to striving for personal freedom and self-realization, and to the discarding of traditional restrictions by feudal serfdom and guild rules. These issues surfaced not necessarily by revolutionary action. Government reforms contributed significantly.

Though in retrospect many of these developments can be seen as positive, inevitably they had negative side effects. They weakened, sometimes even destroyed, the old concept of solidarity and transfers-in-kind. Institutions like the guilds entered decline. So did obligations of 'masters' towards their 'servants', responsibilities of local communities for their citizens, and last but not least, charitable religious institutions who cared for the poor.[2] In addition, and inevitably, there were wars and economic crises with resultant destruction of resources which could have been used for improving welfare. These detrimental factors led, in their turn, to new social problems. But then again they resulted in new insights regarding the nature of these problems and the means to deal with them.

This dialectic process can be understood better when we recognize two characteristic time lags. The first lag: structural change, economic crises and wars causing social problems; yet the challenges inherent in such structural change, economic crises and wars being recognized only some time later. The second lag would occur between the recognition of problems, and consequent political reaction to these by new government policies and in particular by *Sozialpolitik*.

2. HISTORIC ROOTS

It seems that already in the beginning of the Middle Ages the state participated actively in *Sozialpolitik*. Charlemagne is said to have introduced a tax for the benefit of the poor. He also insisted that the Church should use the tithe to finance caring for the poor. In the high Middle Ages, the main burden of organized caring for the poor fell on the Church, in particular on the religious orders. Nevertheless, the real centre of care and welfare was the family and the clan. Wars and crises, and the advent of the Enlightenment eventually weakened these networks of primary solidarity, and so did the gradually reduced role of the Church. The burden of care shifted to local government, in particular to the cities. These bodies would now build hospitals and poorhouses.

In the 18th and in particular the 19th century, it became increasingly recognized that the dimension of the social challenge exceeded the capacities both of the private and the local government sector. These problems could no longer be left to private initiative and disparate local government activities. State action was required. Prussia was the first to react. In 1794, care of the poor was incorporated in common law, the 'Preußische Allgemeine Landrecht'. Moreover, social policy was not restricted to fighting poverty. The protection of workers and regulation of labour market were also seen as a state function. Again, Prussia in 1839 adopted the first German law to protect young factory workers. Bismarck then developed the system of State Social Security, promulgated in the 'Kaiserliche Botschaft' (Message from the Imperial Throne) of 1881.[3] This resulted in legislation for compulsory health insurance in 1883, continued with the institutions of public accident insurance and old age retirement schemes. Numerous other measures followed during the next five decades.[4]

It is a characteristic of the German system of social security that it was created 'from above'. This is what Bismarck did, by a combination of conservative-liberal ideas based on the philosophy of the Prussian state. Accordingly, the state has to develop a country and to provide appropriate public services for the well-being of its citizens.[5]

Now to the period after the Second World War, which again illustrates the sequence of disastrous events being followed by formulation of *Sozialpolitik*. Related time lags are part of the picture. The consequences of the Second World War, as of previous calamities, called for social reform. Two major reforms of the retirement pension schemes were legislated in 1957 and 1972. Since built-up concealed inflation, a result of the war, did not allow the setting up of a new funded system, an unfunded one was introduced in 1957. Strictly speaking, this was no longer an insurance scheme but, implicitly, a transfer process based on the 'Generationenvertrag', *an inter-generation agreement*.

The underlying rationale of this remarkable principle assumes that the present active working generation should pay the pensions for those already retired; the following generation will in turn pay for their pensions once these are required. Additional benefits made the scheme even more attractive. Yet at the same time there were the makings of financial difficulties: payable pensions are only partly a function of previously paid contributions, but are topped up each year in relation to increasing incomes of the active working generation; a considerable financial burden.

Public Assistance was reformed by the Federal Law on Social Support (BSHG) of 1961. This established an innovative principle in Germany: public assistance has to be granted *ex officio*, that is, an individual entitlement right was created. Furthermore, to supplant paternalistic implications the term *Fürsorge* (taking care) applicable to the safety net for those not covered by social insurance was replaced by *Sozialhilfe* (Social Aid).

Throughout this long history we can observe a two-fold trend: the imposition of beneficent structures from above, much on the Prussian model, and pressure by citizens and their local bodies resulting in their participation in the exercise of responsibility.

3. INTERPRETING THE IMPACT OF SOCIAL ISSUES ON PUBLIC FINANCE

i. Adolph Wagner (1835–1917), one of the leading German public finance and social policy experts, argued that there exists a *law* according to which public activities and state expenditure will increase to respond to the *refined needs* of a developing society.[6] He distinguished between two major types of such increasing demand: one serving the purpose of law and power ('Rechts- und Machtzweck'), covering the *classic* state functions including the military one; the other serving culture and welfare. The latter includes social policy. 'Wagner's law', formulated in several versions between 1892 until 1915, seems to have been working until present times if one takes the increased share of public expenditure in GDP as an indicator.[7]

ii. Following Wagner, Peacock and Wiseman (1961)[8] argued in their study for the UK from 1890–1955, that it is wars and social crises in particular that cause an increase in public spending. They stress, however, that the process does not develop in a continuous form, but as a stepwise *ratchet displacement* effect: expenditure would be increased in order to fight wars or crises, but after wars and crises ended, the expenditure levels are not reduced but remain high until the next shock pushes them up again.

iii. Crowley (1971)[9] showed that if one takes the frequency and intensity of European wars during the period 1020 to the present as an indicator of costly public activity, there was neither a linear process as suggested by Wagner nor a continuous stepwise one as per Peacock and Wiseman, but rather a sequence of long-term cyclical swings, with alternate periods of 'laissez-faire' (low activity) and 'public control' (high activity). Admittedly his methodology is a crude one for lack of expenditure data over a long period, and being restricted to military activity. Yet, in the light of the findings of Beck (1979)[10], Crowley's analysis confirms the conclusion that it is indeed the social consequences of wars and crises that contribute to a large extent to the increasing public expenditure shares in a large number of countries. Following wars and the destruction they wreak, succeeding governments come under strong pressure to introduce legislation that grants public transfers to those who were direct or indirect victims. This pressure increases if, as has been the case in Germany after both world wars, the new government is not capable or willing to serve the public debt and to guarantee the stability of the national currency. Additional pressure results – the German experience – when the government introduces monetary reform which partially expropriates the holder of monetary claims including those of bonds, resulting in stark disparity between them and others who own land or material capital assets. Under the circumstances it becomes unavoidable to expand the public social security system.

4. A FRAMEWORK FOR ANALYSIS: THE EXTENDED COST APPROACH

I proposed initially the regular occurrence of two time lags: the first between the emergence of new social problems and their recognition, the second between recognition and political action. They may be understood as periods of gestation. In each case there must be a sufficient number of people, particularly people with sociologically significant functions, who share the recognition. This in turn implies awareness of ethical values, as it is in the light of such values that recognition takes place. In a pluralistic society this does not necessarily mean that all those concerned need to hold the same religious or the same humanistic convictions. Measures recommended and resultant social policy can differ considerably, depending on whether one's ethical base is orientated more towards individualism or more towards collectivism; whether it is based on faith or on atheism. Some may prefer greater scope for responsibility of the individual, or of small homogenous groups, others may tend towards engaging large groupings, in the extreme case central government. It suffices that the different value positions converge towards a common perception of human dignity and its implications. Most important is the fact that this analysis underlines the significance of not only a sociological but of an ethical dimension as intrinsic to approaching economic difficulties.

Integrating ethical value dimensions in economic analysis is not an easy task. There exists, however, a specific extended cost approach based on the seminal work of Buchanan and Tullock (1962)[11], that is very useful in this respect. Their approach allows the conception of, in addition to the traditional 'resource cost', a second major cost category which I have called, following Pennock (1959), 'frustration cost'. These latter costs reflect the negative repercussions of majority decisions on citizens with a different set of values and beliefs. By differentiating between efficiency and equity, this approach bridges the gap between a traditionally narrow economic evaluation and evaluations based on a larger set of values, like in theology, sociology, political science and law, and the derivation of overarching principles of constitutional democracy and of fiscal federalism.

Let us illustrate this with the help of the well-known *principle of subsidiarity*. This notion articulated in the papal encyclical *Quadragesimo Anno* in 1931 has become common coinage in political debate. In the present context its relevance consists in supporting the significant role to be played by small units in relation to bigger ones (for example, person and family vis-à-vis society, local units vis-à-vis central government). Though subsidiarity is considered to be an important philosophical and socio-ethical principle (*'gravissimum illud principium'*) rather than an economic one, it is possible to make it operational in the sense of the extended cost approach. Thus decision-making rights attributed to individuals, families, small groups or government at the local level enable these entities to bring their values and preferences into policy formulation. As a consequence, frustration is minimized. Alternatively, when a decision is taken by somebody or some institution far removed from the person or the problem involved, and possibly according to a different set of values, *frustration* results. *Resource costs*, for their part, relate to time, personal effort and money required to investigate and execute solutions. The challenge is to find a cost-minimizing trade-off between frustration and resource costs.[12]

The correspondence principle, formulated by Breton and Oates[13], represents another principle of fiscal federalism. It says that an optimal supply of a *public good* (for example, social policy) will only be obtained if, within the legitimate decision-making body, there is identity between decision-makers, tax payers and beneficiaries. If in such a body those who pay tax are in a minority and the beneficiaries or their representatives are overrepresented, the level of social policy decided will be too high.

This is illustrated by the German decision-making process for social assistance. The legislative responsibility is assigned on a *concurrent* basis to the Federal Diet (Bundestag) with co-decision-making authority of the Federal Council (Bundesrat, representing the Länder governments). It is, however, the local councils (Gemeinden) who have to execute this law and to finance more than 90 per cent of related expenditures. Bundestag and Bundesrat have legislated on norms and criteria that result in a payment of about DM 12,000 per annum for people entitled to full benefits (who pay no tax). This amount is seen to represent the subsistence minimum. A tax payer, however, is only allowed to deduct DM 6000 as minimum subsistence allowances. Given that income tax revenues are shared between the superior bodies and the local ones (Gemeinden) in the relation of 42.5:42.5:15.0, to raise these allowances to a more equitable level would represent a revenue loss to Bund and Länder of DM 0.85 for every DM 1.00 increase, but only 0.15 to the Gemeinden. Not at all astonishing that the legislating process produces results not in tune with the real social aid issue and the income tax issue. The lesson to be learned is that whenever one of the principles of fiscal federalism is violated, distortions will result. The principle of optimal differentiation of responsibilities comprises two variants: differentiation between full and partial competence, and between exclusive and concurrent ones.[14]

Where a *full* competence is allocated to one level of government, this level can operate without any special restrictions. Federal systems where a full competence is allocated either to the federal or to the states (Länder) level, can be described as *competitive federalism*. But whenever full competence is divided into partial competences (for example, legislation, administration, financing) and if these are allocated to different levels, a tendency towards *cooperative federalism* will emerge. Under these conditions, no single level of government is able to use its (partial) competence independently since it does not dispose of all the preconditions to deliver the particular public service at issue. In the German context, with its strong preference for equality, such a structure can have undesirable consequences, especially when the correspondence principle is violated. The decision-makers at the (federal) level disposing of the legislative authority, for instance for social policy, can be tempted to be too generous when the costs are borne at another level.

5. STRUCTURES OF POLITICAL COMPETENCE AND SOCIAL EXPENDITURE

Article 20 of the Constitution (Grundgesetz; GG) lays down that the Federal Republic of Germany is a democratic and social federal state. This led to the notion of *Sozialstaat*: a state governed by the principles of social justice and fairness, in parallel to the notion of *Rechtsstaat*: a state bound to the rule of law.

Article 70 GG states that legislative competence is vested in the Länder with the exception of specific competences reserved to the Bund. The latter is entitled to legislate in matters regarding the creation of equitable living conditions throughout the whole territory and of maintaining legal and economic unity. When the Bund decides to exercise this prerogative the resulting new federal laws will 'break' and, if possible, replace the existing Länder law.

When in 1961 the Bund made use of its right and replaced earlier social legislation, it followed the tradition, and still left executive and administrative competences at local level, whilst at the same time declining financial responsibility for Social Aid. Only a number of specific

Transfer through Taxation 37

Table 3.1 Public sector ratios in selected countries 1989-1990

	Total public expend. % GNP /GDP 1990	Total revenues in % GNP/ GDP 1990	Central/ Federal 1989	States/ Länder/ Kantone 1989	Regional and local gov. combined 1989	Local gov. only 1989	Social security 1989
Germany	49.0	37.7	31.9	22.2	–	8.7	36.3
Japan (1989)	31.5	30.6	46.3	–	25.8	–	27.9
UK	41.5	36.8	70.7	–	10.6	–	17.6
USA (1990)	36.1	30.1	40.0	18.7	–	12.1	29.1
Sweden	59.9	57.7	55.6	–	28.0	–	16.4
Switzerland	30.2	31.2	28.9	22.0	–	16.3	32.7

Note: The shares of social security contributions are lowest in Sweden (16.4 per cent), but the UK is not far away (17.6 per cent), whereas Germany has the highest percentage (36.3 per cent). These last figures seem to indicate that a higher percentage of total social security expenditure in Germany is financed by a special earmarked tax, whereas Sweden and the UK seem to use more normal taxes for that purpose.

Source: Bundesministerium der Finanzen (1992), pp.311-16.

forms of aid are now financed by the Bund (for example, for war victims, for immigrants, for Germans in foreign countries, for the so-called tuberculosis aid)[15].

Thus of the total expenditure for social policy of DM 163 billion in 1990, 27 per cent is financed by the Bund, 37 per cent by social security contributions, 13 per cent by the Länder, and 23 per cent by local authorities. Note that whereas Social Security Insurance is financed from *contributions* by employers and employees (normally each party pays 50 per cent) plus a financial transfer from the Bund, the cost of Social Aid has to be covered almost completely by local authorities.

For international comparison, Table 3.1 presents key figures for the public finance systems of selected countries.

Next, some information about the Social Policy Budget in West Germany for 1989, 1992 and 1994 is given in Table 3.2. According to this table, total transfers increased during these five years in absolute terms by 62.48 per cent, in terms of GDP shares from 30.61 per cent to 33.31 per cent. However, their percentage share in total public expenditure (including social security) decreased from 64.77 per cent to 62.92 per cent. The reason is that social policy expenditure growth (+ 62 per cent) was stronger compared with the growth of GDP (+ 49

38 Welfare and Values

Table 3.2 Social policy budget in West Germany, 1989, 1992 and 1994

	1994	1992	1989 (West Germany only)
GDP (DM millions)	3,321,100	3,075,600	2,224,400
Total public disbursement (DM millions)	1,758,205	1,614,454	1,051,079
Total public revenues (DM millions)	1,652,511	1,491,602	1,038,408
Payments			
– in DM millions	1,106,185	1,001,388	680,811
– % of GDP	33.31	32.56	30.61
% of Disbursement	62.92	62.03	64.77
Funding			
– in DM millions	1,141,883	1,017,490	714,101
– % of GDP	34.38	33.08	32.10
% of Public revenues (without public borrowing)	69.10	68.22	68.77

per cent), but lower compared with the overall expenditure growth (+ 67 per cent). On the financing side, both the GDP shares (from 32.10 per cent to 34.38 per cent) and the total revenue shares (from 68.77 per cent to 69.10 per cent) increased.

Table 3.3 below gives an overview of the development of the main social policy expenditure categories from 1988 to 1993 in West Germany.[16] As can be seen, all categories have not only increased in absolute but also in relative terms. As percentages of GDP, they reached 20.37 per cent in 1993 compared with 18.78 five years earlier. The lowest increase in absolute terms show the children transfers (+ 54.4 per cent) the highest (+ 65.39 per cent) pension expenditure.

This picture must be evaluated against the background of a large number of measures having already been taken during the relevant period in order to reduce claims for social support and the fact that it had become extremely difficult to impose additional cuts. Part of this trend seems to have been caused by the German reunification and by different regulations in West and East Germany.

As mentioned earlier, splitting up competences may be good democracy but makes for distorted decisions. Thus the federal legislator could be relatively generous in respect of the needy, because at that level the resulting financial burden does not have to be shouldered.

Table 3.3 Main social policy expenditure categories in West Germany, 1993 and 1988

	1993		1988	
GDP (DM millions)	3,159,100		2,096,000	

Disbursements (Transfers)	(DM millions)	% of GDP	(DM millions)	% of GDP
State Health Insurance	211,781	6.70	1,344,376	6.41
State Accident Insurance	23,349	0.74	14,038	0.67
National Insurance	3,342,741	10.85	207,238	9.89
Child Benefit	16,657	0.53	10,788	0.52
Income Support	48,919	1.55	27,010	1.29

6. OUTLOOK

It is extremely difficult to escape the impact of long term developments which almost always increase the public sector's call on GDP and personal incomes. In the case of Germany, there may even subsist some hidden 'bad conscience' factor. So many people lost their lives or have been otherwise negatively affected by wars and crises, that it seems to have become an obligation of politicians to do more to improve the living conditions of those who survived. As long as growth, employment and prosperity prevailed that was not a big problem. To expand the welfare state when people have been ready to work hard, to reconstruct what had been destroyed and to reserve a substantial part of the increase in incomes, profits and wealth in order to finance solidarity was achievable, reasonable and possible. These good times, however, seem to have come to an end.

Now, doubts as to the sustainability of the generation agreement, to which I referred earlier, are given an edge by the drastic reduction in recent economic growth. Due to the fact that economic growth for 1995 has been much lower than predicted (presumably only one per cent instead of three per cent) and is estimated to remain as low as 0.5–0.75 per cent in 1996, there is a drastic shortfall of overall public revenues of more than DM 80 billion. As in other countries, this has reopened public debate on the retirement pension system and induced proposals to cut expenditure and to increase revenues; in particular to reduce social security expenditure.

The Bonn Coalition government agreed on 25 April 1996 on a

programme that is expected to reduce expenditure by DM 25 billion, of which 20 billion should come from social security. Chancellor Kohl, next day in his statement to Parliament, presented a programme for growth and employment and identified too high a level of direct and indirect (public) labour cost and too generous social security rules as the main causes of the economic problems. The programme contained a large package of expenditure-saving measures. In order to avoid unrest, he stressed that pensions were safe, that they would be adjusted as usual to wages and salaries, but that *inter alia* the pension age would be raised. He announced that an expert commission would be created to make proposals for the reform by the end of 1996 so that the necessary legislative decisions could be made in 1997. He mentioned also that it is necessary to offer a positive perspective for the younger generation that will have to finance the pensions. A commission will have to prepare a reform of the tax system with lower tax rates and fewer exemptions to become effective in 1999.

As was to be expected, the Social Democrat and the Green opposition strongly criticized this strategy. They agreed that tax reform is unavoidable and that tax rates have to be reduced, but proposed to finance the reform by reducing investment allowances and by introducing a levy on large fortunes.

This and earlier debates clearly demonstrate that simply to continue old policies is no longer possible. The cost of the welfare state has not only become increasingly unfinanceable, but also creates substantial burdens for the business sector. If one resorts to Wagner's law and to Crowley's analysis, it looks as if now a turning point in the trend of social security expenditure in Germany has come – as elsewhere. In fact, Germany would be a latecomer in the reform of the welfare state, in comparison with Sweden or the United Kingdom.

NOTES AND REFERENCES

1. The word 'Sozialpolitik' can convey more than 'policy'. In a sense it is akin to a concept like 'welfare state' with its strong overtones of a social philosophy. [Editor]
2. Heinz Lampert, 'Sozialpolitik' (Social Policy) and Detlef Merten, 'Sozialhilfe' (Social Aid) both in: Roman Herzog *et al.* (eds), *Evangelisches Staatslexikon*, 3rd edn., Stuttgart, 1987, vol. 2.
3. Detlef Merten, ibid., col. 3215.

4. Reinhard Richardi, 'Sozialversicherung' (Social Insurance) in: Roman Herzog *et al.* (eds), *Evangelisches Staatslexikon*, 1987, op. cit., col. 3286.
5. Some historians argue that this type of conservative reformism has contributed to prevent revolution, like in France, though in Prussia also substantial privileges of noble families and landlords existed (cf., for example, Otto Büsch, 'Das Preußenbild in der Geschichte' (The Prussian Image in History) and Ulrich Scheuner, 'Der Staatsgedanke Preußens' (The Idea of the State in Prussia) both in: Otto Büsch and Wolfgang Neugebauer (eds), *Moderne Preußische Geschichte* (Modern Prussian History), Berlin, 1981, vol. 1.
6. Wagner started to analyse government growth in 1883; the last version of his 'law' was published in 1911 and reprinted in: Horst Claus Recktenwald (ed.), *Finanztheorie* (Public Finance Theory), Cologne/Berlin, pp.241–6. An English translation is to be found in: Richard A. Musgrave and Alan T. Peacock (eds), *Classics in the Theory of Public Finance*, London, 1958.
7. Herbert Timm, 'Das Gesetz der wachsenden Staatsausgaben' (The Law of Increasing State Expenditure), *Finanzarchiv*, Neue Folge, vol. 21, (1961), pp.244–66. Timm undertook an ex-post reinterpretation of Wagner based on the hypothesis of several time lags.
8. Alan T. Peacock and Jack Wiseman, *The Growth of Public Expenditure in the United Kingdom 1890–1955*, Princeton, 1961, revised edn. London, 1967.
9. Ronald W. Crowley, 'Long swings in the role of government: an analysis of wars and government expenditures since the eleventh century', *Public Finance/Finances Publiques*, vol. 26, (1971), pp.27–43.
10. Morris Beck, 'Public sector growth: a real perspective', *Public Finance/ Finances Publiques*, (1979), pp.313–56.
    The author found that in the majority of countries the increasing shares are due primarily to the development of the transfer expenditure of the welfare state, and not so much to the expansion of the 'classic' public consumption function.
11. James Buchanan and Gordon Tullock, 'Calculus of Consent – Foundations of Constitutional Democracy', 1962.
12. Dieter Biehl, 'Fiscal Federalism in Germany', in: Anne Mullins and Cheryl Saunders (eds.), *Economic Union in Federal Systems*, Sydney, 1994, pp.151–93.
    The subsidiarity principle and the correspondence principle are two out of nine principles of fiscal federalism dealt with.
13. Albert Breton, 'A theory of government grants', *Canadian Journal of Economic and Political Science*, vol. 31, (1965), pp.175–87 and Wallace E. Oates, *Fiscal Federalism*, 1972.
14. Biehl, 1994, op. cit.
15. Merten, 1987, op. cit.
16. Due to a number of special regulations applying to the new East German Länder, it was not possible to obtain comparable figures for them; the above figures, therefore, only apply to the old Länder in West Germany.

4 Economic Restraints
Ian Steedman

There would be little point in any proposals for social provision of various kinds of goods and services which did not attempt to take seriously the economic constraints on such provision. Such constraints simply do exist and do matter and to pretend otherwise would be to engage in self-indulgent fantasy. Moreover, in so far as economic policies can tighten or relax such economic constraints, there can be a political economy dimension to the limitations faced by proposals for social provision and these limits too must be recognized, even if they are somewhat fluid and hard to pin down. (Recognition of such political economy aspects, however, must not lead one to suppose that economic constraints are simply reducible to political constraints; they are not, as will emerge below.) The purpose of this chapter is to draw attention, in an informal and non-technical way, to at least some elements of the relevant pattern of economic constraints – and it will serve its purpose only if its elementary and introductory nature is acknowledged. Certainly no economist will find anything of interest in this chapter.

We shall begin by considering a 'closed economy' – that is, an economy which has no exports, imports or other economic transactions with the rest of the world – and by paying little attention to any directly economic role of government. Then this latter role will be considered more explicitly. Finally a more realistic 'open economy' will be discussed, account being taken of foreign trade, international financial movements, and so on.

A CLOSED ECONOMY

No matter what combination of goods and services is to be produced and no matter by what mixture of market processes or government taxation and expenditures the outputs are to be allocated between final users, it remains the case that over a given short period of time there are definite limits to the levels of output and consumption which are possible in a closed economy. Amongst the factors limiting those levels will be the available supplies of different kinds of labour; of different kinds of land, mineral deposits, and so on; and of the given stocks of already existing machines, plant and equipment. What can be produced with all these different available inputs will also, of course, be limited by the current knowledge of scientific principles and of their varied technological and engineering applications. And yet further limitations to possible output levels will stem from customs, work practices, management styles and many other less tangible but still relevant factors. No proposal concerning the provision and distribution of goods and services merits serious consideration if it in effect advocates that more must be available, in a certain period of time, than can in fact be produced subject to the varied limitations to possible output levels.

Over time, of course, the available resources may be subject to change. The supplies of labour of various kinds can change due to population change, to an increased (or decreased) tendency for certain social groups to participate in the labour force, to changed educational norms and retirement ages, and so on. Land supplies will usually be subject to less change, of course, but known mineral deposits, oil reserves and so on need not necessarily be reduced by extraction, since that effect may be more than offset by new discoveries. Machinery of different kinds can be accumulated (or destroyed) and scientific and technical knowledge can be increased. All these changes, together with any development in the less tangible but still relevant factors mentioned above, will mean that achievable levels of output will be liable to change from one time period to another. In modern capitalist economies, of course, the *maximum possible* output often grows from one period to another due to capital accumulation and technical change – even if actual output (see below) does not do so. But this in no way alters the fact that over each time period there are definite limits to the possible output levels and hence to the possible consumption levels of goods and services.

The crude sketch given so far might appear to suggest that only quantitative change is involved in economic growth. In fact, qualitative change is often involved and, indeed, that has not really been denied above. Thus the labour force, for example, cannot be adequately described, even for our present purpose, in merely numerical terms. How well educated are the members of that labour force? How much on-the-job training and experience do they have? Do their customs and traditions embody rigid or flexible attitudes to changes in work methods? These and many other questions about the 'quality' of the labour force are clearly highly germane to the question of how much can be produced with the available resources. Again, the extent of scientific and technical knowledge cannot sensibly be represented by merely numerical indices and modern machinery is seldom qualitatively identical to old machinery. (It is not just 'more of the same'.) And it will hardly need to be said that consumption goods (and services) also often change in nature over time. Once again, however, recognition of this further complexity in the limitations to possible output does not mean that such constraints have melted away; they are still only too real.

We now need to focus on the fact that actual output can – and often does – fall short of maximum possible output, with the result that there are even tighter constraints – constraints within constraints, one might say – on the availability of goods and services than those discussed so far. Before doing that, however, we shall stop to outline one way in which economists seek to assess how effective a free market economy can be, or can fail to be, in meeting people's wants. The language used in the next section may seem rather more formal than that employed in most of this chapter and any reader wishing to do so may skip to the subsequent section without loss of continuity.

PARETIAN WELFARE ECONOMICS AND LAISSEZ-FAIRE POLICY

Following in the tradition of the Italian economist Vilfredo Pareto (1848–1923), economists have developed a formal argument to prove that, under a number of precise and strong assumptions, a competitive, free-market economy will produce an outcome such that, given the available resources and technical knowledge, no reallocation of resources or of consumption outputs could make anyone better-off without making at least one other person worse-off. When fully and carefully spelt out, this argument is, in its own terms, simply correct. It by no means follows however (and no competent economist takes it to follow) that a *laissez-faire* policy of minimal state intervention has thereby been demonstrated to be always the best economic policy. For one thing, the conclusion of this argument – like that of any other logically valid argument – depends upon the assumptions made at the beginning. And in the present case it is by no means self-evident that all the assumptions involved are descriptively realistic with respect to actual economies. (Which they do need to be in welfare economics, whatever might be the case in other branches of the subject.) A careful examination of the implications of moving the assumptions in the direction of realism can then become the basis for recommending intervention of various kinds in the working of the market system. There is also another and quite different reason why the logical validity of the 'Paretian welfare economics' argument does not entail the indefeasible correctness of a *laissez-faire* policy. This is that the argument has little to say about income distribution. To make the point with a ludicrously extreme example, suppose that production is efficiently carried out and that all output is allocated to just one person. It will then clearly be impossible to make anyone better-off without making one other person worse-off! Thus even if Pareto efficiency is taken to be a *necessary* condition for the satisfactory working of an economic system, few are likely to take it to be a *sufficient* condition. The distributions of wealth and of income may also be held to matter and the distributions thrown up by the unimpeded workings of the market may not be found acceptable.

There is naturally far, far, more that could be said about the Paretian approach to assessing the efficiency of a market system but here we may simply draw attention to two features of that approach which bear directly on the argument of Chapter 14 below. One such feature is that Paretian welfare economics theory generally assumes that, no matter what bundle of goods, services, leisure time, and so on, a household possesses, there will always exist at least one other such bundle which it would prefer to have. (The 'axiom of non-satiation'.) The second feature referred to is the standard assumption that a household's ranking of different commodity bundles as more acceptable and less acceptable (the household's 'preference ordering') is quite independent of the working of the economic system. Both the 'non-satiation axiom' and the 'autonomy of preference orderings' assumption play an important role in the standard Paretian arguments and careful reflection on that axiom and that assumption is thus in order: some preliminary moves in that direction are made in Chapter 14. But it is easy to see at once that if consumers' preferences depend, in part, on what is produced then there may be some circularity involved in assessing economic performance in terms of how well the economy's output meets preferences.

(Before returning to the main line of argument in this chapter and considering actual output as opposed to maximum possible output, we should at least mention that some advocates of the free market system have little patience with Paretian arguments, basing their advocacy on the claims that a free market is essential for liberty and for making the best use of individuals' very varied knowledge, skills and innovative capacities. It must not be thought that defenders of the market necessarily rely on Paretian arguments – and it is perhaps increasingly common for them not to do so.)

ACTUAL OUTPUT

As noted in the last section but one, the constraints on the provision of goods and services may be even tighter than those set by resource supplies, technical knowledge, and so on – these latter constrain the maximum possible output but actual output may fall short of what is technically possible. It is not uncommon for there to be fairly widespread underutilization of both available labour and available plant and equipment. Hence the cause(s) of this shortfall of actual output relative to maximum output could be said to constrain the provision of goods and services. But what is that cause (are those causes)? Insufficient competition in product markets ('monopoly power'), lack of flexibility in labour markets ('trade union power'), inadequate levels of effective demand ('too little purchasing power'), and so on, have all been held to be (partially) responsible for the shortfall in output at one time or another, by one group of economic commentators or another. This is certainly not the place to assess the respective validity and significance of these different claims but it may still be noted that they lie behind different kinds of economic policy, for example, policies to increase competitiveness; policies to weaken trade union power; fiscal and monetary policies to influence the level of effective demand.

Even on confining our attention to the role of fiscal and monetary policy, we find that the last 60 years (since Keynes's *General Theory* of 1936) have been marked by considerable controversy and notable changes of emphasis concerning that role. Some even deny the existence of such a role, claiming that a government's fiscal and monetary policy can have little influence on aggregate output or levels of unemployment. Some others question whether a government can control the aggregate money supply, for example. But even those commentators who agree both that government can steer monetary and fiscal policies and that such policies have definite effects on the level of economic activity may nevertheless reach different judgements about the desirable mix of monetary expansion, tax reductions and increases in government expenditure, say, to increase effective demand. (Such policies all have implications for the national debt. These cannot be discussed here – but it may be noted in passing that the recent series of privatization exercises will inevitably come to an end, since no government can reduce its ownership of physical productive assets below zero.) What are some of the limits to a government's capacity to expand effective demand (given that it has such a capacity)? One concern is that expansionary policy may, at least under many circumstances, fuel inflation and some are then worried about the distributional implications for those living on fixed money incomes, or about the implied increase in aggregate taxes as those with rising money incomes move up into higher 'tax brackets'; others regard any costs of inflation as worth paying for the stimulation given to the overall level of economic activity. A more immediate limit may be found, of course, in those political views and attitudes which are resistant to increased government spending, on the broader grounds of political philosophy. No-one who fears the power of government and/or extols the virtues of individual initiative and self-reliance is likely to be a generally enthusiastic supporter of expansionary economic policy based on increased government expenditure; at most, such a policy will be reluctantly accepted as the least bad available alternative. However, an expansionary policy based on a reduction in taxes might be more congenial to such a person. The fact remains that rather general views about the political process can act as constraints to government policy and hence, perhaps, to actual output of goods and services.

More crudely political conflicts are also germane, since government taxation and expenditure policies will often have (more or less direct) distributional implications. An expansionary policy based on increasing the income taxes of a particular social stratum whilst also increasing (by a greater amount) government spending on, say, education, health or welfare which principally benefits a different social stratum is, quite obviously, a policy involving the possibility of conflict. There could be pronounced resistance to the payment of increased taxes and hence an electoral threat to the government. In such a case, the relevant attitudes of the taxpayers in question place a limit on government economic policy and hence, perhaps, on actual output of goods and services. Of course, it is not a foregone conclusion that the taxpayers will have the attitudes just referred to; they could be well-disposed to the payment of extra taxes if convinced that that payment corresponds to an expenditure policy of which they approve. This is highly relevant to the theme of the present book – as is the fact that these would-be generous taxpayers will not in fact be convinced that there is any clear link between their increased taxes and an increase in particular government expenditures which they would support. (As so often, goodwill – however necessary – is not enough; knowledge is also necessary.) A different kind of conflict of interest can arise around, for example, a government promoted expansionary policy of road-building or (in the past) of building nuclear power plants. Some will benefit directly from the newly created employment opportunities and others will benefit from, say, the reduction in their daily journey times when driving to and from work. But yet others may object strenuously to the environmental impact of the new road, the power station, or whatever it might be; such objections may be politically influential enough to place a limit on certain government expenditures and hence, perhaps, on the actual output of goods and services. There are, thus, various kinds of constraint on government economic policy even in a 'closed' economy; further constraints will emerge in the next section.

AN OPEN ECONOMY

We conclude our brief sketch of 'the economic constraints' by turning now to the case – the realistic case – of an economy involved in economic transactions with the rest of the world. These transactions will typically include exports and imports (not forgetting the slightly less obvious cases of tourism, shipping, insurance services, and so on), short term financial flows (in response perhaps to exchange rate changes or to temporary inter-country interest rate differentials) and longer term international investment flows (for example, when a Japanese company builds a factory in the UK). Like many other advanced capitalist economies, the UK economy is both very open to such international transactions and, indeed, increasingly open to them. This results partly from the requirements of such institutions as GATT and the European Union, partly from the UK government's wish to expose domestic markets to the pressures of international competitiveness and partly due to the sheer power and dynamism of the world-wide capitalist market system. Such economic 'openness' places significant limitations on the range of economic policy options genuinely open to a government – and this not only with respect to the 'effective demand' influencing policies mentioned in the previous section but with respect to economic policy more generally. If rapid domestic expansion causes imports to rise much faster than exports, as has often happened in the UK, the government may be forced to check the expansion. If the authorities seek to lower the domestic rate of interest, in order to stimulate domestic investment, this may provoke large outflows of financial capital. In fact almost any policy which changes taxation, or interest rates, or inflation, or the legal framework of economic activity, or productivity growth – or, indeed, which even provokes fears or expectations about such matters – may generate powerful and swift responses on the part of individuals and firms that are free to hold their financial assets in Britain *or elsewhere*, to set up factories in Britain *or elsewhere*, to purchase goods from Britain *or from elsewhere*, and so on. The UK government is often in no position to dictate to the individuals and firms in question what they will or will not do, or where they will conduct their business. Its choice of economic policies, therefore, has always to be made bearing in mind how all these 'international' economic agents are likely to respond and this inevitably restricts its room for manoeuvre very considerably. (The same is true for other governments as well, of course.) In conjunction with the greatly increased competition now faced by the 'older' economies of Europe and North America from the economies of South-East Asia and the Pacific Rim, these considerations have led some to claim that governments are now almost powerless to influence the direction of domestic economic development. Even if such claims are exaggerated (and they have inevitably been disputed), they are probably *only* exaggerated, it being true that the capacity of governments to determine economic activity levels and to direct the trends of economic change is itself severely constrained. This was already shown by the notorious 'Stop/Go' era of UK economic policy in which bursts of growth were repeatedly halted by balance of trade problems – and the constraints today may well be more severe.

Just as it would be futile to advocate social provision of goods and services which the economy is simply not capable of delivering – there really are economic constraints – so it would be futile to demand that government achieve outcomes which it is simply not capable of delivering – there really are constraints on government economic policy. To reject pessimism and defeatism may well be wise but to reject realism is plain foolish.

Part II
Self and Community – 'Doing Theology'

5 A Platform – Moral and Spiritual Values
Rupert Hoare

The brief which I was given for this chapter included the words: 'a moral and spiritual platform'. The word 'platform' conjures up in my mind an oil rig, or to be more specific, a mobile, floating platform, operating in a gale in the middle of the North Sea. It is operational, pumping oil, receiving helicopters, and providing a floating home; it is reasonably stable, but the sea is turbulent, and it could drift, or even capsize. At least life feels like that at the moment for most of us, and we are reliably told that we are going to have to live with that sort of turbulence for the foreseeable future. A turbulent world and the uncertainties that come with it are the context of the deliberations of this book. Such turbulence is probably not the best context in which to look for the enhancement of the moral qualities of civic responsibility and generosity. To change the metaphor slightly: such a turbulent context would move us rather towards 'battening down the hatches' and riding the storm out, as best we can, everyone for themselves. And I do wonder whether in fact such an attitude underlies much of the individualism which now pervades our society.

Theology is of course at home in such conditions. To the theologian turbulence speaks of creativity, faith and testing, judgement, and is to be expected if not necessarily welcomed. The image of the storm recurs in the New Testament, and the ark is itself a venerable symbol. But it is the attitudes with which such adverse and turbulent circumstances are met which make up much that is of central importance to theology, and where theology has a contribution to make.

Yet our secular world does not readily grant theology a hearing. Notwithstanding, I find myself taking seriously Bishop Peter Selby's advice that it is worth attending to what is going on in the Church, – and I imagine he would broaden that to any faith-community – on the grounds that what was happening there was likely to reflect and even to illuminate what people were wrestling with in the secular world around us.[1]

MEETING SOCIAL NEEDS WITHIN THE ANGLICAN COMMUNITY

I will therefore refer to five things going on now in the Church I serve:

1. Because of escalating costs, through diminishing inherited reserves and increasing numbers of retired clergy requiring pensions, a thoroughgoing restructuring of the Church's life is in progress; there will be fewer professional clergy, and a corresponding greater sharing in responsibility by lay people; at the theological level there is a rediscovery of the primacy of the whole people of God, that is, the whole community together, and every member's active part within it, and a corresponding uncertainty about clergy roles. There is recognition of the necessity of on-going training and education for both clergy and laity throughout life, and a constant demand for more opportunities to learn about the faith; people are learning by teaching; clergy are having to share and hand over power in order to enable others; anxiety and stress levels are high, but there is a real sense of a shared enterprise and calling, without much clarity at the moment about the form the Church will have taken in say ten years' time (humanly speaking).

2. At the same time, over the past eight years, the Church Urban Fund has managed to collect some £20 million, over and above the increases needed to keep the institution afloat. It has thus shown itself capable of shifting resources to points of greatest need, in order to use them to initiate and foster new work. The total sum raised is not huge, but the exercise itself demonstrates very clearly that people can be mobilized to raise funds for disadvantaged groups within society; Church of England members have shown a sense of social and civic responsibility, and acted with generosity, in respect of people outside their own particular community. It is a late 20th century example of what theology has known as apostolic faith at work, stretching back through the Church's history to the early days when St Paul made his famous collection for the church in Jerusalem. This was not so much a case of generosity in the sense of Humean benevolence,[2] but rather of corporate solidarity within the Church through which specific needs in certain parts of the community could be addressed. Such action was seen in terms of justice rather than beneficence. But it was possible because of individual members'

generosity. It parallels links made between materially richer and poorer dioceses and parishes, in which each side discovers it has gifts with which to enrich the other.

3. The third thing to which attention should be drawn is the movement called Community Organizing, which amongst many other projects, and not without criticism, the Church Urban Fund is supporting. Here is a method of empowering disadvantaged and discouraged people particularly in industrial and post-industrial societies to organize themselves and to begin to take control of their lives, in the face of today's otherwise overwhelming principalities and powers. Community Organizing works with faith communities, Sikh, Hindu, Muslim, Buddhist, Jewish, as well as Christian, because of the value systems such communities enshrine. Well established in the USA, it is now taking root in this country (in a British form), in Bristol and Merseyside, and beginning its work in the Black Country and East London. It works by identifying and utilizing common or mutual self-interest rather than by generosity in material matters, though it certainly requires generosity in terms of time and effort and commitment by all involved with it. I will return to the contrasting values of self-interest and generosity it highlights later in this chapter.

4. Mention should also be made of the movement within the European churches that goes under the banner: Justice, Peace and the Integrity of Creation. Increasingly within the European churches, it is being seen that questions to do with the better ordering of society can no longer be addressed independently of the need to preserve, renew, reclaim, and sanctify the earth as such. (I write from within the Black Country, where areas of waste land are so polluted that they have to be fenced off out of bounds to human beings.) Pollution affects other people besides the polluter, and thus shows us the inadequacy of individualism on its own.

5. The fifth development which I see as informing the life and thinking of the Church has to do with the way we see community life dynamically, involving all age groups in interaction with one another and human life as such a process, movement, growth, from the cradle to the grave. The emphasis is no longer so much on specific and discrete age groups, as on moving from one period of life to another. So, for example, the focus now is on ageing, not old age; on making the transition from childhood to teenager to

young adult, and so on, rather than on any of these as separate periods of life complete in themselves.

SOCIAL NEEDS WITHIN THE WIDER COMMUNITY

I come now to questions of definition relating to the book's theme: 'meeting the escalating costs of social needs'. I take it we must use 'social needs' in a very wide sense, so that it includes needs arising from unemployment, poverty, homelessness, to mention three major negatives of our experience, as well as the vast positive public exercise of education. To these has to be added the formidable area of crime, crime prevention and punishment. And as far as health is concerned, there are particular questions relating to escalating costs of particular advanced forms of treatment.

There is, however, also a narrower definition of 'social needs' which has become important since the move to replace hospitalized care as far as possible by care in the community. Sir Roy Griffith's Report,[3] and the subsequent White Paper *Caring for People* (1989) distinguished between health care (and needs) and social care (and needs). The former is the responsibility of the health authorities and the latter, following Sir Roy's recommendations, are the responsibilities of the social services departments of the local authorities. In this context, social needs are those needs of people (known in our market orientated world as consumers or even customers, or service users)[4] who require care in the community over and beyond the strictly medical (which would relate to physical or mental disease, or injury, or handicap – to use a poor term).

Whether the arrangements are working out in practice is another matter; the *Report of the Commission on Social Justice*, described 'the condition of community care' perhaps predictably, as 'a nightmare'.[5]

Most would agree that the thoroughgoing introduction of the project 'Care in the Community' is a step in the right direction although it is also becoming clear that society is going to have to maintain greater secure hospital provision than was anticipated at first. 'Care in the Community' consciously enlists the support of other agencies in the community; it recognizes more fully the crucial role of the informal carers in the total provision of care; and it moves the local authority into an enabling role, and away from its predominance as provider of services, upon which people become too dependent. But Care in the Community also explicitly recognizes the reality and importance of community as such, even if it operates with a variety of understandings of the term community, which I will explore below. It suggests civic responsibility and generosity may be qualities which a society such as ours is ready to affirm to some degree, even with its highly individualized view of human life.

At the same time the new arrangements and its underlying philosophy moves the community into new and uncharted waters of collaboration and partnership which are unstable in themselves, with a lack of clarity about accountability, or their relation to the elected representatives of the local community as focused in the municipal council. 'Social partnerships' as they are called are now the order of the day in England and may be elsewhere in the UK. The one I know best is the Dudley Partnership Board, which brings together the Training and Enterprise Council, the local authority (officers and elected representatives), the health authority, representatives from industry, the voluntary sector including ethnic minority groups, and the Church. The Board is very much to do with meeting social needs in Dudley, in the widest sense, and has found itself playing a key strategic role in relation to central government's single regeneration budget in the borough. Accountability to the local community is secured first by being tied in to the local authority (but with the authority as only one player amongst others) and by committing itself to ongoing, thoroughgoing processes of consultation. It does not directly focus on the escalation of social costs, but it is directly concerned with addressing social needs effectively and thus improving the quality of life of all who live in the borough.

I have focused so far on social needs in the local community of borough, or county, or town. But our starting point does not specify the community we are to attend to; it could be the borough; it could be the nation-state, or the so called developed countries of the western world, or of the European Union, or further afield. We will need to be clear which community we are primarily talking about. In theological terms (and, of course, industrialists conscious of the growth of the industrial might of the Pacific Rim would agree, as would organizations such as Christian Aid working with the poorest countries of the world) I would argue that while it might be quite proper for us to focus on, for instance, the nation-states of the European Union, we cannot cut ourselves off from the rest of the world when thinking of the costs of social needs. The overseas aid programmes should not, from the theological standpoint, be considered as a separate afterthought to the meeting of social costs at home.[6]

However we handle that problem, it may be useful for us to identify elements in the social needs of the countries within the European Union which may be peculiarly significant to that particular country. For instance, in Germany there are significant social costs relating to reunification and also to the extensive immigration from the East into Germany, in addition to those the rest of us face in relation to asylum and immigration (sadly seen increasingly as a problem of cost and not a wealth-creating opportunity).

But in addition to those areas of life I have already referred to, more endemic to the countries of the European Union, will be social needs springing from violence, particularly violence in the home, and abuse of various kinds, and disabilities incurred through accident or injury, or bad practices at work. To these must be added the costs of the penal system, the prison service, probation officers, and so on; as in education and health care, the UK government is trying to contain costs by the introduction of devolved budgeting to individual establishments, with the threat of privatization where expenditure targets are not attained.

Yet the biggest growth area of social needs and costs must lie in the increasing number of elderly, and very elderly people, that will need care and support in the community. In 1996 there are over one million people in the UK over 85 years old, and that number will continue to rise. At the same time the numbers of people able to take on the crucially important role of informal carer (nearly seven million at the moment) will not keep pace with the increase of those needing care.[7]

Hence the problem: costs of social care are escalating and likely to go on doing so. Care in the community is not, in itself, a cheaper option, nor should it be adopted as policy because it could enable the state to cut its own provision of care while hoping others will pick it up.

LIMITED RESOURCES – PRIORITIES OF ALLOCATION

Just as there are many different parts to the overall provision of welfare, and many different spheres of the social life of this nation (and other developed countries of the West) which are each of them adding to the total costs of that provision for very differing reasons and causes, so there may be a number of different ways of meeting these escalating costs, perhaps unrelated to each other. Some social needs will be more easily recognized to be the responsibility of the state than others; some will appeal more easily to a sense of civic generosity than others (always bearing in mind the danger that civic generosity could deteriorate into patronizing charity which does nothing for social cohesion). The context is the realization that escalating costs cannot simply be absorbed indefinitely. The political will is not there, at least at the moment, in either of the two large political parties, to address the problem by raising direct taxation. And this brings me to a theological point. Theistic belief places infinite resources in God, and not in us, either collectively or individually, nor in planet earth on which we live. In the UK, Mrs Thatcher helped us see that the state did not own a bottomless well of resources on which we could draw. But I do not think that cured us of the illusion that infinite resources were there to be grasped; we simply looked in a different direction, and located their source in the market, in individual or corporate enterprises. 'The sky's the limit' was the slogan we lived by in the 1980s.

Of course, we can 'add value' – by our own efforts, and by working together with others. We can even 'create wealth', I think, thereby adding, by our work, to the total sum of wealth in the world. But not infinitely, and not indefinitely. Resources are used up; the earth's future is itself limited; one day it will either have returned to the sun, or otherwise come to an end. Only God is infinite; and God remains the boundary of our striving; we remain finite creatures, with finite capacities, who have to live within our finitude. The story of the Tower of Babel still applies.

However immanent God may be within the human world, I believe God is also beyond it and remains so. Contrast this with Hegel in that extraordinary work of his, *The Phenomenology of the Spirit*,[8] where he articulated the view that, whether individually or corporately, the divine spirit was to be found incarnate within a developing world; no longer should we look beyond; the spirit was to be realized ever more fully within. In any external objective sense beyond us, the God 'out there' who had, to use Hegel's language, depressed our spirit and produced an unhappy consciousness within us, was dead. Particular interpretations of Hegel's thought have led to a mind set that believes all boundaries can and should be overcome, and that the infinite spirit can be definitively realized amongst us.

In less exalted terms Jonathan Boswell in his recent book *Community and the Economy* makes a similar point about the spirit of indefinite enlargement that pervades both individualist *and* collectivist ideologies that are so pervasive in our culture: 'A further and ubiquitous idea tends to be (usually implicitly) subscribed to by believers in all of the above despite their many conflicts. This is the notion of an indefinite enlargement, acquisition or conquest of resources, whether in terms of inventing new things, exploring space, or acquiring more individual or collective wealth'.[9]

In contrast he insists on a set of principles of the primacy of community as a higher value, with which all notions of indefinite enlargement as the goal of human activity are really irreconcilable. What matters supremely for the tradition he represents is the fullest possible flowering of persons in relation to other persons; he speaks of it as the principle of associativeness in liberty. Where that becomes primary, all else including the market becomes subordinate to it.

COMMUNITY AND RESPONSIBILITY

Boswell's work is one example of the way in which, at the very end of the 20th century, various notions of community are again coming into focus; but community is conceived of in very differing ways, and I would like now to mention five of them, in a scale of one to five, measured by the thinness of the sense of community implied by each.

Sir Roy Griffiths displayed a fairly thin notion of community in the Report to which I referred above, outdone only by the subsequent White Paper, *Caring for People*.[10] In the White Paper's view the value of community lies in its providing the environment in which individuals can continue 'independent living' (2.12); each person has his, or her, front door, behind which (one assumes) they can continue to be in touch with family or friends. Living in the community is the highest guarantee of independence and freedom, which are without doubt, in this view, the highest values of human life. Care in the Community (to quote Sir Roy Griffiths, himself quoting a Department of Heath and Social Security statement) means to 'enable an individual to remain in his, or her, home wherever possible, rather than being cared for in a hospital or residential home'.[11] There are, of course, in this view, groups and other individuals and volunteers (including advocates) whose availability is, however, taken for granted.

Moving to a somewhat fuller, though still fairly thin view of community you come to the *Report of the Commission on Social Justice*. Individual choice and personal autonomy remain key objectives. 'The welfare state must be shaped by the changing nature of people's lives, rather than people's lives being shaped to fit in with the welfare state; the welfare state must be personalized and flexible, designed to promote individual choice and personal autonomy.'[12] However the Report clearly recognizes the social or communitarian aspect of the community or society as a resource which is, or should be, more than the sum of its parts. Its fourth proposition on social justice is 'to reconstruct the social wealth of our country. Social institutions, from the family to local government, must be nurtured to provide a dependable social environment in which people can lead their lives. Renewal must come from the bottom up, as well as from the top down.'[13]

Then comes Community Organizing, to which I have referred above. It works primarily with disadvantaged and marginalized groups of people, seeking to enable them to move themselves from dispersed and powerless fragmentation to vital and powerful community action; from a thin and vacuous experience and concept of community to one which is extremely strong. It therefore works with a dynamic, process view of community. Religious beliefs implying that change for the better is possible, that strong community can come into being, and injustices be overcome, lie at the heart of its operation, working as it does with faith communities. It does so by building a community where there was none in an organized, active, sense, out of one-to-one encounters in which people are brought to identify their own self-interest, and to see how it fits the self-interest of the others in the group, in the self-interest of the whole. It focuses on specific matters which are debilitating people's lives. It is 'up-front' in confronting those who wield power, its major instrument of effecting change being the organized assembly of massed groups of people, who by their disciplined organization change the situation so that it becomes a matter of the self-interest of the powerful to attend their meetings, normally held on disadvantaged people's own home territory. In the process they create a strong sense of community, and develop active and direct forms of citizenship (amongst groups where the 'democratic deficit' is normally very apparent). The espousal of self-interest, in such a setting, has a very different value and feel to it than it does where it is all too inward looking and evident in more affluent areas.

I am not sure that Community Organizing would want to talk about generosity in the public, civic, world at all. They might regard it as a virtue that had its place in the home only. On the other hand, they are certainly concerned with the revitalization of a sense of citizenship within society, but place a high value on the robust pursuit of self-interest within that civic world. To my mind the citizen, as statesman, in the polling booth, has to ask what is in the interests of the community as a whole, and has to subordinate his, or her, own self-interest to that wider interest. But within the life of disadvantaged sections of the community civic responsibility can rightly demand the robust pursuit of that sectional interest for the righting of evident injustices. Not to assert the sectional interest is to succumb to a state of docility in such circumstances which simply colludes with and reinforces the status quo.

The fourth view of community I have referred to above; it is expressed by Jonathan Boswell and sees, to use his language, 'fraternity, association in liberty, and participation' as the essential values or principles that do (or should) make up community wherein people find themselves and their own personhood in relation to others. So all social groupings, and social events, are valuable in themselves as fostering persons-in-relation-to-one-another, rather than in some external end which the group is seeking to achieve.[14]

But locating value in the relation between people puts this view in direct contradiction to that of much of the thinking of the Right in recent years: contrast John Gray in his book *The Moral Foundations of Market Institutions*: 'it is in any case bizarre to suppose that a purely relational property could have intrinsic value'.

Nothing should distract us 'from concern with what alone matters in political morality – namely the well-being of individuals'.[15] Boswell's view is also in direct dispute with the White Paper referred to above which insists in focusing on 'objective setting and monitoring towards outcomes and away from process'.[16] But he would also appear to be in dispute with Community Organizing; for in his view friendship is a crucial quality of community that builds persons-in-relation. For Community Organizing, such qualities as loyalty and friendship belong in a private sphere, to be found in the home. And the home is sharply contrasted with the public sphere of political action and citizenship, concerned with the establishment of accountable contracts, and the exercise of power – reference to which I have not yet found in Boswell's book.

I now want to contrast all those four views with what I see as central to Christian theology's understanding of community and the individual and the relation between them. First, it takes a process view, witnessing to a movement from the here and now to what is to come. It takes very seriously division and alienation and fragmentation in human life but knows that this can move into a greater unity and harmony. (I admit but leave on one side for the moment we have a bad record in allowing this movement into harmonious community to come to fruition.)

It recognizes very clearly that such healing, or movement into community, is costly and difficult. Indeed the paradigm it works with is of the redeemer losing his place in family and community, losing his friends and support group, until he was totally isolated and alone. Individuality pushed to its ultimate, in the passion and death of Christ. You cannot get thinner than that: community concentrated down into one dead individual. But the Christians came to see this total stripping bare of the Christ of all power, all human support, to the point of the cry of dereliction from the cross, as despite all appearances being done representatively for the rest of us, and as in fact handing on and handing over power sufficient to change the world – as it in fact did. In his aloneness, Christ came to be seen as our advocate; thus at the heart of Christian theology are the notions of the representation of us all by the one man, and the exercise of power as involving a letting go and handing on to others, at extreme cost to himself. The Christians came to see this as 'for our sake', and accepted him as representative in the fullest possible sense.

We have not recently done justice to the centrality of this notion of representation (although Dorothee Sölle wrote a famous book on the subject some years ago).[17] But I believe we can take this relationship, one person standing for and speaking for another, or for groups of others, in such a way that it does not disenfranchise or disempower them but precisely the opposite, as a paradigm for our exploration of the much fuller democratic community which we are in need of. The advocacy (and advocacy was recognized by Sir Roy as a legitimate role for volunteers) that is at the heart of the Christian faith shows us a way of refinding the solidarity of one human being for another which our current individualism makes impossibly hard for us. Witness much modern drama: for instance Beckett's *Waiting For Godot*.[18]

This individualism is very deep seated (Nietzsche understood that and the pain of it) and I doubt whether Boswell's communitarianism can supersede it. But when one person continues to hold his, or her, ground to the point of death, and knows themselves to be doing that 'for' someone else, or for others, and those others come themselves to see it to be so, that it was indeed done for them, then the isolation of individualism is overcome and a new way into community comes into being. Here is civic generosity and social responsibility raised to an altogether higher level – and Christ's is by no means the only human example of it, but (from the Christian point of view) his selfless generosity is also the supreme example of the generosity of God himself. And the other side of Christ's action which differentiates it from a paternalistic benevolence, also needs to be brought to expression: it is one of the great themes of, for instance, Augustine's City of God: the power of God known in the humility of God, which empowers others and overcomes what he saw as being of the essence of sin, namely, being dominated by the desire to dominate.[19] In other words, the desire to take hold of, to establish and hold on to power, rather than to share it and pass it on. The desire to hold on to power by individuals is of course in the end illusory; it overlooks the centrality of ongoing process in human life; in the end, one has to let it go, as one ages and dies. Christian theology (though not often Christian history) makes the handing on of power a matter of celebration and calls it victory. So it is.

And it is also the basis of community, which is itself a developing process. Power sharing in some form or another and the handing on of power, are essential. In a less overtly theological setting, Aristotle quietly makes a similar point in *The Politics*, when he repeatedly says that leaders have to take it in turns to hold power and lead. One has to give way to another.[20] Where that principle is not accepted (or when community is seen in static terms) all collaboration becomes inherently unstable, for underlying it are inevitably hidden rivalries and an unspoken jockeying for power. Moreover professionals can only release power in those around them, when they are prepared to share it themselves. This requires honesty and humility but at the same time – and this is the sticking point – a recognition of one's own power and responsibility to those one represents. That has to be worked out in terms of practical contracts, agreements, ways of working, which accept and use the exercise of power for a given time, but within an underlying covenant between those working together for a common good, which knows that power has eventually to be shared and then handed on.

FROM THEOLOGY TO PRAXIS

Theology works with processes of change, not to speak of turbulence; it knows of a present which needs superseding, a new beginning which is breaking in on the present, giving us glimpses of what is to come; it gives us imaginative pictures or visions of the future, but then directs us back to the present, without forgetting what could be. It directs us to 'become what we, in the purposes of God, already are'. It also speaks of that as vocation, and relates vocation first of all to the community as a whole, and only secondarily within that context to individuals, and last of all to those to be ordained, though clearly ecclesiastical practice has largely confused that priority.

At the moment that sense of being called to contribute to a greater good is scarcely there as a description of how people normally feel about themselves within the society of which they are a part. But it is far from being completely absent. The Housing Association movement is run, I believe, by 25,000 volunteers. Volunteers abound in the life of this country, not least among the younger generation. However it is so often a case of searching round for volunteers, and of the same people being ready to volunteer for ever further voluntary tasks. There is no pervasive concept of voluntary national service on the part of each citizen, as fundamental a dimension of active life as is casting one's vote in the secret ballot of an election or readiness to do jury duty when requested (and I admit a substantial minority don't bother to vote).

In the short term at least, an overtly religious motivation seems unlikely to arise in the hearts and minds and wills of many of the population of our western societies. But I hope that Care in the Community may be a starting point for reawakening a much broader vision of what the community as a whole, whether of the nation, or of a borough, or village, or of the European Union might be able to become. In that sense the publication of Sir Roy Griffiths' Report (with its explicit recognition of the essential place of the local authority's social services departments) was a turning point from the individualism of the 1980s to the more communitarian perspective that is beginning to re-emerge in the UK in the 1990s.

Care in the Community is about shared health, and health is something which inspires people into action. Health practitioners are beginning to see their roles in more communitarian, disease preventative, health promotional terms, involving community, working together. Indeed participation in community, in decision making, is now recognized as a basic human need.[21]

All sorts of experiments to foster such participation in community are now under way within the world of health authorities, general practitioners, and so on. This work has been drawn to my attention in the Borough of Dudley by the work of a general practitioner, Dr Malcolm Rigler. Here is someone who, while continuing his normal general practice work, has been instrumental in bringing the wider community together to promote health. He does so, for instance, through art, by making available computerized information, by bringing together social services, chemists, librarians, above all schools, and churches; in order, one might say, to decrease his workload in treating sickness, by fostering health in the community. He uses artists, to help those who come to his surgery feel good as they come into the waiting room. He describes one patient who walked into the waiting room, surrounded as it is by posters, paintings, fish tanks, plants, and people doing all sorts of things together, feeling, as she put it, as if she had 'died and gone to heaven'. Perhaps the ultimacy of this reaction was not exactly what he intended, but the surprise and delight the woman felt was in itself a tonic for her. A very different response to the one of anxiety he had perceived so often in his patients, and he honestly says, in himself, prescribing tranquillisers for them and for himself, as he sought to cope with his own anxiety about them. The opening up of his professional work to his patients, encouraging their learning so that they could take control of their own health, by giving them the information they require and receiving from them their own stories so that these could be shared one with another, and the expressing of health through the work of art and artists, all these things have the potential to turn a fragmented and lonely community into one where people are beginning to take hold of their own lives and create a healthy community of which it is good to be an active member. But to embark upon such a process involves a sharing of power. Speaking of the use of art in medicine, David Hart, literature officer, West Midlands Arts, wrote: 'The crossing of professional boundaries is not easy. It is one of the vital things to learn from the experience so far that we "professionals" have very little time or brain space or emotional energy to let go a little of our role and our expertise and our familiar strategies, in favour of co-operating in listening to each other and to other people. The participation of new patterns in the relationship, the articulation of what has been constrained or taboo, the allowing of the rough edges of experience to show, these are necessary in building a new kind of community. They are also, of course, the essentials of artistic work.'[22]

In conclusion, I would return to the theme of the community as a whole. Care in the Community as a programme goes a step in the right direction. It orientates back into the community, but it does so with a very impoverished notion of citizenship (indeed for much of the government's publications 'citizen' seems confused with 'consumer'). And Care in the Community still gets things the wrong way round; it starts with the professional social workers focusing on needs. It starts with the professionals then goes to those with needs, seen as customers or consumers, then to their carers, then to the private sector, then to the volunteers.

We have got to start the other way about, if we are ever to become what, in embryo we already are, an active democratic and healthy community. Start with children, who will become citizens, who will then become carers, and will end up, if all goes well, as cared for again by others. As citizens, they are also volunteers, sharing in the widest sense in promoting the health of the community, acting as advocates for the disadvantaged; they are also decision makers, as electors, representing others, and represented by others; for a good deal of time they will be wealth creators, sometimes in paid employment, sometimes not. All will be members of an interwoven network of interdependent community, constantly learning from one another in an ongoing educational process. In time they will themselves be informal carers of others requiring the support of the professionals, whose place, as in the life of the Church, is last not first among them, as those who serve. In time they will come to need care themselves before they die. So the order is: citizen, informal carer, volunteer, the cared for, and only then professional carer. In this sort of rediscovered community lies health, and with it an increased sense of civic generosity and responsibility, which could even produce the will to meet the escalation of social costs.

NOTES AND REFERENCES

1. The remark was made in a private meeting which the Bishop addressed.
2. See for example, *David Hume Enquiries*, 139ff., 1777 edition.
3. *Community Care: Agenda for Action*, 1988.
4. *Caring For People: Community Care in the Next Decade and Beyond*, HMSO, 1989, 3.4.3; 3.1.4.
5. Report of the Commission on Social Justice, *Social Justice: Strategies for National Renewal*, Vintage 1994, p.295.
6. Cf. Report of the Commission on Social Justice, p.22.
7. Report of the Board for Social Responsibility, *Ageing*, 1990, p.16 following.
8. Hegel, *Phenomenology of Spirit*, 1807.
9. J. Boswell, *Community and the Economy, The Theory of Public Cooperation*, Routledge, 1990, p.32.
10. *Caring For People*.
11. *Community Care: Agenda for Action*, 3:6.
12. Report of the Commission on Social Justice, p.223.
13. Ibid, p.21.
14. Boswell, op. cit, especially Chapter 3.
15. John Gray, *The Moral Foundations of Market Institutions*, IEA Health and Welfare Unit, 1992, p.35.

16. *Caring For People*, 6.2.
17. Dorothee Sölle, *Christ The Representative*, English Translation, SCM, 1967.
18. Samuel Beckett, *Waiting For Godot*, 1952.
19. Augustine, *City of God*, I Preface: III 14; XIX 15.
20. Aristotle, *The Politics*, for example Vi 2 1317 b2.
21. J. MacDonald, *A Historical and International Perspective*: Occasional Paper 64 of the Royal College of Practitioners, Community Participation in Primary Care 1994.
22. *Arts in Primary Heath Care*, 1994.

6 Jewish Tradition and Ethos of Generosity
Meir Tamari

INTRODUCTION

The issue of escalating social costs has occupied almost all the economies of the free world since the early 1980s. These costs began to absorb an ever-increasing percentage of the national budget, leading to increased tax, to a feeling of having to fund fraud and wastage, and disagreement with the funding of lazy or addicted people living on welfare. Much of the impetus for the Thatcherite, Reagan and the other right-wing collected personalities of the 1980s and early 1990s can be seen as an attempt by the citizens to rid themselves of these rising costs.

It is true that welfare costs express themselves in financial terms and affect fiscal policy, they affect development, and the cost of government. At first glance it seems therefore plausible to see welfare costs as an economic problem. In effect, however, despite these economic aspects the basis of the escalating costs lies in cultural, religious, or other ideological factors. The escalation of such costs flows from the greed both of the recipient and of those funding the costs. If this is indeed the case, then any solution to such costs must be sought in ways and means of curbing this greed. The issue is not one of limited economic resources. If that were the real issue it would imply that social responsibility and welfare would be non-existent in poor underdeveloped countries and would be maximized in the wealthier economies. There does not seem to be any historical proof that this is true. Primitive and underdeveloped economies have been able, very often, to provide for the old, for the sick, for the inefficient members of society, albeit at a level commensurate with existing economic activity. On the other hand, historically, many wealthy societies do not seem able to cope with the needs of these same groups. There is no basis therefore to assume that economic growth alone will solve welfare issues, unless accompanied by restraints on greed.

SOCIAL OBLIGATIONS

Judaism teaches that all wealth originates from G-d, who created the world in such a way that human needs would be satisfied not by miraculous happenings, but through normal every day economic activity. This wealth, provided by G-d, is part of a greater Divine plan which provides the needs of all creatures in G-d's world.[1] The wealth which flows from this Divine source is meant to satisfy not only the needs of the possessor, but also to provide for the needs of those less fortunate or weaker members of society.[2] This is G-d's method, as it were, to channel wealth to those sectors. So, individuals and society have an obligation to provide some of their wealth in order to solve social issues. This may take two forms, one of them philanthropy, flowing from a personal obligation to dispense charity; and the other from an enforced transfer of wealth from one person to another through taxation. Judaism insists on both forms. Philanthropy alone, whether of individuals or of corporations, often tends to remain a pious wish, while legislation alone can often be merciless, or even not viable without a spiritual consensus. Both these obligations devolve not only on Jews operating within a Jewish society and relevant to other Jews, but also to non-Jews. It is considered that the obligation to give charity in both these forms is part of the Noachide obligation included under the parameter of establishing a just society. This Noachide obligation is part of the Seven Noachide Laws, obligatory in Judaism on all men. The classic example of non-Jewish society's transgressing this, is the story of Sodom which was overturned *inter alia* for its inability to share its wealth with the less fortunate. It should be noted that the Biblical story stresses the wealth of Sodom.

Philanthropy has the merit that it involves the giver in the social, spiritual and physical problems of the recipient. It is, however, dependent on generosity and this requires one to break one's greed and in Jewish thought this is something that all people are not always able to achieve. Therefore, in accordance with the general Jewish tradition and legislating patterns of behaviour both in ritual and in social issues, there is a parallel obligation enforceable by the rabbinic courts on society to levy taxes for social purposes.[3] These taxes are not theft by the state, nor are they immoral, but constitute a religious obligation placed on man to support and assist others.

THE SCOPE OF OBLIGATION

There is no concept in Judaism of deserving and undeserving poor. The reason for the person's needing assistance is usually irrelevant, so that even people who are in need of social assistance through faults of their own, are entitled to such assistance. Two examples will suffice. A person who ended up in a debtor jail for borrowing money which he was unable or unwilling to pay back, was entitled to be redeemed by the community even though his imprisonment was due to his own fault. This was limited to a second and a third time. After that there is no more communal assistance, unless the imprisonment involved a danger to life, in which case the number of times redeemed is irrelevant because of the obligation to save lives.[4] The second example is the more recent responsum that a person who is addicted must be provided with food so that he does not die of hunger, and we are obligated to prevent people from dying.[5]

This social obligation is not restricted to monetary assistance. Sometimes the individual giver does not have money to provide the assistance since any individual's financial assets are limited. At the same time, one is commanded to give whatever assistance possible. This may take the form of good advice, of providing a job, or of lending money to somebody in order to start up their own business. Indeed, this is regarded as the highest form of charity, since it breaks the poverty cycle, prevents people from becoming welfare recipients, and enables them to escape the welfare system.[6] It is interesting to note, that in many countries government assistance in helping people to establish their own businesses has been a major form of combating unemployment. The individual has a further obligation. In those cases where assistance is needed, one is obligated to draw the attention of the authorities, municipal or state, to the recipient's situation so that they may provide the needed welfare.[7] Bearing in mind that the highest form of charity is the provision of a job, this would seem to place Judaism in favour of macro-economic policies aimed at providing full employment or preventing unemployment.

To raise tax for purposes of charity implies an understanding that society has an obligation to provide for the food, clothing, housing, and so on, for those unable to provide for themselves. Under the tax system envisaged by Judaism, taxes have to be approved by majority vote, whereby the majority could force the minority to participate in funding of communal needs. There are, however, areas in which the minority can force the majority to fund those needs specified by Jewish law, thus overruling the will of the majority. Welfare and charity is one such area. *This means that a majority cannot decide that it is going to do away with the provision of social services and charity in order not to overburden its tax structure and rather make these a function of individual philanthropy.* So too, price control, rationing, subsidies, the provision of interest-free loans for the sake of establishing businesses, are all additional aspects of the community's obligation to assist the weaker members of society.

Over and above all these obligations, it must always be borne in mind that Judaism talks of doing charity rather than giving it. The whole system requires kindness and love, not only assistance.

It must be pointed out that in Jewish thought there is no such thing as a poor community.[8] The scene of the wealthiest nations in history being unable at present, to fund the needs of the relatively small section of the population would not be duplicated.

Parallel to the wide network of communal and individual assistance, seen by Judaism as the obligation of those who possess wealth, it is important to stress that there is also a parallel constraint flowing from justice. Justice demands that the poor, weak, inefficient members of society are only to be helped, not to be made rich or equal, through a fiscal transfer of wealth.[9]

So, there is no obligation in Judaism to provide for an average standard of living, however this may be defined. It would seem therefore, that Judaism, as part of its brake on escalating social costs could not accept the usual, modern definition of poverty which corresponds to some average standard of living. All assistance provided is minimal, aimed at keeping the recipients alive and functioning. This minimum would have to be considered in the light of medical knowledge regarding the amount of calories a person requires, social knowledge about the amount of space a person needs, the same would apply to clothing; and all of this would be geared to a minimum standard. So too the question of subsidies, in whatever form, would seem to have to be geared to the basic needs of recipients who cannot provide these for themselves, rather than something allocated to the whole society. If subsidies to transport, to basic foodstuffs, and so on, are given to all people, then this is a subsidy also for those who are not entitled to any subsidy. So Judaism would favour the targeted allocation of funds to satisfy the needs of the individual. All of these restrictions would cut down waste and reduce the cost of welfare to the economy.

Naturally, this would involve the question of means tests. Judaism has gone on record in support of such means tests as long as they do not refer to basic foodstuffs, since by the time the society has decided who is eligible the individual might have died.[10] All other needs can be allocated on the basis of means tests.

RECIPROCITY: THE RECIPIENT

As pointed out at the beginning of this chapter, not only is it greed on the part of the wealthy which seeks to reduce welfare costs, but there is also greed on the part of the recipients which seeks to increase such costs. The idea that society does not have the obligation to make the needy wealthy or even average is a major contributor to maintaining welfare costs at a reasonable level. Furthermore, Judaism has always seen shame attached to receiving assistance. This does not mean that the recipient may be shamed or discriminated against, or in any way degraded. Care is taken to make the allocation of charity as comfortable and as easy as possible, even while stressing that it is charity. The law expressed in the Bible of leaving the corner of a field is an example of this.[11] Spaces of special time were fixed by Jewish law for the aged, the young and the women with children to cater for the needs and weaknesses of these groups.[12] Despite this consideration, the poor were obligated to come and harvest their own corner and it was obvious to all, that this gleaning, and other agricultural gifts to the poor, were gifts in the full sense of the word and not something that had been earned simply by being poor. The Rabbis said a man should flay a carcass in public, a demeaning form of work, rather than accept charity.[13]

Alongside this shame, which is in effect the price that the recipient pays for the assistance given by society, there is a further consideration that sees theft from the public as a much greater sin than theft from private individuals.[14] A person who steals or defrauds somebody else can achieve atonement by giving back that which he had stolen and expressing his sorrow. However, one who steals from the public purse or from a community, or from society, has no way to return the theft as there is no way to find the individual members from whom they have stolen. So, there is a terrible spiritual damage done to one who cannot do penance for what was done. It is true that second grade repentance, or alternative forms of repentance are suggested by the Rabbis, but these are all inferior to the real penance which involves giving back that which had been stolen to the person from whom it had been stolen.[15] This is Judaism's most powerful educational tool to prevent abuse of the welfare system.

Maimonides writes that just as it is an obligation to give charity to those who need it, so it is forbidden to give to those who do not need it. Conversely, those who falsely pretended that they had problems, or pretended that they were entitled to welfare, were considered robbers in the full sense of the word. Furthermore, there is a type of fraud consistent in taking benefits which are intended for individual aid and then selling them or allowing others to use them. This is also considered a form of theft in all its spiritual and religious connotations.[16]

In all these different ways, Judaism militates against the creation of a welfare mentality that makes 'living on welfare' a viable alternative to breaking the poverty cycle by the efforts of the recipients themselves.

JUSTICE AND MERCY

The Jewish balance between the mercy expected from society and the demands of justice placed on the recipient, may be seen by the application of Jewish law to the case of somebody who could not pay back the interest-free loan given to them. The Bible enjoins the giving of such a loan but, at the same time, obligates the recipient not to waste the money given, nor to delay payment. In the case of one who was unable to pay it back, the lender was first asked as an act of charity to waive his rights. But if he did not do this, the full force of the law was brought to bear on the debtor to pay back the debt. This may seem stern. But consider that the lender, in fulfilment of his obligation, has lent money which enabled somebody to set up a business or to break the poverty cycle, and so on, but does not wish to give it as a gift; hence the moral obligation on the debtor to pay it back. In this case the debtor's assets would be sold but leaving him once again with the minimum needs of food and clothing and a pallet to sleep on, his essential religious requirements, but no more. When the debtor becomes poor, society is obligated to assist him, as we have explained above, removing the obligation of the individual creditor, who, however, as a member of society, will of course participate in the social costs.[17]

CONCLUSION

A great thrust of moral education is essential in order to assure, in today's conditions, the provision of a viable safety net for the poor, weak, aged, sick or addicted. This type of education must be designed to convince firms and individuals of the necessity for philanthropy, but also for taxation and the adoption of macro-economic policies to further welfare. If such an education is not provided as a matter of urgency, natural egoism and selfishness will continue to militate against a solution resolving the welfare problem.

However, a similar moral education is needed to prevent the development of the welfare mentality and the demand by recipients for average standards of living which cause welfare costs to escalate.

Without such a process of moral education it will be impossible to prevent the escalation of welfare costs to a level which cannot be viable for most societies, or to prevent vociferous opposition to the type of economic policies geared to providing welfare; an opposition that will lead to drastic reductions in welfare funding.

PRACTICAL SUGGESTIONS

There are practical measures that flow from this moral education.

- Budget cuts that threaten the basic requirements of the weaker members of society are not acceptable. Fiscal policy may require cuts in other government expenditures and/or an increase in taxation.
- Firms and individuals are to be encouraged in philanthropic ventures, perhaps even through provision of public sector matching funds or tax benefits.
- Public funding should be provided for making interest-free loans for establishing new businesses by the unemployed or by displaced entrepreneurs.
- Negative income tax would be preferable to subsidies.
- Welfare fraud needs to be regarded as a severe social crime and statutory measures should be set up to deal with it.
- Clear-cut objectives of providing basic requirements, determined objectively, need to supplant unviable measuring criteria.

SOURCES

1. Kli Yakar, Ex 23:11; also Sefer Ha Chinukh, Mitzvah 332.
2. S. R. Hirsch, Ex 22:24.

3. Shulchan Arukh, Yoreh Deah Section 250; also Mishnah Torah, Mat'not Anryim, Chapters 7 and 9.
4. Mishnah Torah, Mat'not Anryim, Chapter 8, halakhah 13.
5. Aser Le Chah Rav, Section 123.
6. Mishnah Torah, Mat'not Anryim Chapter 7, halakhah 1-2.
7. Shulchan Arukh, Yoreh Deah, Section 248, Ramah.
8. Mishnah, Shekalim, Chapter 3, Mishnah 2.
9. Mishnah Torah Mat'not Anryim, Chapter 9, halakhah 9 and 13; also Chapter 7 halakhah 3.
10. ibid, halakhah 6.
11. Lev. 19:9-20, Deut. 2:19-21.
12. Mishnah Torah, Mat'not Anryim, Chapter 2, halakhah 17.
13. Pesachim 112-13.
14. Shulchan Arukh, ona'ah u grievat Da'at section.
15. Meinat Einaiyim comment.
16. Mishnah Torah, Mat'not Anryim, Chapter 10, halakhah 19; see also Pitchei Choshen, Hilkehot Genievah Section 1.
17. M. Tamari, *The Challenge of Wealth*, NJ, Jason Aronson Inc., 1995, Part Two, Chapter One.

7 The Idea of the Public Good
Religious Conviction and the Interdependence of the Individual and Society
James O'Connell

> *The state comes into existence for the sake of life; and it continues for the sake of the good life.*
>
> Aristotle
>
> *Rats and roaches live by competition under the law of supply and demand; it is the privilege of human beings to live under the laws of justice and mercy.*
>
> Wendell Berry

INTRODUCTION: THE COMMON GOOD AND THE STATE

Every society in which people accept solidarity with one another, recognize interdependence and foster participation formulates in one form or another a concept – the common or public good – which expresses those broad ends that members of the society pursue together. The notion of the common good embodies the conviction that the good of individuals is ensured in the pursuit of the good of society.[1] This notion is in one form or another contained in the world's great religions. Within Christianity, the two-fold precept of Christ on love of God and love of neighbours (two sides of the one obligation) drew on and summed up its Judaic heritage. It was expressed again in Islam. This obligation works through Hinduism in which the absolute permeates all that is contingent; in Buddhism it finds expression in reverence for all that lives; and in Confucianism it is embodied in the acceptance of a strong social and family ethos.

In relation to the public good the state or political association (and government as its authority) plays a special role in fostering predictability and trust in society; it is the association through which persons and groups organize themselves to maintain good law and just order, to uphold conditions for respecting personal rights and duties, to promote prosperity and the conditions for it, and to ensure the defence of the realm. The state meets essential needs in society but it is not the whole of society. Even where it assumes coordinating powers, it still has to respect the autonomy of the family, religious groups, and other social, economic and voluntary groups.

In a democratic polity such as ours we possess the freedom and initiative to make personal choices; and we cooperate with others not only to meet needs that individuals cannot meet singly but to create social and economic effectiveness and establish linkages of justice and compassion. Through such achievement the well-being of our society redounds to the benefit of its members even as we pursue our most individual ends. Similarly, on an interstate scale our own country has come together with other countries in the European Union as well as within various international organizations and has given up dimensions of sovereignty to achieve with other countries levels of security and prosperity that we and others could not achieve alone.

THE IMPLICATIONS OF SOCIAL CHANGE

During social change, especially the kind of rapid social change which we are presently living through, the political and social organization of society is constantly being modified through the impact of technology and new skills. More than in the recent past, individuals run risks in their sense of personal identity and economic security as technology and expertise, including new genetic research and controls, change the nature of life and work; and they experience tensions in interpersonal relations as new organizational forms and shifting relations between groups bring with them greater, but sometimes uneven, access to prosperity, revised roles for the sexes, altered life styles, and new forms of recreation.

For some time, crucial social transformations in our present industrial and post-industrial order in Britain were relatively gradual and concealed three significant developments.

First, Britain had over two generations become more educated and prosperous and, consequently, more middle class.[2] In fact, some half of the British population is now middle class. The new groups were predominantly engaged in non-manual work, aspired to home ownership and took up shareholding. With the decline in the industrial working class came also de-unionization and a further rise of those service industries in which there was considerable casualization and part-time employment.

Second, while the newer members of the middle classes have been recruited from abler and upwardly mobile members of the working class, those who have least profited from social change have been other working class persons and families who have historically been less formally educated, less well-to-do, and less articulate than the established middle classes, who are diminishing in both demographic numbers and political influence, and who in an information age face more than ever before a skills gap in gaining upward mobility. Significantly the share of total national income in Britain (after housing costs) for the lower 50 per cent of the population fell during the last 20 years from nearly a third (32 per cent) to one quarter (25 per cent).

Third, linked to the segmentation that was taking place in society on the basis of a new spread of skills some of its former solidarity began to break down and sections began to pursue interests of their own with less reference to the broad community. At the same time government which saw itself as the guardian of the new entrepreneurial classes[3] legislated to alter the tax system, reducing the demands on the more prosperous, shifting the tax burden from direct to indirect measures, increasing consumption and promoting wealth accumulation for the overtly entrepreneurial and the well-paid. In this context, an unwillingness (or perceived unwillingness) among large numbers of voters to pay higher taxes for educational, health and other services and an insensitivity to the poverty of many families converged to tempt government and its supporters in the press to play down those ways in which the common weal of all citizens was linked and to give lesser force than before to arguments for longer term investment in educating the workforce, in improving and extending public services, in maintaining the economic infrastructure, and in alleviating social misery.

Middle class opinion leaders create the broad climate of public attitudes in our society. In the recent past a 'culture of contentment' came to prevail. Part of this culture contained a degree of resentment against taxation, especially taxation that funded welfare costs and eased the lot of those who had not succeeded economically. Alarm over a demography that predicted huge numbers of older people entitled to pensions and health care and a deliberate effort to keep taxes low prompted efforts to reduce benefits for pensioners and families and to offer lower support to hospitals and schools than the national income would have permitted.[4] Many also sought in practice to protect themselves against the inadequacies of the state health and retirement systems through taking out private health insurance and making pension investments; and while the great majority of the middle classes stayed within the state education system for their children, they sought the best part of it for themselves through residential choice.

However, the technological changes that earlier affected adversely workers in manufacturing sectors, and particularly those located in heavy industries such as steel, shipbuilding and mining, have begun, particularly through the computer revolution, to affect sections of the middle classes and to create feelings of job and other insecurity among them. In other words, this new and expanded middle class, which in any case was psychologically less confident than earlier middle class groups, also found itself less secure in its attainments. Its members came under threat from the penetrations of the national economy by the globalized economy; and they became confused in their work loyalties as financial priorities given to shareholders and short-termism in the business outlook engulfed them much as similar policies had earlier swept aside manual workers. A culture of contentment has, in fact, proved to be brittle and temporary for many who had expected their employment and income security to last indefinitely, and who were unprepared for a consequent growth in personal and family indebtedness.

Not least, to the dismay even of thinkers on the left, the state apparatus has in many respects – for all its necessity – proved inept and intrusive in dealing with the poorest in society.

THE DEBATE ON THE PUBLIC GOOD, PRIVATE WELL-BEING AND TAXATION: THE BALANCE OF EFFICIENCY, OWNERSHIP AND REGULATION

Those social and economic changes that we have remarked on have been taking place during a political period in which serious efforts were being made to privatize society and the state. The failure of the British economy to grow as fast as other Western economies and Japan was blamed on the size and operation of the public sector. Unease among ruling groups over the perceived (and in many cases real) lack of efficiency in state enterprise resulted in the sell-off of state-owned enterprises, including natural monopolies such as water and gas, to private companies.[5] While much of the initial effort to privatize came from those who wanted greater efficiency in public monopolies, the drive quickly came under the control of free-market ideologues who not only broke up well coordinated economic units in the name of competition but also refused to put in place adequate regulation of the privately owned utilities.

In the prevailing climate of opinion, competition between the two largest political parties has emphasized less and less the services that the state might provide and has instead concentrated attention on the taxes required to pay for them. The British electoral system facilitated trends towards curbing the reallocation of resources and reducing levels of welfare payments; and its voting patterns have cowed the current opposition into coming close to almost neurotically insisting that they will never generally raise taxes. Ironically the lack of a will to promote employment policies and government concern to put the control of inflation and interest rates ahead of unemployment and possibly growth has prevented an overall drop in welfare spending.

Out of the distrust of public service came imposed regulation and internal marketing in health and education that resulted in a proliferation of managers, consultants and paper. Simultaneously, while there was a rise in private affluence for some (for example, more personal book-buying and home appliances), there was a decay in public provision (fewer books in public libraries and dirtier streets) for all. This privatizing era has been gradually coming to an end. But technology and certain forms of management ethos are still bringing about employment retrenchment. It is little wonder that a sense of failure has taken hold of the country; and seldom has the national mood as well as morale in the civil service, health service, schools, colleges and universities been so low.

A growing awareness of slow British economic growth, a belated realization among middle class persons that their employment, health provision and retirement security are under threat, and a wider understanding that between a third and a quarter of families with children live below the poverty line are now among those factors that are prompting supporters of all political parties to rethink policies and priorities. In this sense, the United Kingdom appears to be gradually returning to a more general Western European consensus. In countries such as Sweden, Germany, France and Austria the welfare state – though under pressure from taxation costs – is still seen as the finest social achievement of the post-war era. Thus, even when in the latter part of 1995 Chancellor Helmut Kohl sought to reduce government spending and cut welfare benefits, he did so in the context of a 50-point programme that included increasing investment and reducing regulations for firms; and he acted within an overt ideology that sought growth so as to maintain the social market and basic welfare benefits. In France, strongly as President Chirac's government has sought to prune public spending to meet the conditions for a single European currency, it has backed away from doing much more than snipping at the outer margins of welfare benefits. Only in Britain and the United States, among the major Western countries, was politics played out with insistent and multiple references to dependency cultures and with implied suggestions that a new and highly individualist enterprise was in place.

GUARDIANS OF THE COMMON GOOD: GOVERNMENT AND ACTIVISTS

There are many guardians of the common good, ranging from trade unionists to poets. In this section I want to concentrate on two – and in some measure overlapping – groups: government and faith-groups.

Government and the Common Good

The analysis of this chapter suggests a society and a period where social and technological changes are crowding in upon us, where society is becoming more segmented through differences in skill possession, income diversification, and differing life styles, and where it is less clear than it used to be that in the great majority we recognize our interdependence, rely on solidarity, and accept a common belonging. Yet if against this background most citizens retain a sense of the common good and give legitimacy to means used for achieving this good, what do – and what will – they require from political association (the state) and from ruling groups within the state (government)? I want to argue that four broad challenges lie before government in pursuing the political dimensions of the common good: maintaining peace, meeting the desire for prosperity, supporting social justice, and fostering compassion.

1. A government has an obligation to maintain peace internally in restraining violence and crime and externally in contributing to international cooperation and rejection of war. But internally this obligation does not require that Britain should continue to fill prisons indefinitely with petty criminals, to remove from judges discretion in individual cases or to neglect rehabilitation measures within prisons; and externally it imposes no requirement on Britain to pursue a major rather than middle power role with corresponding expenditures.

The Idea of the Public Good 83

2. A government faces a commitment to efficiency in public services as well as creating supportive conditions for corporate and private endeavour. But if the state and administration are committed to social and economic efficiency, they have in the process to be committed to careful regulation of the market, investment for the future, and concern for the infrastructure and the environment. In this connection, supporting and creating employment is a factor in respecting the dignity and enhancing the welfare of citizens. It can also in the longer run reduce public spending.

3. A government has to concern itself with justice in society and be pledged to social and legal equity; and it has to convey that concern to its citizens. Indeed the core issue in contemporary democracy is the extent that 'market outcomes must be accepted (in the name of efficiency) or corrected (in the name of equity and justice)' (Claus Offe). If justice is the bond of rule, where society is perceived as unjust, many will not only question their allegiance but will also withhold their best endeavours.

4. A government – and obviously a society that is made up of many religious and other voluntary groups – needs directly and indirectly to foster care and compassion for the disadvantaged. In a society in which such concern did not properly exist, more advantaged groups might make short-term social and economic gains. In the longer run, however, all its groups would have to live with social loss, including having a national workforce that was insufficiently skilled, a population with grossly uneven life expectations, and younger people with too little hope and tempted into crime. The affluent would not avoid the impact on consciences of media coverage of the degrading life-world of a large section of society; and they would suffer the identity and moral problems arising out of demeaning divisions within the society.

From an understanding of these challenges to a future British government, one central political responsibility takes on shape: convincing a national audience that public initiative, investment and coordination remain crucial to our society and must be paid for. It matters much less whether government itself undertakes tasks directly or retains the right to supervise contracting out measures. If public performance has, however, to conform to norms of efficiency, it also depends fundamentally on working with a sense of community or social homogeneity, even in a segmented society. For that reason, good government and politics entail convincing middle class and prosperous voters especially that they gain not only in national efficiency by eliminating the waste of human potential among the less well-off sectors of society but that a wholesome society fosters solidarity in remaining sensitive to justice and grows humanly in exercising compassion. In a profound sense in Britain and in Western Europe generally – both within and between political parties – there is a battle on for the minds and consciences of middle class persons who divide between those who retain a committed sense of social community, wish to combine efficient public action, national social insurance and the fundamentals of income distribution, and accept to be taxed accordingly, and those who profoundly distrust the 'interventionist state', cherish a 'politics of resentment' against welfare costs, want to provide privately for themselves, and vote to pay lower taxes.

In practice, any government that seeks to lead will have to explain carefully to its people that it needs to undertake measures to support retraining and to make life tolerable for those obliged to wait for jobs or between jobs. It may also need to explain to people that spending on schools (pupils, teachers, equipment and buildings) is investment in the future as are environmental planning and firm, if supple, regulation of public utilities. Similarly, government may need to remind its people, particularly those who are growing older, that private insurance can never replace a publicly run health service and never cater adequately for chronic ill-health.

Above all, good government will convince people that lower consumption and wisely spent taxation represent sensible economic investment that translates into deferred gains as well as into an infrastructure of public support that binds a community together in order, justice, compassion and shared aspirations. If it is true that we should pay as little tax as possible, it is also true that we should pay as much tax as we need to. Indeed one may sum up the values underlying this chapter in saying: efficiency draws on our rational endeavours; justice establishes basic integrity in our relations with one another; and compassion develops the empathy and care that make us most fully human.

Finally, in our contemporary globalized society a well-to-do and still morally Christian country such as the United Kingdom cannot confine the notion of the common good to its own boundaries, but in cooperation with its European Union partners and other developed countries needs to reach out to developing countries in just trade, compassionate aid and far-sighted investment policies. Such an approach deepens human solidarity, promotes the social and economic welfare of all peoples, and consolidates world peace.

Society as a Community of Communities: The Role of Faith Groups in Politics

The unavoidable commitment of Christians – and other religious groups – to politics arises out of the obligation to love our neighbours. This obligation does not stop within the sacristy of the church but pulsates through the whole of life, that is, wherever people live before God. It does not normally entail that religious bodies as such play a partisan role in politics, though religious persons may well have to do so but it does mean that these bodies contribute to the making of political culture and use their organizational resources to guard the common good as well as further their own particular goods.

What role then is there for the churches and for Christians in the immediate future of our politics? It seems to me that there are three such converging roles.[6] There is, firstly, a role of *broker* that comes out of a sense of the values of the gospel in the context of a pluralist world that has many and manifest contributions of its own to make; secondly, a role of *prophet* that comes from the ability of the churches in every generation to beget thinkers and activists who draw on their religious faith to make a commitment to their fellow humans, who find a fellowship with like-minded persons within and without the churches, and who are willing to challenge entrenched attitudes and institutions; and, thirdly, a role of *captain* that comes from the capacity of the churches to use their organizational structures for secular purposes as they have traditionally done in spheres such as education, medicine and agriculture as well as from the ability of individual Christians to take part in active politics and social organization. A word is in place on each role:

Brokers: A longer-term challenge for Christians is to encourage thinkers to listen to another, to remain themselves open to persuasion from wherever truth may be found, to deepen awareness of the problems of an era, and to enter into an enterprise in which there is a common pursuit of truth and justice and a sensitivity to all sections of the national and world community. This enterprise needs to include all those who are brokers in our time: among others, bishops, theologians, intellectuals, journalists, broadcasters, people who write letters to the newspapers and the radio, teachers who work with integrity, volunteers who undertake mediation and arbitration initiatives, and weekly preachers in the pulpits who speak in favour of fellowship, avoid confrontationalism, and reject demonization of opponents. These are the people who collect information, reflect on it, put forward new ideas, persuade opponents to consider entering into negotiation or arbitration, and argue the case for justice and peace. They are also those who exert themselves to persuade their more well-to-do fellow citizens that most people in our society have reached a reasonable standard of living; that a relentless desire to increase consumption comes from centuries old attitudes that are no longer immediately relevant,[7] and that for the immediate future self-disciplining initiatives to divert resources towards longer term investment and just and compassionate distribution/redistribution of assets can build communities and safeguard the environment and its resources. Only through sensible brokerage can we create a society in which there is a sense of identity and belonging and which refuses undue segmentation. Within this kind of approach, also we can rationally debate the role of longer and shorter term manufacturing investment, work out means of enskilling young people, contrast the worth of universally available benefits with means tested benefits, elaborate fair pension plans and argue the worth of health for the whole community.

Prophets: Churches that do not have saints or prophets are impoverished churches. Yet in organizations in which the great majority, including the clerics, are relatively ordinary people who serve institutions as much out of tradition as out of conviction, sanctity can more readily be recommended than required. Prophets are those who move to the margins of society, who accept to be disdained and even reviled, and who make those society-sized gestures that prompt ordinary members of society as well as its rulers to look sensitively and without complacency at issues. A society that has no prophets is an impoverished society. In recent times, the prophetic tradition has surfaced in a dominantly secular way within the environmental movement. In the churches it has come to life especially in supporting the 'option for the poor'. This option has meant for many not just the decision to work for the poor but to identify with them by sharing their lot and working in collaboration with them rather than just for them. Liberation theology has mainly dealt with justice but the genius of using the term 'liberation' has emphasized that those who are not free – who have not freed themselves – cannot secure justice, even if it is handed to them. It is easy to understand liberation theology in the Latin American context but it cannot be confined to that context while there are poor families and individuals living in our own country. At their very best, the efforts of those who belong to the various strands of the prophetic tradition – development, poverty, environment, gender – converge and strengthen one another. There are dangers in the prophetic tradition and prophets are not easy people to live with but there are far greater dangers in not cherishing it, ignoring it or trying to stifle it.[8] Those in the churches who belong to it follow Christ closely who was rejected by the establishment of his time and who died outside the walls.

Captains: If brokers think and communicate, and prophets preach and act, there must also be those who compete for and share in decision-making: the 'captains and the kings' are the politicians and the public administrators who wield authority in states; and the political activists at every level who exercise influence on parties and lobbies. Those who are concerned about the public good cannot abandon political decisions to other people: they cannot leave the dirty work to others while they whitewash their consciences and remain in the interstices of society. It is essential that there are persons, imbued with a sense of public service, who serve apprenticeships in politics and who act politically in spite of all the compromises and scheming and organizing that infuse the competition for power, the possession and sharing of power, and the uses of power. Similarly, we need administrators who organize the public services and who work out soberly and honestly social and economic benefits and costs. In the last resort crucial decisions on the good of society and state depend on the integrity, competence and collaboration of politicians and public servants.

In practice, most people are a mixture of all three types – broker, prophet, captain – though a mixture varying according to each individual and each society. One can think of a politician such as Brandt who has also played a broker's role and a splendid administrative theorist such as Beveridge who combined prophetic and practical vision; one can mention a writer/broker like Merton who was a gifted prophet and an economist such as Galbraith who combines outstanding technical expertise with a fully human compassion; and one can recall a great Jewish prophet like Isaiah who was a most shrewd politician and a modern Indian one like Ghandi who never missed a political trick. Fortunately too, there are those at every level and every sphere of society who combine roles and qualities and help to leaven the social whole.

CONCLUSION

The conception of society being used here is relatively simple and analogical: a society is any broad group of persons who interact with one another in a patterned way. It does not exclude the overlap or the interpenetration of groups and members or the way in which every individual belongs to more than one group or society. For such reasons, one may refer to – among others – Scottish society, British society, European society and, in our time, global society. Behind this analogical concept of society lies the view that society itself is made up of differing groups – family, religious, linguistic, national, cultural, economic, political – as well as the hope that those groupings that make up a society will ideally form a community of communities. In other words, a will-to-community reaches out from patterned interaction to engender familiarity, belonging and concern – or, if you wish, friendship. The medieval philosopher, Thomas Aquinas, put this view succinctly in a statement on peace: 'Peace is indirectly the work of justice, which removes the obstacles, but directly it is the work of friendship' (*Summa Theologiae*).

To finish: the concept of the common good formulated in this chapter comes out of a religious conviction that we belong to God and to one another in a community of creation and reconciliation. In belonging to one another we have rights and obligations; and we and others grow in security and freedom, in justice and in friendship through respecting rights and meeting obligations. Society at its best is the union of human persons with God and with one another.

NOTES

1. I want to thank Peter Chambers for incisive comments on an earlier draft of this paper.
2. I realize that the term 'middle class' though usually obvious enough in practice frays at the margins. I take it broadly to mean those included in the A and B groups, many in C, and some of D. These categories are very broad: category A includes mostly professionals such as doctors and lawyers and other such groups; B includes upper and intermediate occupations that range from teachers and farmers to company directors and journalists; C takes in skilled occupations that are non-manual: police officers, bus drivers, and so on; D takes in skilled/partly skilled manual workers; and E unskilled people.
3. Many political commentators have commented wryly on the policies of a government that argued that the rich should get more money through paying lower taxes to give them incentives to work and that the poor should be prompted to work harder through receiving lower remunerations and benefits.
4. While middle class people might in their own and the general interest accept,

The Idea of the Public Good

for example, that every car driver should hold an insurance policy, they take for granted differential insurance levies for different areas (linked in practice to postal codes) that cost them proportionally less than those who live in inner city areas and council estates.

5. Few parts of the government's privatization programme proved more popular among the direct beneficiaries than the sale of council houses to their tenants who in one swoop were able to break free from the obscurantist rules of many local councils and while purchasing below the market price enter into the ranks of house owners. The Left opposed the sale of such houses and incurred the hostility of the new owners. The size of the sell-off greatly reduced the housing capacity available to councils for dealing with the impoverished and the homeless; and governmental fiscal dogma prevented the councils from investing the proceeds of sales in new housing. Those who had implacably and without nuance opposed the sale had not however adverted to social changes that had rendered obsolete the massive council-owned states of the recent past. If it was difficult for the Right to overcome the prejudices of dogma, it was difficult for the Left to break free from the practices of a previous era.

6. Readers may recognize a contemporary version of the traditional interpretation of Christ as priest, prophet and king.

7. Many, if not most persons, in developed countries are driven by a passion for forms of growth that comes out of attitudes engendered by the historic human struggle against hunger, disease, and natural disaster. Human attitudes and desires have not yet come to terms with the ease and abundance created by contemporary technology. Given this situation, it seems reasonable to argue that while, for example, advances in health as an area and computing as a technique, should and will and must, continue, it is not, however, rational or sensible to go on ravaging the environment for relatively peripheral advances in transport, cosmetics and comfort or for the well-to-do to seek marginal advances in living standards by withholding resources from the poor, whether the poor within their own society or the poor in the developing world.

8. There are temptations that may harm or diminish prophetic witness. It is possible to spell out briefly some considerations. Prophets must, first, be reluctant: they undertake a hard and dangerous task that is not to be entered on lightly. Second, they need to think through their social objectives, seek to elaborate a political strategy of action and gesture, and advert to the effects of their activities on various levels of public opinion. Third, those who take on the task of prophecy must take it on out of love: if they must preach danger and doom, they must do so with tremendous concern; and they must so love their society that they are willing to make sacrifices for it.

8 Theology and Sharing the Economic Cake
Peter Vardy

PROLOGUE: QUEEN OF SCIENCES

Several chapters in this book, particularly those by Andrew Dilnot and Ian Steedman, deal with the seemingly inexorable growth in government spending and the widening gap between the aspirations of the electorate in Western democracies and the economic ability to deliver. There has been a failure of political will to deal with the problems, but more than this, generally accepted political wisdom regarding our institutions has also failed. Theology could, in principle, instigate innovative thinking and aid an approach to the problems rather than add to them by a failure to take seriously the practical realities.

Theology used to be described as the 'Queen of the Sciences' – due to its inherently unifying role. If God created the universe, the study of God and God's relationship to creation could inform all aspects of human enquiry. Yet today theology is relegated to the sidelines and, to the outsider, theological speculation is often seen to be a game played by insiders which appeals to what was said within 'tradition' and what can and cannot be said today whilst remaining faithful to this mainstream heritage. It is easy to regard it as a self-contained language game with little more than esoteric interest and with no impact on the real world. Likewise philosophy has, in some quarters, become obsessed with linguistic analysis and has lost sight of the need to address issues of practical concern to individuals.

Nowhere is this more the case than in economic morality where most philosophical theologians show a remarkable reluctance to face empirical facts.

1. THE HARD ECONOMIC FACTS

i. We live in a global market. The movement towards free trade has brought enormous benefits, not least to the third world. Manufacturing capacity can and, in many cases is, being progressively moved to areas where costs are lower.

Theology and Sharing the Economic Cake 91

ii. The demand in the West for services from government grows inexorably. Despite all attempts to cut government spending as a share of GDP, even a halt in the growth of expenditure has been difficult to achieve.
iii. The pressure to increase public services (ii) combined with a relatively static growth in GDP (i) means that all Western governments are caught in a trap – they are democracies and are responsible to the will of their people and their people want two conflicting things: they want more spending by government and they want to pay less for it.

These issues are being dealt with elsewhere in this book in some detail – my concern is to reflect theologically on the situation the Western world finds itself in as a consequence, and to consider whether alternatives are available.

2. A THEOLOGICAL REFLECTION ON THE CONTEMPORARY SITUATION IN THE WEST

Religious thinkers often contribute to the economic problems by failing to be realistic. They, rightly, recognize the moral need to respond to the weakest in society. This is admirable – but does not give sufficient consideration to the hard fact that countries with economies that are, relatively, weakening are no longer in a position to meet all the desirable objectives. For instance, in January 1996, the Anglican Primate of Australia and the Australian Cardinal issued a joint statement calling on the Australian government not to follow the approach taken by New Zealand which had resulted in an economic turnround in that country at the price of a reduction in government spending in key areas. As so often, no suggestion was made as to alternative ways of approaching Australia's manifest economic problems.

The example illustrates the challenge posed to theologians to speak constructively and comprehensibly, not merely in terms of abstract principles. Christianity has always claimed to be an incarnational religion – it is not 'otherworldly' in that it has never preached a flight from the real world. It claims that God became a human being and lived with human beings. Jesus' parables talk of employers and workers, of farmers and moneylenders – he lived in the real world. In consequence, Christianity calls people to compassion for the weak and vulnerable. Traditionally it holds fast to the rich Old Testament idea of justice which includes compassion for widows and strangers and is concerned with structural injustice.

This down to earth, experiential approach has inspired for example, Liberation Theology, which produced radical new insights into the relation between God and human beings. It rejects the Aristotelian starting point of Thomist philosophy of religion which posits a simple, timeless and spaceless God; instead Liberation Theology arrives at a God who can suffer with creation. It emphasizes a commitment to a this-worldly view of salvation and concentration on issues of justice. Liberation Theology proclaims the idea of community and looks to ordinary people to revitalize the political system. It must be recognized, however, that while some Liberation Theologians do offer political guidance, their message has not been able to deflect the countries of Latin America from embracing the economic path of a balanced budget and tight fiscal and monetary control as the only way to overcome their difficulties, even though a heavy price has to be paid by those who cannot find work or who are at the bottom of the economic pile.

One thing most religions do proclaim is a global perspective – all human beings are to be seen as children of God and 'our' family or nation does not deserve any privileged position. A free market economy has been shown to maximize wealth creation and thereby can lead to wealth being transferred from the 'haves' to the 'have nots'. Provided this principle is applied responsibly it need not be considered incompatible with this perspective. It is clear that free trade, taking account of comparative advantage in different economies, increases the output of all countries, while, protectionism, which is based on a crude theory of protection against perceived absolute advantage, reduces the GDP of all the countries involved. The price of free trade may mean changing job patterns and redundancies but this flexibility may be the necessary price for economic strength and without such strength desirable social outcomes cannot be achieved. Until a better economic theory is produced, this system coupled with democracy may indeed be the best available way forward.

The contribution of philosophers and theologians must include the corresponding issue of how limited resources should be allocated fairly and effectively, both within any particular economy and more widely. Theological considerations must show that advocacy of any system that puts the interests of the wealthy in a superior position to those of the poor is intellectually, morally and religiously flawed.

3. DADDY DOES NOT KNOW BEST

I said at the beginning of this chapter that a slowly growing GDP and a rapidly rising demand for services cannot be squared. No simple solutions will overcome the problem: there is no easy (nor difficult!) way for a government to dramatically increase GDP nor to cut back on demand for services. Therefore we require structures which do not depend on 'the government' solving the problems of society but instead force individuals to confront the needs of others – with the acceptance that some individuals will choose to ignore these needs because of self-interest.

Justice and fairness are fundamental to any religious understanding of human society. The needs of the weak and those who cannot help themselves such as widows, orphans and strangers were clearly recognized in Mosaic law. All religions accept the importance of a strong commitment to these groups. However this commitment must be an individual commitment – it cannot be displaced onto 'society' or the government and the idea that it can has been responsible for many of today's problems and difficulties.

The idea that 'the government' is the primary bearer of responsibility for the well-being of citizens rests on an unspoken assumption, which for too long theologians, philosophers and politicians have acquiesced in. This assumption essentially derives from Plato reasoning in the context of society as understood in his days: namely that the mass of people are weak and cannot make their own decisions. Plato sought to solve the problem by proposing an ideal state in which philosophers/guardians acted in the best interests of society – daddy knew best.[1] The 'masses' would be told a fable which would convince them that those with 'gold' souls should govern. Plato's proposed republic, seen in today's perspective, was based on a lie. The same is the case of modern democracy, when it avoids confronting people with real problems, in the belief that any political party that does so is doomed to defeat.

St Augustine, writing in a post-Constantinian world in which Christianity had become the recognized religion of the Roman Empire, also endorsed the dominant position of the state – particularly the military aspects of it. In his turn, St Thomas Aquinas, whose political reason used categories evolved in the Holy Roman Empire, supported the established order of divinely appointed kings, feudal barons, freemen and slaves; the idea of individual political responsibility was scarcely apparent. It was not until the Reformation and the Enlightenment that the strong sense of individual responsibility called for in the Christian gospels was once more on the intellectual agenda – although still not on the agenda of governments.

Plato, Augustine, Aquinas and many others have all supported 'leadership from the top' but in the world more than 2000 years later, we can see that such leadership is under severe strain. Leaders are too often self-interested; conversely, 'democracy' too often enables people to avoid personal responsibility by blaming problems on 'the government'. In that light, *democracy is the best way that has ever been devised of killing personal responsibility*. As the numbers of people voting are so large and each individual's vote apparently counts for so little, personal responsibility is radically undermined. Responsibility for the ills of society can be passed from individuals to 'the government', to an anonymous and unidentifiable 'them' which has the chief advantage of not being 'us' or 'me' so that individuals do not have to feel personally responsible. Today's 'democracy' still remains a fiction – candidates are selected by political power blocks within parties; independent thought is discouraged; the role of the media and marketing is essential and the world has become so complex that most individuals are unable to arrive at a balanced judgment.

My contention is that if leadership from the top has failed, the only way forward is to place responsibility back where it notionally already belongs – namely with the individual person. Democracy is far from a perfect system, but a democratic form of government which really takes the ideal of democracy seriously may be the 'least bad' method of government that is available, at least in countries in the West. If this is accepted then policies have to be put forward that (1) are innovative; (2) might be 'saleable' to the electorate; (3) actually transfer responsibility back to individuals; and (4) have a chance of 'success' (and how one defines 'success' is going to be a central issue).

What is proposed in this chapter is a recognition that government from 'on high' is, in the Western world, increasingly failing – it has achieved a great deal but competition for limited resources is now imposing severe strains. I suggest that a model to meet this challenge can come from a theological understanding of the responsibility of each individual – a responsibility that cannot be transferred to the 'them' of government. Reintroducing this sense of responsibility is a challenge for theology and a challenge of moral leadership. *Without it there is no way forward.* There is, of course, no guarantee that trust in the human capacity for acting responsibly is justified. However, it would be a denial of the message of most religions to accept that human beings are not capable of free choice; and that they are not capable of choosing neighbour over self.

4. REINTRODUCING A SENSE OF PERSONAL RESPONSIBILITY

The English Hegelian philosopher, F. H. Bradley, saw people obtaining their identity only as members of a social group and decried the idea of the single individual. The ethical aim, he considered, should be to conform to one's place in society. A human being is a part of society and society is far superior to the particular individual. Society is an organism and each person must realize him or herself as part of this organism. This is, I believe, a fundamentally unchristian and atheistic viewpoint.

The contrary position is held by Václav Havel, who was imprisoned by the former communist government for four years. In his book, *Living in the Truth*, he tells the story of a Prague greengrocer during the communist years who displayed in his window a sign saying 'Workers of the world unite'. No-one took any notice of this sign, as similar ones were displayed in every office and shop. Its real message was *'I will conform. I will not rock the boat. I will be a good citizen'*. One day something in the greengrocer snaps. He takes down the sign and decides to speak up for his friends who oppose the system. He does not become a revolutionary, but he is no longer prepared to acquiesce and to be silent. As soon as he does this, his fate is sealed – he is removed from his job and sent to the canning factory, he and his family will no longer be allowed to take a week's holiday in Bulgaria. Yet the greengrocer has acquired a sense of responsibility. He now stands as an individual responsible to something ultimate which is independent of his psyche, the community and accepted convention. Havel terms this 'living in the truth' and maintains that the willingness to take this stand by an individual is what can overthrow any tyranny, any autocracy.[2]

I wish to maintain that this sense of personal responsibility is the essential ingredient needed to resolve the tension between increased demand for government spending and restricted revenue. It amounts to the recognition *that conformity to culture, to the accepted conventions is not enough* – Bradley was mistaken. We are individuals and we must exercise our individual sense of responsibility to something ultimate – whether we call this God or the Absolute. There has been a failure, aided by 'democracy', to take this dimension seriously. There has also been a failure by theologians, philosophers and others who should provide intellectual leadership to take up this challenge. For too much contemporary theology, the idea of God as a 'Thou' to whom the individual is accountable is absent. Much Roman Catholic theology since the second Vatican Council has, rightly, emphasized a strong commitment to social justice, but it has also emphasized the idea of the 'people of God'. This can be misrepresented, and has been by some Catholic theologians. Even so, the concept appears attractive – it emphasizes the communitarian nature of religious practice and concern for others within the community. However, the great danger is that God may become irrelevant; God may come to be seen as a construct, a reality found only within the form of life of the believing community. To non-theologians such a conclusion may seem surprising, but the biggest challenge faced by traditional theology and religion today is not from atheists but from other theologians and believers who have radically reinterpreted the understanding of the nature of religious truth claims.[3]

5. RELATING 'I' AND 'THOU'

Fr. Gareth Moore OP takes a radical stance in his book *Believing in God*; he sums up his position in the final sentence: 'People do not discover religious truths, they make them'.[4] Don Cupitt takes a broadly similar approach. To Cupitt, Christianity is a fictitious story like other fictitious stories. In a world which Cupitt considers essentially meaningless, he chooses to live by the fictional Christian story and in so doing gives his life meaning and value – but there is no ultimate meaning, no ultimate value. On different assumptions, the distinguished professor of theology at Cambridge, Nicholas Lash, maintains in his book *Easter in Ordinary* that experience of God can *only* be mediated – that is, experienced through the natural world or through other people.[5] He totally rejects (in extreme language at times) the idea, maintained by William James and many others, that it is possible for the mystic or the saint to be aware of God directly.[6] This can be interpreted as Lash effectively rejecting the idea of a 'Thou' to whom an individual is *directly* accountable.

This position, whilst intellectually attractive in some ways, is a denial of an essential Christian, Islamic and Jewish insight – namely that *there exists a Thou who, although largely unknowable in essence, can be addressed as 'Thou' and to whom each individual is directly responsible.* It is this claim that, I suggest, is the central insight that the religious believer should bring to the current debate about economic resource allocation. *The real religious demand is a call for each person to become a 'self', to become an individual responsible to God.*

Talk of an 'I/Thou' relationship between God and individual human beings is essentially in tension with another religious idea – that of obedience by creature to creator. However, Christianity has always maintained that human beings can be drawn to something in a way that goes beyond mere obedience. Jesus called his disciples friends and, whilst never in any way undermining the supremacy of God, showed that the relationship between God and humans can be conceived in parental terms. However, one has to grow into awareness of this possibility. In theological terms, this is what becoming a self involves: to begin to realize that it is possible to live as an individual in relationship with God.

Some, of course, do not accept that there is a God and deny the existence of any 'Thou' to whom one may relate. This, however, does not undermine the idea of personal responsibility – it may be the relationship to some Unknown which the person is reluctant to name or even to an amorphous idea. The Christian claim is that, after death, each individual will have to account for her or his life and that this accounting will not be so much based on what has been believed but on how life has been lived. Kierkegaard said, 'As you lived, so have you believed' and the person who lives a life of responsibility, of care for others, of denial of self and of compassion and forgiveness may be found to be closer to God than the 'believer' whose beliefs do not radically affect his or her life. To a large extent this is a matter of authenticity, but authenticity is not found by 'doing what one wills' but by having a centre to one's life which cannot be moved by contingent circumstances, which does not depend on one's job or one's peers or on any of the temporal concerns that dominate our world. True authenticity and, indeed true individuality can only be found by living in relationship to God no matter what the outward pressures or constraints. It is here that the real challenge of responsibility bites and may give rise to a new way of understanding the ethics of the economic world.

Becoming a self rather than conforming to the crowd is an uncomfortable and sometimes painful process, but only the person who takes this route will be able to take his or her share of the responsibility that is fundamental. It may mean standing alone in opposition to the crowd;

it may mean whistle-blowing on unacceptable corporate practice; it will certainly require accepting our own responsibility for our neighbour's welfare – where 'neighbour' is understood in a very broad sense. *In too many cases, theologians concentrate on dogmas and creedal formations, they dwell on the factual claims of religions or participation in the religious practices or worship of the group with which they identify.* However, transcending these practices is the need for each person to take seriously his or her position as a self which is accountable for everything that is said or done. Society cannot be transformed by 'the great and the good' who, for the greater part, are unlikely to take seriously their position as selves ultimately responsible for their actions to a Thou, which some term God. Wittgenstein said that if we would change the world we must first change ourselves and this represents a fundamental insight which is, today, all too often neglected.

For an illustration of practical responsibility it is useful to look at Japanese culture. To say that this culture is corporatist may be a caricature, but this caricature has validity. Japanese management structures have been changing – the aim is to cement loyalty to the firm which in the past has promised a cradle to grave assurance of employment. Loyalty is considered a crucial attribute of all corporate employees and this loyalty is rewarded by security, just as religious loyalty is rewarded by a feeling of security and of 'belonging' to the club or group. Many US and some British firms have attempted to follow Japanese practices and in some areas these have produced significant increases in efficiency. Loyalty is an important virtue, but traditional Christianity affirms that beyond any human loyalties lies a higher demand – loyalty to God. Even if one does not believe in God, then still a sense of personal responsibility to whatever is considered as ultimate is fundamental to being human and this sense of responsibility needs to be fostered and developed.[7]

6. TAKING RESPONSIBILITY SERIOUSLY

Preaching 'personal responsibility' may achieve little. Practical – and this means fiscal – steps are necessary to put flesh on the idea of personal responsibility. There is no guarantee, of course, that individuals will accept this responsibility but any approach that deserves to be called Christian needs to take the idea of personal responsibility seriously. My proposals for a way forward start with an acceptance of the assumptions set out at the beginning of this chapter – particularly that GDP cannot be sharply increased, and that there is no political consensus for increasing government spending. The way forward may fall under three headings:

i. To cut government spending back radically and to ensure that it is a safety net only available for those in need. This would mean, in Britain, abandoning free medical treatment except for those in real need; doing away with family allowances for all those whose income is above a certain (fairly low) figure; expecting parents to pay for schooling for their children unless they are below the poverty line; moving towards individuals funding their own pensions and long term medical care provision. The problem with this suggestion, if taken in isolation, is that it would not appeal to the majority of people needed to elect a government as these are the people who most benefit from state handouts. Also, by not taking seriously the needs of the weak and the marginalized it seems the reverse of a Christian approach. It therefore needs to be combined with other proposals.

ii. To cut taxes substantially to reflect the savings made under (i). This would be popular and would be the *quid pro quo* for the cutbacks above. I would envisage a severe reduction in taxes so that central government became minimalist – saving, incidentally, considerable administration costs. This, alone, should have a salutary effect on GDP growth. However, at the same time all individuals should be required to contribute a fixed percentage of their income to fund their future pensions and long term health care (cf. Chapter 15). This measure could, in common with others, be introduced on a gradualist basis. These pensions could be invested through a number of private pension schemes and, on retirement, the individual would receive the pension she or he had 'set aside'. The same requirement would apply for long term, chronic health care – Germany has recently introduced a payment of one per cent of income (rising next year to 1.5 per cent) to pay for this cover. It will be paid for partly by doing away with a public holiday so the cost to employers should be minimal. The aim should be to transfer to the individual (and the family) entire responsibility for her or his short and long term needs. This, however, does not address the needs of the poor and the weak – for whom the government would still provide a basic safety net. This net alone, however, is not enough.

iii. The third element is an innovative one – namely to provide a mechanism for people to elect to pay additional taxes ranging from, say one to five per cent of income. This election could be made for a three or five year period and the taxpayer could choose among broad categories as to how these funds should be expended – for instance on inner city education; on relieving poverty; on third world aid; etc. Some incentive, apart from an inner feeling of virtuosness, would be needed to encourage people to pay higher rates and some form of 'Prince of Wales' or 'Medal of Congress' award could be available (marked by badges on cars or lapel labels) which would indicate whether the individual was a 'one per cent extra giver' or a 'five per cent extra giver'. It is true that altruism should be its own reward but, sadly, this rarely happens and many will require recognition for their generosity.

Combined with this approach would be increased allowances for corporations to become more actively involved in their communities – contributing, for instance, to inner city regeneration. The private sector is still the most effective vehicle for bringing about change – indeed at the time of Perestroika in the USSR more would probably have been achieved by funding private enterprise Western firms to open supermarkets in the capital cities of the former Soviet Union and to source supplies locally than by the huge handouts by the West to support what was, largely, the *status quo*. Increased allowances would, however, be conditional on obtaining something equivalent to the 'investor in people' award which would ensure that individuals within the organization were developed to the maximum potential and that they could assume responsibility for their actions within the corporation.

The key point is to make individuals aware that they must assume responsibility for the needs of society and that it is only if they are willing to fund worthy projects that these projects are supported. No longer would it be possible for people to say that 'the government must do something' because the funds to enable this to happen can only come from people's optional contributions. The aim would be to follow Václav Havel's injunction and bring people to accept their responsibility for others in the community and in the wider world. The power of government to cure the ills of society would be recognized and the power to care and to foster change would be passed back where it really belongs with individuals. This approach is, I believe, in accord with the insights of Liberation Theologians and with the faith that traditional Christianity has in the ability of people to make their own decisions and to take responsibility for them.

Despite Mrs Thatcher's assertion that 'there is no such thing as society', it seems obvious that individuals live in societies which are substantially composed of economic, social and political structures. Therefore, structural alterations are necessary to aid the proposed changes. I would see these as falling under the following headings:

- In recent years, power has tended to move to the centre with local communities having far less influence and control over their local affairs. This trend needs to be reversed and democracy needs to become localized at the same time as the role of central government is diminished. This will involve radical changes in the relationship between the centre and local communities.
- The short term approach of many investment institutions and bankers needs to be changed. Financial markets tend to emphasize short term factors at the expense of longer term development and fiscal measures are needed to discourage this approach. One of the reasons for the success of the disparate Japanese and German economies, is that they support a culture which supports long term investment strategies. This is partly coupled to a commitment by workers to employers and employers to workers. There is a recognition of mutual dependency which is often ignored in Britain and sometimes in the US.
- Corporate voting power has to be restored to individual shareholders – in recent years, in Britain, a larger proportion of shares has been concentrated in the hands of institutions leaving individual shareholders with little or no say. In Britain, many shares are held through PEPs and these frequently remove the right of the individuals to vote the shares. In the US, there is a far greater awareness of the power of individual shareholders, and directors recognize their responsibilities to them. This trend has not been followed in Europe. A move towards greater individual responsibility has to be accompanied by bringing shareholders to accept that the companies which they own have a moral obligation to the communities in which they operate.
- The influence, in Britain as well as other countries, of quangos and other bodies which exercise great power and yet which are under the control of unelected and unaccountable officials has to be severely curtailed. A radical shift in responsibility to a much more local level ought to take place. The arts, sporting policy and the allocation of scarce resources have increasingly to be switched to a more local level. Cake distribution must be the responsibility of those who consume the cake – with the risk that some people may be greedy.

Changes such as these will, sadly, be resisted by those faith groups and their theologies which are built on hierarchical models and which prize conformity much more highly than individual responsibility. A revolution in society which starts from the bottom is hardly likely to be supported by such institutions. However, the insights behind this proposal can claim at least as strong a Christian heritage as those which claim that the government must solve the ills of society. I am well aware that such changes are too radical to be readily acceptable. Reaction to proposed political change is inevitably painfully slow; but economic facts may force changes. Sometimes economic imperatives may rise to the aid of social justice and overturn a system which is increasingly failing to meet the demands made upon it.

NOTES AND REFERENCES

1. Plato, *Republic*, translated by H. D. P. Lee, Penguin Classics, Harmondsworth, Penguin Books Ltd, 1955.
2. Søren Kierkegaard, in *The Present Age*, makes a similar point when he forecasts that democracy will lead to the disappearance of moral authority. There will be no way for a person to find any orientation when 'the crowd' is king. There will, Kierkegaard forecasts, be a decline in fellowship, a contempt for autonomy and all responsibility can be passed to the 'them'. His solution, like Havel's is to depend on the single individual.
3. Cf. Peter Vardy, *The Puzzle of God*, HarperCollins, 1995.
4. Gareth Moore, *Believing in God*, T. & T. Clarke, p.287.
5. Nicholas Lash, *Easter in Ordinary*, SCM Press, 1988.
6. See William James, *The Varieties of Religious Experience*, Collins, 1977.
7. Simone Weil echoes this when she says that there is 'no guarantee for democracy, or for the protection of the person against the collectivity, without a disposition of public life relating it to the higher good which is impersonal and unrelated to any political form', *Selected Essays*, p.220.

9 Looking Behind the Scenes
Self-interest, Civic Generosity, Altruism
Peter Askonas and Cho Ngye Kwan

Our Theme

The everyday approach to economic and social issues, whether one is concerned with political ideas or pragmatically with problem solving, is to consider a string of phenomena as they do function or should function. Politicians, economists, and the citizenry at large will rarely look beyond to enquire *what they are*, or *why they are*. In this chapter we want to ask such questions; notably about interpersonal drives and especially about altruism.[1] What are the latter's intrinsic dynamics? How does altruism relate to civic generosity and to self-interest? What is the potential for enhancement of its role in civic behaviour – is enhancement possible?

1. HURDLES, PLATFORMS, COMPASSES

As soon as one sets out to think these questions through, one is faced by several major obstacles. First: we are venturing into *terra incognita*. At the centre of our analysis are notions like self-interest, and hence *self*. For all their familiarity, do we know what they signify? Are *selves bodies*, biological entities shaped exclusively by their genes? Is *selves* the same as *mind*? What is mind? What are drives and motivation such as self-interest: responses to stimuli, and release of tensions generated by obstacles? These type of questions abound; we are far away from an even marginal comprehension of the subject.

Secondly: Bishop Rupert Hoare (Chapter 5) stresses the significance of a platform on which to site the framework for civic values. Yet there are several platforms tossed about on today's turbulent waters, each with a cluster of related devices; or, to extend the marine metaphor, there are at least two flotillas. And to everyone's bewilderment their compasses point in different directions. Adversaries? Competitors? Fellow-adventurers?

Now substitute for *platforms* the term *world views* and you will describe the two dominant ones broadly like this:

- one position is based on a spectrum of convictions saying that all of existence functions on principles akin to complex mechanisms; these are accessible and ultimately decipherable by rationality. Any alternative explanation is relegated to the realm of make-believe.
- the other assumes that a transcendent principle underlies all that is, one which is sufficient to itself and ultimately beyond explanation by human deduction or expression by language.

The former, rationalist view has found its way into an array of political and economic theories, especially those of social philosophies from the sixteenth century onward. Since then it was further developed by making use of principles derived from biology, genetics and other natural sciences; and also by introducing disciplines like sociology and various branches of psychology. More recently, consciousness studies and some philosophies of mind are providing additional and fascinating material. An enormous body of understanding has resulted, and though any serious thinker must acknowledge how incomplete this is, it can go some way to empower today's citizens to shape a social environment in which welfare could progress.

Now to the latter world view. This operates through a mode of knowing which can be described as a surging of the mind or, simply, as the intuition of faith (a grasp of things not yet seen),[2] or simply as primary insight. Etienne Gilson coined a most perceptive phrase for this mode of knowing: *la raison raisonnante*.[3] Again, we are provided with principles and a mode of knowing which will guide us when formulating a behaviour pattern for social and economic activity.

Both views mediate weighty implications, especially for social policy, personal responsibility in civic affairs and the role of economics. Their two antinomous starting points lead to two correspondingly irreconcilable interpretations (read *platforms*):

- civic behaviour is the outcome of determined (and determining) causes and needs – for example, social cohesion as a condition for advancement and satisfaction of individuals and groups and ultimately for the perpetuation of kin and species;
- civic behaviour is orientated by indefinable but often acutely experienced values, including what might be called 'values in themselves', values which transcend tangible ends of here and now.

But let us stop for a moment. It is currently much debated whether these two positions are truly irreconcilable. Can they not shed light on each other? A number of contemporary thinkers argue under the banner of *Realism* that to reason from a primary *inward* insight is a necessary precondition for any thought system. An orientation derived from belief in an undemonstrable cause does in no way preclude an extensive understanding of this world resulting from rigorous reasoning based on observation and verification of *what happens*. We are not far from a key concept of pre-cartesian enquiry: *fides quaerens intellectum* (faith reaching out towards reason).

For example, Mary Midgley, as befits a contemporary moral philosopher, crusades for this type of search: there can be cooperation between reasoning which takes account of evolutionary principles or a mechanistic understanding of consciousness, and other modes of perceiving/believing (Midgley will use terms like *feelings* rather than faith). She excludes the *a priori* assertion that motives can be reduced unavoidably to an empirically definable substrate. 'We are beings that *naturally care* directly [that is, intrinsically] for others, as well as for ourselves [our italics and brackets].[4]

In a different field, a compendium with the title *Self Interest* (Jane Mansfield, ed., 1993)[5] questions the hitherto sacrosanct dictum that each economic act is motivated by self-interest. Several contributors to the book introduce the possibility that utility maximalization dictated by rationality is not the sole driving force in the economic operation of the *polis*, though none go as far as to be explicit about alternatives.

If you look for a more explicit reference to transcendent reality as point of departure for reasoned perception, say, of social interaction, this is provided by John Milbank in his magisterial *Theology and Social Theory*. It is invidious to pluck a brief quote from such a comprehensive study; but this is all we can do here. Thus Milbank commenting on continuity between rationality (in historic narrative) and metaphysical insight: '*all the modern discourses force theology to stand transcendentally above human community...*' and '... to give a causal account of social reality... is really to ascribe meaning in a manner that goes beyond any "objective" justification'.[6]

There is therefore a good case for a formula explicating civic behaviour which reflects interaction of meta-rational and rational modes of knowing:

- civic behaviour is set in motion (*inter alia*) by the attraction and impact of transcendent values; and, in spite of being often obscured by sheer complexity, is operative in processes which can be deciphered by rational examination.

This wording can serve as the basis for a model of self-interest and altruism which derives its dynamics from that which is experienceable in the first place by faith, and which functions in time and space in an order accessible to human sciences. We acknowledge that these basic assumptions remain an anathema to some other inquirers in this field, but we are attempting to find a language sufficiently resonant to make emphazising, debate and a common search feasible.

2. HOW ALTRUISM, GENEROSITY, SELF-INTEREST FUNCTION

An attempt to speak with relevance about complex interpersonal drives has yet to cope with a further difficulty. Their complexity exists at different levels. There is the level of function; observable modes in which drives manifest themselves; for instance generosity, which comprises a large range of behaviour patterns. There is also the level which we will call *roots*, an amalgam of transcendent and other values as well as circumstantially determined causes. We will first examine our subject at the former level.

Self-interest, generosity and altruism make up an intricate system, difficult to unravel. And yet these and related labels are habitually tacked onto persons and activities blithely, without any qualification. For example: 'Tax evaders act from self-interest (read: greed)'; or 'Tax evasion is forced on us in spite of ourselves, as the alternative to hardship'. Or: 'to support xx is a matter of self-interest', or 'to support xx is a case of altruism'. Yet each situation is a combination of circumstances, personal make-up, prevailing ethos and intangible dynamics. Rarely will it comprehend all that is at issue.

Perhaps too few words are available to designate a wide diversity of drives such as those covered, for instance, by the title self-interest. This adds to the temptation to fudge complexity. A more thoughtful and differentiating mode of describing the full facts would have to convey:

- that human motivation is a vast compound of coexisting drives; that different drives rarely function isolated in a pure state, which makes their identification and assessment tenuous;
- that these drives interact and constantly modify one another.

Figure 9.1 Some models of self-interest

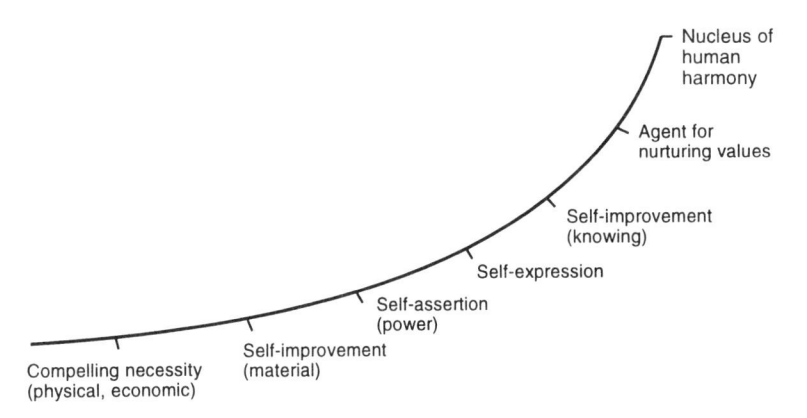

- Nucleus of human harmony
- Agent for nurturing values
- Self-improvement (knowing)
- Self-expression
- Self-assertion (power)
- Self-improvement (material)
- Compelling necessity (physical, economic)

3. A HIERARCHY OF MOTIVES

In order not to be daunted by complexity we have to introduce an element of structuring. Hierarchy of motivation and correspondingly hierarchy of self-interest can be useful concepts in this regard. An example: everyone would agree that the motivation for taking care of a sick friend is superior to that for playing the lottery. (Hierarchy has for some a connotation of unhelpful rigidity. But hierarchy could also be understood as a playing field, equipped with basic qualitative indicators about levels of response; or degrees – lower and higher motives. This kind of hierarchy is not automatically self-defining but will allow for the unpredictable, the innovative, for manifestation of creative spontaneity.)

This concept of hierarchy has been applied to needs and corresponding behaviour by the philosopher and psychologist Abraham Maslow. A progression of needs is set out, starting from the primary biological ones, and ascending through others, such as need for safety, belonging, esteem, to need for *self-actualization*.[7] Here we propose a somewhat similar pattern in respect of various types of need-responses, especially self-interest and its eventual refinement in altruism. This is indicated by Figure 9.1. We add our emphatic reminder that all such representations are only crude abstractions.

In common usage self-interest has a pejorative flavour. A more subtle implication becomes possible by introducing distinctions between modes of self-interest. Thereby we come to appreciate the possibility

Figure 9.2 Towards enhanced humanity

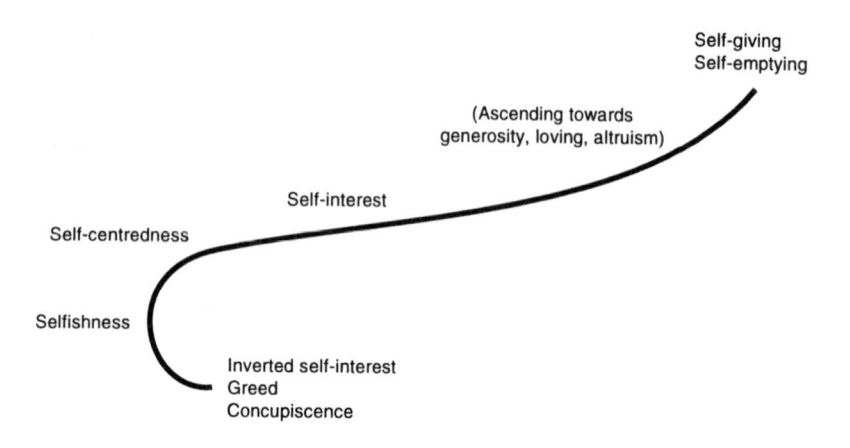

```
                                              Self-giving
                                              Self-emptying
                              (Ascending towards
                              generosity, loving, altruism)

                     Self-interest
   Self-centredness

   Selfishness
                     Inverted self-interest
                     Greed
                     Concupiscence
```

of progression from *lower* to *higher* modes. Accordingly self-interest is not necessarily tantamount to disregard of others.

This is most apparent in the last of the modes. Here the *self* for which we are – or should be – concerned is not a self-sufficient ego, but a gift and a point of departure. Its true value consists in the capacity for identification with others and The Other. Indeed one ought to speak more forcefully not just of identification but of immersion. Described alternatively, the self in this mode is that centre of *my* person where human development is initiated. *I* can have no impact on the development of *you* unless *my* self is undergoing development and maturing.[8] Paradoxically this advanced process of self-development may be experienced as diminishment of the self. To paraphrase a key concept in Chapter 14; a matter of 'wanting less and giving more'.

Figure 9.2 introduces further differentiation, indicating the stark reality of regressing self-interest (with which we cannot deal in this chapter), but also the alternative option of progression towards altruism. Here too different behaviour modes coexist, though all bundled into the same designation *altruism*.

We would have to extend this graph beyond the margin of a page to convey a lifelike feel of civic behaviour. The area where self-interest and altruism overlap and become ambivalent would have to take over much of the space. So extensive is the intermingling of self-interest with altruism, that it becomes very difficult to differentiate. A prominent sociologist, R. Goodin, goes so far as to say that differentiation is not only impossible and in any case irrelevant; what matters is that

Looking Behind the Scenes 109

outcome provides the least noxious possibilities for social coherence.[9] But then, he gives a nil rating to a possible transcendent cause. Meanwhile, to illustrate ambivalence, here are two illustrations of social patterns both with the label, altruism.

Reciprocal altruism. This is based on the assumption of a quasi-contractual nature regarding mutual interdependence. In order that you do something essential for me, I must do something for you (even to the point of sacrifice). Classic Kantian reasoning; with the implication of an obligation to help those in distress as part of the general obligation tying human beings one to another in view of their common nature as moral agents. Much of social morality, especially since the eighteenth century, rests on variations of this theme. One such variation brings in the social convention theory: obligations to do something for someone else albeit without direct benefit to themselves, *on the condition* that others are tied by the same obligation where similar criteria exist (Harman, 1977).[10]

Another mode of ambivalent altruism can be observed in an example of the far-eastern social ethos. Robert McLaren relates the anecdote from a Japanese university much frequented by Americans. At the examinations for a course in English, a Japanese student was not allowed the use of an English dictionary; whereupon one of his American colleagues exclaimed: 'but that is not fair'. McLaren points out that such a statement would lack meaning to the Japanese. Their appeal would be on the lines: 'but he (the Japanese student) is so *kawaiso*, meaning *pitiable*. Implied is entitlement arising out of disadvantage; respectively obligation by the advantaged to support the one who pleads *kawaiso* (McLaren, 1984).[11] We can see how that principle leads to relationships between superiors and inferiors and to consequent requirements obligatory on the former. (Translating the story into a different environment: what about the ship's master who must be last to leave the bridge? An obligation for the privileged toward those who are inferior in rank or talent?)

From all this it is evident that altruism, just as self-interest, is not exclusively 'this *or* that', the genuine article being the one which conforms to one particular perception and all alternatives being no more than outcrops of inadequate reasoning. On the contrary, it is a case of this *and* that. In this guise it functions within rationally definable processes (say, a set of utilitarian social structures). Yet there is also altruism of a different order manifest in unconditional outreach towards the other, with roots. One might use the simile of two distinct streams to drive one turbine. The one reflects evolutionary and to some extent intelligible dynamics, the other a transcendent reality with the capacity to break through the limiting pathways of the power plant. The resulting events may culminate in acts of self-giving, self-emptying and so on. This double image illustrates the fact that separate drives are intertwined to the point where outcomes are unpredictable.

How Civic Generosity Fits In

So far nothing has been said to explicate civic generosity, the central subject of our book. We have stressed that all forms of interpersonal behaviour reflect a rich mix of possibilities. Seemingly disparate components, self-interest and altruism, can both be operative in civic generosity. Referring to Figure 9.2 civic generosity can be located in the area where self-interest and altruism merge. In a sense that implies ambivalence. Yet it needs stressing that this ambivalence ought not to induce anyone to discount civic generosity. A simple illustration: a person may embark on a generous initiative from ulterior self-regarding motives (and, as Frank Turner points out in Chapter 13, thereby generate a distorting power relationship). Yet there is the potential for subsequent widening of horizons, whether we call this change of heart or maturing. And even when no development of this order takes place its potential counts. What did not emerge in one set of circumstances may come to fruition in another.

4. ROOTS

Reaching Out

> 'Whenever I come across the phrase "reaching out" my imagination reaches back into memory and vision. I find myself once again standing in the Sistine Chapel... I feel, as much as I see, the power-filled finger of God, stretched out to Adam who in this instant *is*'[12]

Reaching out is a powerful description of generosity. It leads to a realm made accessible by metaphysical concepts and metaphor. In the first instance reaching out conveys how a Primary Cause, a Transcendent Reality, or in an unambiguous term, God, imparts his/her being to us; and with that being imparts attributes like goodness and generosity. That is outreach by God. But outreach can also tell about human generosity; as movement from self towards the other.

Looking Behind the Scenes 111

This is a perennial theme of theology.[13] Aquinas incorporates the image into a comprehensive pattern when he speaks of God's *giving*: the gift of God's *being* to his/her creatures. Or again, as God's *presence* in rational human beings, and particularly in the righteous.[14] Nicholas Lash puts it vividly: '... the enablement ... that human beings ... conform their treatment of each other ... to the pattern of God's outpoured peacefulness'.[15]

Milbank speaks of God's gratuitous imparting of him/herself using words like *'God's love for what he creates implies that the creation is generated within a harmonious order intrinsic to God's own being'*.[16] And quoting the post-modern philosopher Gilles Deleuze: '... *a full participation in the suspension downward of hierarchies (the aiding of others by charity)* ...'.[17] Yet another formulation, by Václav Havel: '*I have always felt ... a boundless and unmotivated sense of responsibility* [arising from] "*existence beyond our existence*" ... *into which we are primordially thrown* ...'.[18]

Lastly some lines from a poem by Dietrich Bonhoeffer. It was written in prison not long before his execution and conveys his intense awareness of God's generous self-giving even at a time when human beings experience abandonment:

'God goes out to all and to every man in their sore need
gives himself as bread, soul and body to feed;
alike for Christians and pagans his dying deed ...'[19]

Outreach, outpouring, gift, mirror-like reflection, sending; 'imprint' – the creativity of God, making its imprint on the human self and conversely our generosity making an imprint of goodwill on 'the other'. A wealth of such metaphors has been formulated within the various spiritual traditions; each conveying with a specific nuance what generosity and altruism is and does.

Yet another word can be helpful. The German *Mitleiden* conveys vividly what is at issue. (*Compassion*, the English equivalent, leaves us slightly at the margin of what is meant; the word makes us sympathetic beholders, no more.) *Mitleiden* is outreach and commitment; no questions asked. We enter into the other's experience with disregard of ourselves. Just as in Bonhoeffer's poem.

It must be borne in mind, though, that *Mitleiden* has been again and again idolized and thereby turned into a black farce. This happens whenever there is morbid dwelling on suffering: when, for some persons suffering becomes the exclusive redeeming condition of life. It then gets distorted into all kind of sterile self-torture (literal and figurative). An ineradicable manichean streak marks western culture; 'all creation, humanity foremost, is corrupted through and through; the joy of living and giving is dangerous if not outright reprehensible; an act cannot be virtuous unless it hurts; therefore to derive ostensible satisfaction from one's own beneficence deprives it of true value'. A somewhat lighter touch should help to get the balance right.

Listening to the language of outreach and transcendence can be inspiring for some; it will invite resistance by others. Sceptics most of us, we do tend to reduce human motives to the lowest value denominator. A hyperbolic formulation might therefore run like this: 'Outreach, far from being an expression of altruism, is a dramatic form of self-interest. If there exists a transcendent principle – a Creator – to reach out toward him/her (or to his/her creatures) is no more than the desire (perhaps an unconscious desire) for self-affirmation'.

This position cannot be dismissed lightly. But consider the counterproposition. Outreach with all that this implies in terms of self-giving is acknowledgement of limitation and of dependency. Not a case of pandering to *The Other* because of what this will do for *me*; but acknowledgment of *The Other's* (and 'the others') being and his/her full significance. Correspondingly two reactions are possible. If you will, reduce outreach to mere questing for a condition whereby the self is asserted for its own sake. Alternatively, recognize that by virtue of altruistic outreach the self can become transformed from a self-regarding and self-preserving object into a subject called person which uniquely generates relationship, see *Summa*, Ia,Q32,[20] also Lash.[21] Both options tell about dynamics and counter dynamics in human existence. One however is the richer one.

5. TENSION, ESSENTIAL FOR BALANCE

To ascribe vital significance to civic generosity and even more so to altruism, and to assert the potential for their enhancement is not the same as to indulge in facile optimism. Countervailing drives and circumstances are too evident. Human performance is often unspeakably grim and cannot be wished away. But neither can we allow today's pervasive climate of moral pessimism to obscure the potentially ennobling constituent of our humanity.[22]

For example contrast two passages from Havel:

'... once I try – here and now... not excusing myself by saying that things would be easier elsewhere... to live in harmony with the voice of Being... I suddenly discover that I am not the only one, nor the first...'[23]

'... When I recall the dozens and dozens of hours I have spent over the past year in meetings about the constitution, the thought that these negotiations may drag on... makes me cringe in dismay.'[24]

The first text, written from prison in darkness, evidences hope; the other – at a time when some of Havel's hopes had been realized, acknowledges darkness emanating from in-turned self-interest. A story of irremediable failure? A statement of the ineffectiveness of altruism? But read on:

'... a state based on ideas... is meant to extricate human beings from the straightjacket of [political and economical] ideological interpretations and to rehabilitate them as subjects of individual conscience, of individual responsibility...'[25]

Havel testifies that ideas and belief have, especially in adversity, a dynamism which withstand even the bane of success – that is, the success of negative self-interest.

Can we conclude, therefore, that there are reasonable prospects for actual enhancement of civic generosity and altruism in our social affairs? Once again a question with various possible conclusions. Here are three:

- An outright No. 'We have had enough of utopias', so say some positivists.
- Perhaps. Altruism is contingent on environment and can be 'managed' to be of greater utility.
- Yes – with a 'but' built in.

We ought to test that 'but'. There are indeed countless instances of responsibility some with far-reaching impact. But when it comes to the totality of personal human dispositions and the spectrum of individual make-ups – some speak rather loosely of 'human nature' – there is no hard evidence that this has changed in the history of the past 7000 years or so. On the other hand when we consider responses by cultural or economic groupings to needs of others, including needs far away, there is evidence of rising norms. What might have been the popular response to Oxfam in the days of Columbus?

It could be argued, then, that dispositions of societies actualize, however inconsistently, that which is latent in personal being; and in reverse, that the personal potential for self-giving finds release as result of the communal behaviour which it helped to shape. In consequence we might speak of maturing – *crowds* becoming *communities*.

So, civic generosity and altruism are not static. They have the capacity of being enhanced – and of course also of being degraded or disfigured.

Such seemingly optimistic interpretations require one final caveat, at least from the angle of some of the major religious faiths. Even when human altruism and all its manifestations are recognized to reflect the transcendent principle at the heart of existence, these motives in themselves are insufficient to produce more than a momentary breakthrough. To expect limited human beings to achieve more than occasional and restricted social progress would be yet another facile abstraction. Altruism and its expressions will always depend on being sustained/empowered by that same transcendent principle of which it is a reflection and which is beyond prediction.

6. CIVIC GENEROSITY TODAY AND TOMORROW

Throughout, our discussion has concentrated on model building, a paper exercise as some might call it. In Chapter 18 we will offer several practical suggestions on how our model of civic generosity can be transformed into public policy, and how thereby its transcendent roots are authenticated by experience.

Meanwhile, we have attempted to show that enhancement of civic generosity as a significant factor in social and economic mechanisms is not only a possibility because, in the light of our particular world view, it accords with the fundamentals of *how things are meant to be*. This statement includes acknowledgement that civic generosity expresses, even though only inadequately, the Creator's freedom to give. Yet included in that proposition is an additional acknowledgement. Built into created existence, including of course economic and political processes, there is necessity and contingency. And these limit the enhancement of which we are speaking here.

We are compelled therefore to recognize that civic generosity and, even more, true altruism, is and for the time being will remain, a minority project. That means a restricted not a dominant role; and also a role performed here and there, not universally. But that must not be seen as an insignificant role. On the contrary. Minorities have provided drive and transformation for social patterning throughout history.[26] Evidence abounds. Sometimes a minority assumes the figure of the *elect*, usually in the wilderness, the chosen people. This is a biblical theme, established in current theology as *the exodus people*. Sometimes they are the dissidents, innovators or even revisionists, those at odds with the establishment. The concept is expressed fittingly by the Hebrew word for 'remnant'. *The remnant*, the minority who not only persist in a seemingly lost cause but provide the vital impact for its continuance and eventual vindication.

Hence good ground for confidence.

NOTES AND REFERENCES

1. This is the natural habitat of the behavioural sciences. Yet our own approach is primarily theological.
2. '*Faith is the certainty of things not yet seen*...', St Paul, Heb.11:1.
3. A recurring notion in Gilson's writing. cf. *L'Être et L'Essence*, J. Vrin, 1948, cp.IX.
4. Mary Midgley, *The Ethical Primate*, Routledge, 1984, p.182.
5. J. Mansfield (ed.), *Self Interest*, University of Chicago Press, 1990.
6. John Milbank, *Theology and Social Theory*, Blackwell, 1990.
7. A. Maslow, *Towards a Psychology of Being*, Van Nostrand, 1962.
8. Václav Havel, *Letters To Olga*, transl. P. Wilson, Faber & Faber, 1988, p.321.
9. cf. Robert E. Goodin, 'Do Motives Matter?', *Can. Journal of Phil.*, 19/3, p.405.
10. C. Harman, *The Nature of Morality*, Oxford University Press, 1977.
11. Ronald McLaren, 'Kawaiso, Justice and Reciprocity – Themes in Japanese and Western Ethics' in: '*Philosophy East and West*, University of Haway Press, 1984, No.1.
12. Michael Hollins, Preface to H. J. M. Nouwen, *Reaching Out*, Collins, 1976.
13. '*Who am I, and what is my people, that we should be able to give this freewill offering? For all things come from you, and of your own have we given you*' I Chronicles 29:14.
14. cf. Per Erik Perrsons, *Sacra Doctrina*, transl. R. Machenzie, Basil Blackwell, 1970, pp.163-71.
15. Nicholas Lash, *Believing Three Ways in One God*, SCM, 1955, p.88.
16. John Milbank, op.cit.
17. ibid.

18. Václav Havel, *Letters to Olga*, p.321.
19. Dietrich Bonhoeffer, *Wiederstand und Ergebung*, Chr. Kaiser 1955, from Christen und Heiden' transl.ed.
20. Thomas Aquinas, *Summa Theologica*, transl. A. Pegis, 1a, Q32.
21. Nicholas Lash, op.cit.
22. Václav Havel, op.cit. p.349.
23. ibid. The theme recurs in letters 132–41.
24. Václav Havel, 'In time of transposition', *Summer Meditations*, transl. P. Wilson, Faber & Faber, 1992, p.26
25. ibid. p.128.
26. Juan L.Segundo, *Evolution and Guilt*, Orbis, Maryknoll, pp.127 onward.

Part III
Generosity

10 'Enthusiasm'

Conversation with
Jane Tewson
Founder and Chief Executive, Charity Projects and Comic Relief
and
Maggie Baxter
Grants Director
Transcribed by Michael Walsh

Question: We thought that instead of retelling an account of your striking story – telling it at one remove, our readers will get a more intimate feel of it from the spontaneous responses in a conversation. So, directly to the heart of the matter: What prompted your very distinctive approach?

J: It all arose out of my experience of working with people with learning difficulties. I felt there was a real problem in getting resources to the grass roots. I saw a lot of the larger charities not really getting to the people at the bottom of the pile, and to their carers. I thought I might be able to help them. And, with a lot of good luck and the support of the general public, we have been able to do so. It is not us that have done it, it is the general public and the people who advise us.

M: Jane was the driving force behind the organization. She set up Charity Projects basically to raise new money. Our mission statement is still exactly the same as it was ten years ago – to raise new money, to direct it to specific charitable projects in the UK and Africa, and to ensure sponsorship for our costs so that we can say that every single penny the public gives really does go to charity. We educate people about why support is needed, and also that giving can be fun.

Q: In order to raise money you needed money?

J: No. We didn't have any money when we started. We did not have contacts. I had secured sponsorship for my wage and we went on from there. We outlaid no costs to produce anything because we didn't have the money; we hadn't proved ourselves, and it was difficult to get money, but people gave us things in kind, gave us themselves and their products. That is how we started, and how we went on for a few years.

M: It was the idea that you do something for no reward and make something happen that excited and inspired people, and ignited their enthusiasm to support Jane's idea. And that is how it still remains.

Q: Who are the people you managed to involve?

J: I chose to work with contemporaries. I was lucky enough to find an office in Soho, which was donated. All around us were advertising agencies, film production companies, and these were the first people I went to. First I asked them for very small things, if they would donate the postage every day, or a typewriter. That is how we got involved with them. They were names that weren't known, but they just thought 'Gosh that's a good idea; we'd like to help Jane support Charity Projects' mission and wouldn't it be wonderful to get funds to the people at the bottom of the pile?'

Q: You go into a film production company or whatever and say 'I'm Jane Tewson. I want help with this'. Is that how it works?

J: No. I go along and say 'I'm trying to set up something that I feel is very important'. Then I tell them what it is, and say that to do it I need stationery, old furniture, daily postage. It was very cheeky, but it was at a time when people weren't doing this sort of thing, and when you asked for ten boxes of paper clips it was very difficult for them to say no.

Q: Who did you ask? The girl at the front desk?

J: A variety of different people – including sometimes the MD. I sat in Saatchi and Saatchi's reception and waited until I was seen. We are a people's organization, and the people who support us are a whole variety. Though the organization has grown much bigger, we are still a people's organization, and on the whole it is people who get involved in fundraising, not a company. Whether it is in sponsorship terms or in the giving of grants for projects, we are absolutely keen on people getting involved. I think people have a respect and enthusiasm for passion, and given the amount of energy and passion the organization has, it is difficult for people to say no. I find it contagious. If someone wants to help us it is wonderful – I just want to get back into the office and do more.

M: Last week I was talking in Scotland to organizations in the voluntary sector and was very nervous. But the Director of the Scottish Council for Organizations said 'You have such a wonderful story to tell – don't worry. I would love to stand up and tell that story. It is something people can relate to, and feel warm about when you look at the material'. It is true. It is very accessible. It is not a theory, it is getting on and doing something.

Q: How much can you raise for a particular project?

M: We don't raise money for particular projects. It all goes into a pot which is then distributed. So far in ten years we have raised £112 million.

J: We are in the top 20 grant-giving trusts. Two-thirds goes to Africa and one-third to the UK. The original idea was to assist solely the UK voluntary sector, but then there was the famine in Ethiopia and Band-Aid, which was music based. We had been working for about a year and a half with comedians, and they said couldn't they do something for Africa too? They wanted to create support for Africa and the UK long term, not something which raised a great deal of money which was spent quickly, leaving a great hole. I spent some time in the Sudan and Ethiopia and when I came back we set up Comic Relief as a child of Charity Projects. It was organic growth, and the mission statement and the distribution have stayed the same.

Q: It is sometimes said that when people do something for others, they are really acting out of a kind of self-interest.

J: The lovely thing is that, when people give money to Comic Relief they feel good about it. And so they ought. But yes, I think self-interest comes into it. People normally don't do anything unless they have something to gain in exchange.

M: You could say it was self-interest. When my children go to school on Red Nose Day they are interested because it will be fun. The interest for companies is that they are seen to be doing a good thing, and being socially responsible.

Q: Is the corporate attitude different from the personal? My father was quite a generous man, but he would always say that if you give something and it does not hurt, then it does not count. I do not think this myself, but I suspect it is deeply engrained in people – especially in Anglo-Saxons and Germans.

J: I think so. It depends on your cultural heritage, or your religious background. There is a driving force within some people in this organization which is different from that of others. There are those who feel they want to contribute something to society, and they feel that this organization gives them a mechanism for doing so. But for others it is a job.

M: There is also evidence that people like to get something in return for giving money. If they go to a film première they are quite happy to spend money – they are paying for something they want to do. People always want to see something in exchange for what they are giving their money to – not altogether, perhaps, but basically they are giving money to have fun. There are some people who have been involved with this organization from the beginning, and of course they are getting a return of a kind – they enjoy it, they smile when they come in. There are some extraordinary people whose names are not widely known who have worked in a voluntary capacity, and given their all to us. We have been quite spoiled by having such tremendous people around us in every capacity. It is a very attractive organization, and I'm sure those early days were the breeding ground for that attraction. But it is still attractive.

Q: What would you say is the influence of religious backgrounds? For example, many Jews are very generous, I know Catholics give primarily to Catholic charities... but beyond that?

J: When Lenny Henry was in Somalia he said that if people have walked 25 miles to your front door, you could not but help them. Everyone is potentially our neighbour, and we do our bit to help them in any way we can, but it is certainly not out of a religious bias.

Q: It is sometimes said that though a large proportion of people in the West have no real religious affiliation, this sense of a common commitment to each other is in effect the God-experience of our time.

M: It has been said to us that we are a very spiritual foundation. I wonder then how one could define the word 'spiritual' because we cover the whole world, where that word is given such different meanings. But it is interesting that it has been said to me so frequently. We will not, however, support organizations which are evangelical. We were having a discussion recently about the use of the word 'beneficiary'. We don't like it because it denotes a dependency, or otherness.

Jane challenged us right from the very beginning about the use of words, to stop the 'them and us' attitude. There is so much in common between us, whether one lives in a disadvantaged area or not. The money is everyone's.

Q: In the story of the Good Samaritan the Samaritan reaches out to the one who had been attacked because he could see himself in the same situation; whereas those who passed by maintained a barrier...

J: It is terribly difficult to break down this barrier, but it can be done if the spirit is there. We have an enormous spirit, and an enormous capacity to be spontaneous. As an organization we try to do as well as we can. But married to our enthusiasm and compassion is openness. One of the things we have fought to do is to be very open, and to explain why we are doing things. I think that is more and more true of us.

Q: What can we do to enhance this enthusiasm?

J: You can increase the numbers. We feel very lucky, to be able to educate some people why this is such a difficult time in the UK and Africa. If I were in a wheelchair how would I do things? Rather than make rash judgements about people, educate us to think why things are as they are.

Q: There has been a trend to inform and to motivate, but we seem to be no further on.

J: But we are not further back. The joy of this organization is that we have made a bit of an inroad. We feel really proud that this year many children have watched our education package. It's very important to us to feel that we are chipping away, making some progress.

M: Let me give you an example of an education project, one I have experienced from both sides of the fence, called 'Altogether Better'. It is about disability, including disabled children in mainstream education. It is an interactive video pack for governors, teachers, education authorities. I have a child in a school which has just become designated for disabled children. I have experienced parents' absolute, implicit fear for their able-bodied children – will it get in the way of my child's education: people's own interests are at risk, usually, through fear. The teachers are fearful of the disability, but also for lots of good reasons. But say to the children that the disabled children are different

– they don't see it in that way. They see them as their classmates. We can change attitudes, we can support and challenge attitudes. Who does the fund raising, and those to whom the funds go, they have to be interrelated. To increase the numbers involved, and make it relevant to all, that is the challenge. We haven't done it yet. We have so much to aspire to.

Q: Does the lottery effect you?

M: A profound effect. I have an emotional reaction to the lottery as I fear for those who buy tickets and can't afford to. I was talking to a postmaster in my parents' village, and he says people are not buying food to buy lottery tickets. It has such a knock-on effect on our society. In terms of our grant-giving and education, our grants have become less significant. But it does not mean they are insignificant to the groups who will get them – we must not forget that.

Q: So where is all that extra money which is needed going to come from? Ordinary people do not have the money to pay more taxes. Only the wealthy could do so in principle. Is it your experience that they give more?

M: Up to two Red Nose Days ago, the people who gave the most were in Northern Ireland. If we did a survey, we would find very little came from the richest ten per cent.

Q: That is an old, old story. But don't you think that everyone, everyone, should feel compelled to contribute more, one way or another? Those with large emoluments foremost.

J: That is the sort of thing you can say if you are not on the breadline. There are some dangers about a charitable ethos if it comes down to 'them and us'. If people are not able to be financially generous, it is often through circumstance, not through indolence. People often say they want to give, but do not know how to give direct, and would not like to give to a large project. I was once in a very poor Muslim Sudanese village but Ethiopian Christian refugees were welcomed there with open arms. It was one of my most humbling experiences. I often think that the less material wealth you have, the more you give in other kinds of wealth. The suburban middle class aspires mostly for itself, but on a housing estate you will find that generosity is the human response – the human versus the material.

11 After Darkness
Flourishing of Generosity in an Evolving Environment
Martin Šály

BACKGROUND

The story of the Olga Havel Foundation in the Czech Republic is an example of what individual enthusiasm can achieve.

Prior to 1938 there existed in the then Czechoslovakia a vigorous tradition of commitment to non-governmental caring. Such data still available from 1931 shows that at that time 5450 welfare organizations and similar bodies were operative. But when the communists took over in 1948 all such organizations were centralized and subjected to 'politically reliable' direction. They became totally dependent on the state, bureaucratized, and thus incapable of responding to individual needs. It was part of the prevailing ideology that the disadvantaged, like the physically and mentally handicapped, and the elderly were undesirable. Indeed 'disadvantage' could not exist, and hence there was considerable pressure to make such human beings 'non-existent'. The 'benevolent' state would take care of that.

After 1989 the citizens of Czechoslovakia were faced with an enormous number of new and fascinating challenges; the process of transformation into a 'standard' western democratic state had begun. Gradually the centre-right government under Václav Klaus implemented a liberal policy resulting in a more or less standard market economy. Simultaneously, a concern for the social impact of economic policy began to develop. Yet so far this has had a low profile, due to the lingering of past orthodoxy, at least within the public sector. Escalating costs of social needs and the complexities surrounding the search for an innovative approach to meeting the bill are not headline news for the Czechs, though in fact the problem of a rising deficit in the health-care system has assumed critical proportions and requires systematic discussion. Czech politicians as well as the Czech public have to learn a great deal about the complexities of this issue.

Here then is the political background into which burst the OHF (Olga

Havel Foundation). The success story which was to follow is inextricably linked to the personality of the founder. Olga Havel's childhood and adolescence were not propitious: a working class environment in the dark days of the 1930s; the broken marriage of her parents; being constrained to help with the upbringing of her sister's children. In due course she was apprenticed as a stocking mender in the huge Bat́a shoe complex. For a sensitive young person these are natural roots for a growing sense of solidarity with the underprivileged. At the same time she developed a love of the theatre; eventually finding work at Prague's Theatre on the Balustrade with the help of a young man she had met earlier and who had a job as scene shifter, Václav Havel. They married in 1964. The rest is history: Havel's outspoken dissidence, constant persecution by the authorities and imprisonment, his role as the leading personality in the Velvet Revolution, and finally his emergence, unintended by himself, as President. Olga's involvement throughout was profound: not merely by total loyalty in circumstances which would test their relationship severely; but through total sharing in the intellectual search which is a part of being a dissident. Václav Havel's letters from prison provide a fascinating insight into how two very distinct personalities interact, at times in tension, yet with touching mutual dependency. When her husband assumed highest office, Olga remained herself: a deliberately private person, going quietly about what seemed important to herself. In spite of being the President's wife, she avoided state occasions and international media exposure, as much as feasible.

In retrospect one would say: it was imperative that a person with an urge for commitment had to give practical expression to her ideas. In 1990 she initiated her Foundation. In view of the public apathy which had prevailed for four decades, it was a significant undertaking; creating something out of nothing, if you like. The enterprise was to reflect Václav Havel's, and her own, concept of mutual trust and of 'civility'. Its prime aim was, and still remains, to integrate into a changed society the mentally and physically disadvantaged with their families. Over a period of five years $15,000,000 were raised to that end.

A significant resource of the Foundation, at least in its initial phase, was the link with members of 'Charter 77' (the world-renowned underground group of dissidents which had braved the previous police state). In the days of strict 'management of truth' these people, by their continuous monitoring and making public adverse social realities, had acquired a knowledge of the true, desperate state of old people's homes, mental hospitals and other institutions in that sector. Also, they were accustomed to confront and overcome the obstacles of indifference and of bureaucratic obscurantism. Now, the status of some of these persons had been transformed from having to make a living as window cleaners, labourers, and such like, to ministerial rank and other positions of influence. Their moral and practical support for Olga's project was an important asset.

The structure of the new Foundation reflected the new political freedom which was conducive to formulating a wide, and thus looser, concept of social care than that of the more pragmatic programmes attempted in Western Europe. Some of the original OHF supporters saw the new organization's function as 'system integrator', more concerned with reviewing and renewing systemic ideas than with help to individuals. This is why the early texts of OHF objectives may seem to be somewhat sweeping, for example: 'To assist those in Czechoslovakia who are disabled and those who through prolonged ill health or deprived social circumstances are unable to care for themselves'. 'To help, in keeping with available resources, the organization and financing of certain projects which cannot receive help from elsewhere'. 'To influence legislative changes'. It must be acknowledged that this ambitious vision had a considerable impact. Yet a revised version of the objectives edited in 1995 shows a movement toward more specific projects of social care for handicapped, for example: 'Enable the education of the children of the socially marginalized and the handicapped'. And a final version reads: 'To help handicapped people to be integrated among the healthy and to live together with them'.

These are ambitious aims. In more down to earth terms the new organization utilized the money received from donors to purchase medical supplies, rehabilitation aids, computer equipment for the blind, and organize holiday camps for handicapped children. For example in 1990 15,134 handicapped children were able to go to camps in Norway, Greece, Italy, Switzerland, USA and Sweden. Every year, as a special treat for youngsters with handicaps, an outing by steam train is laid on. For many of these children, it is their first train journey.

Other activities followed. A gallery to display arts and crafts produced by handicapped children as well as by adults was founded. Some special projects deserve mention: a Stop AIDS campaign; the initiation of a Pollen Monitoring System; the Education Foundation intended to support education of children with health and social handicaps.

Since its inception, and in keeping with its wide-ranging objectives, the Foundation has concentrated much of its energy on projects which would have an impact on the emerging social and economic structures.

It became involved in a project called 'Healthy Northern Bohemia'. The major producer of electric energy, EZ, one of the most significant air polluters in the Czech Republic donated £2.7 million for ecological programmes in the most blighted region in the Czech Republic.

Clearly, expert management is required to handle this wide spread of initiatives. Up until September 1991, only one professional worked for OHF; the rest were volunteers. But at that point it was decided to professionalize the operation. Three years later, the office, warehouse and art gallery employed a staff of 20 qualified persons.

OHF AND ITS DONORS

When the new organization opened a bank account in April 1990 the first gift to arrive was Kc 100 from an old people's home; the second was from six teachers who undertook to send Kc 50 of their salary every month. These were people who had experienced need at first hand and knew the impact of help. At the other end of the scale there were medium sized and very substantial donations from the corporate sector, frequently tied to specific projects, and also from wealthy individuals. Typically gifts up to Kc 500 numbered 485 per annum; donors of Kc 501 to Kc 5000 would average at 306 per annum; donors of Kc 5001 to Kc 10,000 50 per annum. In 1993 113 donations of over Kc 10,000 were received. Many of the well known corporations at home and throughout the world provided support. There were also major fund raising events; amongst them a concert by the Rolling Stones, and a reception in New York at which internationally known artists such as Miloš Forman, Ivana Trump and numerous public figures were present, and where $62,000 was raised. Early in the Foundation's history, a gift of $100,000 came from a wealthy Czech emigrant. This contributed substantially towards start-up costs.

Notwithstanding the importance of large scale giving, within OHF there prevails the view that the 'small' gifts from individuals have the greatest value. They constitute proof that care as an expression of civic conscience is a living reality. On the other hand it is at least debatable whether many of the large gifts from companies and wealthy individuals result from a similar motivation. Almost inevitably, they are seen as linked to considerations of image projection. Be this as it may, one must acknowledge a remarkable tendency in business and management. Some of the new entrepreneurs – though obviously not all – are discontented with the concept of total submersion in their commercial

Table 11.1 Income from 1990 to 1994 expressed in £ average

Year	Approx. value of financial gifts	Approx. value of non-financial gifts	Total
1990–1	700,000	1,300,000	2,000,000
1992	500,000	2,500,000	3,000,000
1993	1,600,000	700,000	2,300,000
1994	2,000,000	1,000,000	3,000,000

activity; they want to find some ultimate meaning. To support organizations like OHF, may be for them one way to achieve this.

Simultaneously with financial donations, a flood of non-financial gifts were received. They would be passed on to where they matched a need. For instance the first gift to be received, a copy machine from UNICEF AUSTRIA, was placed with the Prague Federation for Parents of Handicapped Children. Another one, a reading apparatus, was given to a school for the optically handicapped in Brno. The range of such gifts appears staggering: medical supplies, clothes, toys, books, telephones, cameras, computers, records, skis, magazines, flowers, slide projectors, ECG equipment, mammography equipment, even cars and buses and horses. Almost anything you care to name. These non-financial gifts gradually became even more important than financial ones. Table 11.1 summarizes income over a five year period.

WIDER IMPLICATIONS

Readers unfamiliar with the Czech scene should not conclude that OHF is the only voluntary aid organization in this country. Already in the 1980s, as a consequence of a slightly improved political situation, new charitable organizations had begun their activities, without accepting state directives. Today, many of them make a point of having worked informally before 1989. After the revolution stopgap legislation gave formal recognition to the voluntary non-governmental sector. Soon that sector became surprisingly active.

Today, the number of non-profit organizations devoted to social welfare is more than 1600. Perhaps ironically, the Czech public, learning to live in the market economy, consider themselves at times to be victims of what they call 'free market in foundations'. In fact, inevitable excesses apart and thanks to common sense we can count hundreds of examples where the voluntary sector, often through small groups works effectively and on a modest scale to meet a never-ceasing flow of needs.

'NO' IS NOT AN ACCEPTABLE ANSWER

The Sources of Success

1. First and foremost there were the personal qualities of Olga Havlová: vision, total commitment, integrity. There was steel in her too, the result of her harsh schooling. She had learned persistence, never to give up.
2. The name. Doubtless, being the President's wife opened many doors. But Olga's commitment to Charter 77 and her independent mind had given her an aura of her own and ensured support not only from former fellow dissidents but from the public at large.
3. Thorough understanding of real needs.
4. Sound management, together with realistic financial decisions, which secured a virtually self-supporting organization. In line with good management practice, Olga appreciated the necessity to delegate and to secure the Foundation's continuity by handing over to a professional team led by Dr Milada Černá.

AND THE FUTURE?

OHF's basic concept from its inception was: 'to help those persons for whom there is no help from the state'. Essentially, this is a political concept. It starts from the assumption that primary social welfare is the responsibility of the state. Nowadays this is a hotly debated issue throughout the Republic. Questions not dissimilar to those raised in Western democracies are being asked: should the state sector move its involvement in care to local levels, nearer to where specific needs are experienced? Should it restrict itself to provision of social security and pensions, leaving a substantial section of care to voluntary organizations and individual citizens?

Probably OHF is still the most popular foundation in the Czech Republic. It also claims to be the most thoroughly informed non-state organization and thereby in a position to assume an advisory function. But a plethora of other bodies have sprung up, often specializing in much narrower types of needs and using other kinds of marketing, including massive media support. This makes it questionable whether the diversified scope of OHF's activities can be the most effective model for the future. Yet there can be no doubt that the Foundation has been an agent of change, change not only in personal responses towards those in need, but in the political pattern of state and voluntary sector competence. The impact of Václav and Olga Havel's quest for The Civic Society, embodied in OHF, is bound to be lasting.

Olga Havlová died of a serious illness in February 1996.

SOURCES

Basic information about non-profit organizations in the Czech Republic, Prague: NROS, 1994.
Non profit welfare organizations in the Czech Republic, Prague: NROS, 1995.
'Goodwill of Olga Havel' in: Mladá fronta, 20.6.1990.
Interview with Olga Havel in: El n 4/42, Prague, 1991.
The Olga Havel Foundation Annual Reports (covering years 1990–1, 1992, 1993, 1994; in February 1996 data covering 1995 year were not yet available).

Part IV
What Can be Done – by Economists and Politicians

Part 6

12a Economic Expansion*
Gavin Davies

Any government, of whichever political complexion, faces the problem of overcoming the power of two parallel revolutions – one in economic thought, the other in political behaviour – which are tying the hands of democratic politicians throughout the world.

Macro-economics changed forever when the academic consensus decided that, in the long run, unemployment and inflation are independent of each other. The beginning of the end came with the 1968 presidential address to the American Economic Association by Milton Friedman. This, perhaps the most important speech on economics in the post-war era, said that governments could only boost output and jobs at the expense of ever-accelerating – not just high – inflation. Since no society could ever accept ever-accelerating, or indeed ever-decelerating, inflation, the remorseless force of logic implied that the only level of output which could be sustained was that uniquely associated with stable inflation. This rate became known as the natural rate, though there was never much natural about it.

This may all sound arcane, but consider the consequences of this single powerful assertion. If it is true, then governments can no longer be held responsible for unemployment, at least through mistakes of macro-economic management. Their sole macro task becomes that of controlling inflation, which might as well be held at a low rate, since there is nothing to be gained from allowing prices to rise more rapidly. The so-called trade-off between jobs and inflation, the very meat and drink of political debate in the Keynesian era, shrivelled up and died. And in consequence, economists started arguing that the control of inflation could safely be left to technocrats, independent central bankers who were one step removed from the political process. This, and many of the other mantras of post-Thatcher orthodoxy, basically stand or fall by the Friedman proposition. Monetary or inflation targets, PSBR objectives, medium-term plans – all of these were direct descendants of that speech in 1968.

For a while, though, people continued to argue that there were still choices to be made about the size of the state, and the burden of taxation.

* This article has been reprinted with the author's agreement from *The Independent*, 7 May 1996.

John Smith's disastrous shadow budget before the 1992 election was based on that principle. But this approach ran into a political revolution every bit as potent as the economic revolution that preceded it. No longer was the electorate willing to support any political party which promised to raise the overall tax burden, though it would not support serious proposals to reduce the size of the state either. This left us with the prospect of a democratic state forever frozen in aspic, with no party ever willing to risk either higher taxes or an assault on the welfare state.

But with no more tax and no more borrowing, what are they left with? A reallocation of spending programmes, reflecting different political priorities? Certainly. New measures to encourage long-termism in industry, and greater incentives to invest, leading to higher long-term GDP growth rates? That, too. Better ways to manage the public services without spending money? Possibly. But quick results in terms of output and jobs? Nobody dares promise that. The economic revolution prevents the use of demand management to increase GDP growth. The political revolution prevents the use of higher taxes to finance extra public spending. Yet the public demands growth in public services well in excess of GDP growth. A recipe for political discontent on an epic scale.

A bit of wriggling room in this straitjacket is essential. Clearly what is needed is more economic growth, with the focus on boosting long-term investment. But this is unlikely to produce measurable results in the short term. So it means boosting economic growth forthwith to ease the fiscal dilemma, without raising inflation, even temporarily. But how can this be achieved?

First by recognizing that the Friedman proposition, while basically right, should not be treated as totally invariant. A research paper published recently by the US economist Laurence Ball (*NBER Working paper No. 5520*) asks a basic question: Does the experience of a variety of developed economies in the 1980s suggest that the huge rise in the natural rate of unemployment seen in that decade was caused by structural supply side factors, or by the decline in demand which was needed to bring inflation down? According to the Friedman proposition, the whole of the rise in the natural rate should have been caused by the former, not the latter.

But this is not what Ball finds. Instead, he discovers that demand factors played a key role in the rising trend in unemployment, with rather less explanatory power being left for structural labour market factors. That alone is slightly encouraging, because it suggests that the same process may just work in reverse, with a prolonged period of gradually rising demand pressures possibly reversing some of the increase in the natural rate. But more interesting is Ball's discovery that one structural factor in the labour market – the duration of social security support for the unemployed in each spell of joblessness – interacts powerfully with demand factors to explain the rise in the natural rate. The implication is that a drop in demand initially creates the unemployment, but that long-lasting state support for each jobless person then translates this into a permanent increase in the natural rate. Without this state support, the jobless (as in America) would be forced to search for new jobs, even at the cost of accepting lower wages.

This no doubt sounds callous, but the present alternative of consigning the unemployed to the permanent hell of life on the welfare is no better. A programme of gradually rising demand pressures might just lead to permanently lower unemployment, provided that social security is adjusted to ensure that the jobless engage in active searches for new work. The introduction of the job-seekers allowance will go some way to reducing the duration of unemployment support, which should help. But the next generation needs to bite the bullet and go further in this direction, albeit combined with aggressive measures to retrain and increase the geographical mobility of the unemployed. If a Chancellor can force this through, then he has every right to ask for the support of the Bank of England in easing monetary policy, and encouraging the expansion of demand. With higher growth, the budgetary problem suddenly looks a lot less menacing.

More labour market reforms, easier money, less unemployment, and more public money left over for the services people really want. A long shot? Perhaps. But without emergency action to reduce the natural rate of unemployment, and then to boost demand through lower interest rates, any government will soon stumble into the same fiscal abyss which faces us now.

12b Need for Economic Expansion
Stephen F. Frowen

The cost of social welfare has escalated to an extent that most governments are confronted with mounting difficulties in their endeavour to meet these obligations out of tax revenue or by borrowing, with the latter constituting a burden for future generations through interest payments due on outstanding government debt. The reasons for the rising costs of social welfare are manifold. In the health sector, for instance, medical advances have been considerable and the results should be at the disposal of those in need. Heavy medical expenses are also incurred by the extension of life, which simultaneously affects aggregate pension payments. All this coincides with governments and monetary authorities of the Western world having shifted their main economic objective towards fighting inflation; but in order to achieve the low inflation rate we now have, governments had to depress their respective economies. The price to be paid for this shift in policy takes the form of a low rate of economic growth with an accompanying increase in unemployment. Thus more unemployment benefits have to be paid, which substantially increases the total cost of social welfare.

As to the financing of social welfare through government borrowing, it would be true to say that even if in principle the UK government did not mind to do so, at least those EC countries planning to join the European Monetary Union (EMU) would have difficulties following this line. For if they did, they would be in danger of failing to meet the Maastricht criteria for entry, as permission to join EMU is limited to countries with a budget deficit not exceeding three per cent of GDP.

What solution is there for ensuring that the bulk of the costs of social welfare can in fact be financed by governments out of tax revenue? And if there is a gap between what governments can finance out of tax revenue and what ought to be financed, how should this be covered other than by borrowing?

Here one thinks primarily of the voluntary sector. Some of the burden already being taken off the UK government arises from people arranging for private education, private health care, and so on. In the case of private health care in the UK, it often takes the form of companies insuring in particular their managerial staff. All this helps but is not sufficient. There is also the question of justice. Is it right for the privileged few to enjoy better health care and superior education? Will the health service and education financed by the state, on which the bulk of the population depends, not deteriorate further the more people are opting for the private sector? Perhaps the scheme proposed by Frank Field in Chapter 15, of a private social security insurance may be a desirable compromise. This would come close to the German system, the *Rentenversicherung*, which is a separate body not under direct government control.

As to the voluntary sector generally, I doubt that those who could afford to participate through donations will be prepared to voluntarily finance a significant part of the existing gap in covering social costs. With few exceptions (some of whom like to see their name immortalized by funding colleges, museums, and so on), the richer people are, the less generous they appear to be. This seems to be due to human nature and human nature cannot be changed – certainly not in the short run and may be not in the long run either. Even 70 years of communism do not appear to have done much to change human nature in the former Soviet Union. Now being 'liberated' and faced with an insufficiently controlled capitalist system, all the inherent selfishness and brutality of human nature has broken out strongly among a significant part of the Russian population, enriching themselves at the expense of others and leaving not only the old, infirm and underprivileged in a desperate situation, but also those still earning an honest living and doing several jobs just to cover very basic expenses. A truly disturbing state.

A more effective way of enabling governments to fulfil their role as protectors of those in need would be through efficient macro-economic measures to stimulate economic growth so that the utilization of productive capacity, income and the level of employment are maximized. The high income level achieved would not only benefit the private sector. When income rises, so will the government's tax revenue at constant tax rates. If the rates are actually increased or made more progressive, the tax revenue will rise by even more. At the same time, higher employment will reduce the government's spending on social security transfers. Thus, the more income and therefore tax revenue rise, while social security transfers drop, the more governments will be able to reduce the gap between urgent social costs and what they are able to finance of these costs out of tax revenue. During the 17 years of Conservative rule, there has been a sharp drop in real terms in spending on public goods and services, such as health, education, defence, justice, arts and transport as a proportion of the gross domestic product (GDP), only to be absorbed almost completely by the extra spending on social security transfers (Flemming and Oppenheimer, 1996). If such a policy required a more relaxed attitude towards inflation – so let it be. Of course, we do not want to get into an inflationary spiral. This would only cause suffering when the day of reckoning comes and excessive inflation rates have to be reduced through drastic economic measures. But why should an economy – such as the UK's at present – be continuously kept in a depressed state in order to keep the inflation rate at below 2.5 per cent? There is nothing wrong, in my view, in allowing moderate increases in the inflation rate, if this helps to stimulate the economy sufficiently to get out of a persistent recession.

The more an economy produces, the more jobs there will be. And if people ought to have a 'right to . . . decent work [and] to security of employment' (see *The Common Good* statement, para. 91, p. 21), then the last we should pray for is a reduction in people's wants, demanding fewer goods and being happy and contented with less. This can only reduce aggregate demand and aggregate investment, and with it job opportunities. A lower growth rate may be beneficial for the environment, but it is likely to be accompanied by a bigger 'gap'. Economic growth and the size of the 'gap' appear to be inversely related. As to the employment situation, there is another pressing problem arising from the fact that the more generous the provision of benefits to the unemployed is, the more voluntary unemployment one gets. There is apparently a point when financially to many of the unemployed it just does not seem to pay to accept employment. Again Germany with its generous provisions for the unemployed is suffering badly from this phenomenon.

The same is true of benefits paid in the case of illness – the more generous the provisions are, the more tempting it is to search for a sympathetic doctor who will provide the necessary medical certificate for staying away from work in the case of only minor illnesses, illnesses which a freelance worker might tend to ignore. In Germany, employees are entitled to receive their full pay during the first six weeks in case of illness. The amount paid in Germany by the health insurance to replace wages in the case of illness came to the equivalent of roughly £30 billion in 1994. Of course, not everybody exploits the social security system, but many do, and the more generous the system is, the greater the danger that it will be exploited.

Some readers may wonder what the difference is, in its ultimate effect on individuals, between inflation and taxation. To answer this point fully would require another chapter, but to put things into a nutshell, one could say that inflation reduces consumers' purchasing power by price increases (but not all prices are affected simultaneously and to the same degree), while direct taxation reduces disposable income instantly with each tax rise. With an increase in indirect taxes, people can abstain from buying at higher prices, as they can in the case of inflation. Also inflation is a gradual and continuous process – not as inflexible as tax changes – and politically less damaging. In fact, only when thanks to a modest inflation the economy and housing market are booming, do people have this 'feel-good feeling' governments are so desperate to create before each general election. In contrast, tax increases – by reducing demand – lead to recession and ultimately a reduction in tax revenue. But anything that favours a higher growth rate will *increase* tax revenue, reduce the burden of paying unemployment benefit and therefore assist in lowering the Public Sector Borrowing Requirement (PSBR) to a more manageable level. The unexpected sharp rise in the UK's PSBR in 1996 was simply the result of tax revenue lagging behind the total of both government spending and the cost of servicing the national debt.

Of course, exogenous factors cannot be ignored. It is difficult, for instance, to raise the growth rate through higher export levels when the world economy (in particular the economies of our main trading partners in the EC) is stagnating. In this case, the option of devaluation (not an option for member countries of EMU within EMU) can be beneficial, but again one does not want to get into a situation of competitive devaluation. Nevertheless, it remains an effective instrument when the cost and price structure between countries is getting out of line. For this reason, we did have a number of realignments of exchange rates within the EMS.

Another problem of a booming UK economy – while major EC countries are still adversely affected by recession – is likely to arise from a deterioration in the British visible trade balance. In this situation, a reactivated UK economy is likely to cause a surge in imports, with exports lagging behind as a result of increased home demand and export opportunities being at a low ebb.

The international rise in unemployment has no doubt been caused by a decline in aggregate demand deliberately created by governments and monetary authorities in the pursuit of price stabilization. A contributory factor has been the unification of Germany. The latter forced the Deutsche Bundesbank to keep nominal short-term interest rates at a high level to counteract the inflationary impact of an initially record level of East German demand. This in turn forced other EC countries to keep their own short-term interest rates high, thereby deepening their own recession (Frowen, 1997). The latest factor contributing to the low level of demand is the attempt of a number of leading EC countries to reduce government spending in order to meet the Maastricht criteria for joining the European Monetary Union and participate in the Single European Currency when the deadline comes. These are all special, self-imposed factors for the low level of demand among EC countries. There are no signs, in my view, that the First World has reached a demand plateau. People's demand in general seems insatiable. Even if some have enough durable consumer goods in their homes, they may step up the number of cars they desire, go for more expensive models, increase the number of holidays, engage in more cultural pursuits, and so on. There cannot be many people in the UK or other advanced countries, even among the middle and upper middle classes, who feel that their income and wealth enables them to satisfy all their demands to the fullest extent. In England, at least some upper class families with young children to be educated in expensive private schools feel quite impoverished. More important, if we think of the increasing number of underprivileged citizens in some of the most advanced countries, with their basic demands at subsistence level being scarcely covered, one cannot speak of a demand plateau. No, the demand is there, even in First World countries, but cannot be affected because income is lacking.

If we look at Third World countries, the economic situation is far more serious. Here income is lacking to a far greater degree to satisfy even their basic demand. Yet, many factories in the UK and other EC countries are suffering from spare capacity. This has the further adverse effect of keeping capital investment at a low level.

Taking a world-wide look, the situation is truly perverse. A desperate demand for goods and services is there but cannot be affected because of insufficient income, while factories are producing less than they could or would like to, and this leading to levels of unemployment in the advanced countries which have become intolerable. The only industry which appears to be booming, expanding at a horrific rate, producing record profits and paying astronomical salaries plus handsome bonuses to their star analysts and traders, is the financial industry. Surely, all these factors do not add up, and show a world which appears to have gone mad. I think politicians would be wise (and more humane) if at last they would take the time to go back to the Brandt Report (Brandt, 1980) and study it very carefully. The Report is ingenious in that both the First World and Third World countries would benefit from accepting its recommendations. Recommended in fact is a transfer of funds from rich to poor countries. This would raise world aggregate demand and would lower the level of world unemployment. According to the Brandt Report, Third World countries would benefit from such a transfer through a reduction in their foreign exchange gap, which at present constrains their development. Industrial countries, on the other hand, would gain through an expanded demand for their export products on the part of the Third World (Frowen, 1991). Ultimately, the more efficient developing countries, helped in this way, might become dangerous competitors, as some of the Asian countries already are, and this danger may explain the negative response of the Western world to the Brandt Report.

All this is closely, if indirectly, related to the issues covered in this volume. There are certainly immense problems in achieving the goal of financing basic social needs, whether by the public or voluntary sector, but these problems can certainly be tackled in a more efficient and humane way than is happening at present, provided there is a social change to the economic system based more on community thinking (Davidson and Davidson, 1988; Boswell, 1990). But this will take time if it can be achieved at all. Meanwhile, some solution has to be found. It is in this sense that, as a first approach, policies on the lines suggested above will, in my view, be a move in the right direction and may be the most effective immediate way towards filling the gap in meeting social costs. The measures proposed are unlikely to fill this gap entirely. The voluntary sector, in whatever form, will therefore remain essential in order to ensure the well-being of the greatest number of citizens and especially of the underprivileged.

REFERENCES

Boswell, J. (1990). *Community and the Economy: The Theory of Public Co-operation*. Foreword by Bernard Crick, London: Routledge.
Brandt Report (1980). *North-South: A Programme for Survival*.
Davidson P. and Davidson G. (1988). *Economics for a Civilized Society*, London: Macmillan; New York: W. W. Norton.
Flemming J. and Oppenheimer P. (1996). 'Are government spending and taxes too high (or too low)?', *National Institute Economic Review*, August 1996.
Frowen, S. F. (1991). '"Rcrum novarum" and the world economy today', in: A. Luciani (ed.), *La "Rerum Novarum" e i problemi sociali oggi*, Milan: Editrice Massimo, pp.75–92.
Frowen, S. F. (1997). 'The dimensions of German economic unification: Keynote address', in S. F. Frowen and J Hölscher (eds), *The German Currency Union of 1990*, London: Macmillan; New York: St. Martin's Press, pp. 1–10.

13 Choking on Growth
A Theologian Reflects
Frank Turner

I

Professor Frowen, in the previous chapter, has considered ways in which a government might seek to meet the escalating costs of social welfare. He argues that the affluent are unlikely to subsidize such costs by themselves contributing voluntarily to health care, schooling, and so on, while at the same time fully supporting public provision for the less affluent. Therefore he looks to economic expansion to generate sufficient resources to fund adequate social provision. Economic growth, runs the argument, will (subject to certain conditions such as constant tax rates) increase tax revenue even as it lessens the burden of supporting the unemployed, so freeing resources for more constructive use.

This expectation that expansion will allow the relatively painless approach to the attainment of social justice is deeply attractive to someone of my post-war, baby-boom generation, brought up to expect a progressive amelioration of the hardships known by my parents. It evokes the post-war welfare consensus so rudely disputed by the subsequent orthodoxy of the 'New Right', which polarizes economic growth and generous social welfare instead of aligning them. Perhaps the fate of this consensus is symbolized by the fact that I write this sentence on the date (6 April 1996) when a lowering of the standard rate of income tax is lowered from 25p to 24p, largely with the intention of stimulating growth!

But Professor Frowen's argument also embodies an intuitively positive view of economic growth as such. In this chapter, therefore, I hope to contribute to the discussion by offering some theological criteria for the assessment of such expansion.

From a certain political perspective this endeavour will crudely beg the question. Isn't economic expansion a self-evident social good? How can anyone presume to 'assess' it, since any act of assessment must logically be grounded on some latent world-view or value-base which relativizes economic expansion by claiming loftily to weigh it against other goods?[1]

On this point, at least, I feel few qualms, for even those who fiercely espouse the cause of free-market capitalism commonly go beyond the claim that it makes us (or everyone) better off and is therefore an *absolute* good, so that there is no more to be said. They usually argue that it also serves some deeper non-economic good, such as 'freedom', and so regard economic success (characterized in terms of expansion) as simultaneously an intrinsic non-moral good and the instrument of a further moral good. Anyone who succeeded in showing that other moral goods might be blocked or destroyed by expansion would therefore bring the integral benefit of expansion into question.

In this chapter I speak as a Christian theologian. What does this imply? In the words of the American theologian Roger Haight:[2]

> Theology today [is] a discipline which seeks to understand . . . the underlying truth of all reality. Christian theology does not merely talk about God. Rather theology attempts to construe all things, the world, human existence, human history and society, as well as God, from within the vision that is mediated to the Christian community by its religious symbols.

As a theologian, therefore, I must work (critically) from within a faith-tradition. Theologians have the task of explaining the community's faith to itself and to the world, of establishing meaning and relevance in terms of common human experience and language.

Now this faith-tradition has long disparaged the individual and collective search for wealth. The Gospels of Matthew (6:24) and Luke (16:13) each contain the saying: 'No one can be the slave of two masters: he will either hate the first and love the second, or be attached to the first and despise the second. You cannot be the slave both of God and money'. 'Money' here is *mammona*, 'mammon'. *Mammon* was the Syrian God of Wealth, so the term comes to convey opprobrium, to refer not to money (or even wealth) as such, but to wealth which has become an idol, an evil influence. The saying recognizes, then, that it is possible to desire or possess money without being its slave: but suggests also that money almost inevitably becomes a serious rival to God at that deep point of the psyche where people choose their fundamental allegiances. This is illustrated by a character in Barbara Trapido's novel *Temples of Delight*: 'he was entirely secular, and all his gods were material ones'.[3]

This Gospel stance may smack to some readers of this book of religious narrow-mindedness. They might infer that I (or even Christians in general) can scarcely be worthwhile conversation partners in the debate about wealth creation.

Naturally the radical stance is not self-validating. Scriptural views of wealth are not uniform. Also, they derive from a cultural context quite unlike our own: precisely, a culture where the ideal of social solidarity stands in judgement over socially divisive entrepreneurial flair, as in Isaiah 5:8 ('Woe to those who add house to house and join field to field until there is nowhere left and they are the sole inhabitants of the country'). Nevertheless, if I am to speak theologically, I must take the Gospel seriously, as well as trying to take seriously the political and social realities of our contemporary world. For the present, let it at least be noted that 'the vision mediated to the Christian community by its religious symbols' holds that wealth, and therefore also the continuously increasing wealth implicit in the notion of economic expansion, be not immune to critique.

I shall argue that the fundamental value which judges economic expansion is that of *fully human life and development*. Since the Gospel calls for us to 'love our neighbour as ourself' and (in the parable of the Good Samaritan) expands the concept of 'neighbour' to embrace all those in need, this 'fully human life and development' applies to the Self and the Other alike and inseparably. Economic development serves good or evil insofar as it serves or threatens this profound value; and economic growth cannot be an intrinsic good or evil at all, still less an *absolute* good or evil, since it is assessed *only* by how it furthers or distorts the deeper human good.

This first formulation about 'the deeper human good' is too vague to indicate what weight any given society ought to attach to economic criteria in general and economic expansion in particular. Even in this form, and though I speak at the level of general principles, it operates critically against any theory which posits economic growth as the primary determinant of a social policy. Where the goal of economic development becomes in practice absolute, or where business ideology becomes socially and politically dominant ('What's good for General Motors is good for America') the full dimensions of the human good are indeed endangered. The absolute commitment to economic expansion constitutes the 'worship of Mammon', and equally falls under St Augustine's condemnation of the 'Earthly City', in the introduction to Book I of the *City of God*: the earthly city is said to enslave people, is itself dominated by its very lust to dominate. In practice, we do not have to look far to identify the victims.

Even if it becomes dominant, economic expansion always remains one social goal among others. Here are three immediate implications:

1. Much depends on which other goals are associated with it. The package 'economic expansion plus social justice', or 'economic expansion as a means to cover the costs of social welfare', is a different one from the package 'economic expansion plus untrammelled individual liberty'. If a society seeks expansion in order to fund social protection systems more adequately, policy-makers will always be alert to improve such systems as resources allow. Whereas if the goal is expansion plus minimal welfare apparatus (as currently in the USA), expansion will inevitably exacerbate poverty as capital investment in technology displaces workers.
2. Economic expansion will always produce a mixed crop of good and evil together, or rather, some people's good and others' evil. Selling arms to a dictatorship encourages violent oppression overseas even as it saves jobs (and boosts some individuals' wealth) at home. Ethical objections rarely carry decisive weight against the safeguarding of livelihoods – or even against the likely loss of markets to competitors. Again, even when expansion produces a seeming predominance of good, it may sometimes rule out the attainment of greater or more relevant goods: for example, ascribing a high value to productivity and believing in an economic meritocracy might well entail disdain for the unproductive and untalented: and that disdain is socially corrupting and counter-Christian.
3. The relative priority of economic expansion as a central societal goal will depend in part on the starting point. A poverty-stricken society urgently needs growth, since a certain freedom from want is indispensable for people to enjoy health and security and the kind of leisure that enriches their lives, to cultivate friendships, to participate in the wider life of their society. (But my argument asserts that what *ultimately* counts is this health, friendship, participation, rather than their arguably typical economic preconditions.) Once a widely shared sufficiency is attained, a rational and mature society will emphasize aims other than growth. We do this without question in wartime, for instance, when individuals who 'profiteer', or companies who aggrandize themselves through exploiting their own country's war effort, are widely despised.[4]

II

So far, I have suggested that economic goals are necessarily grounded in societal aspirations that transcend the economic realm: and that economic policy is invariably integrated with other than economic factors. Yet, economic policies never come neat, without open or latent political content. Economic decisions (whether made by entrepreneurs or by government ministers) always embody decisions about which particular groups will be the ultimate or immediate beneficiaries, even if they also vaguely envisage a wider acceptability.

Further, though, it is crucial to realize that the *framework* of those decisions, the market system itself, is also not a given fact but is the result of choice. As Peter Calvocoressi put this point:

> In an industrial democracy there is commonly a conflict between economic growth and social justice and when a choice has to be made two opposing propositions are advanced. The first will aver that if priority is given to justice growth will be inhibited, the second that if priority is given to growth justice will be delayed. This conflict between social and economic ends can be resolved only by political action.[5]

This formulation is too schematic, because many public actors would aspire to *balance* wider social goods with directly economic ones. But Calvocoressi is surely right to insist on the 'existentialist' nature of our decisions. Our representatives constantly make such choices on our behalf. The economistic world-view that all practical decisions are ultimately driven by the 'bottom line' of growth or profit is a mystification, because it veils the political nature of such choices and so illicitly precludes the articulation of relevant political and cultural considerations.

Consider, as an example, the gradual realignment of personal taxation since 1979. The overall tax burden is much the same now as then, but its distribution has altered drastically, in two senses: in the steep reduction of the higher rates, and in the shift from direct to indirect taxation. The Government might well claim (contentiously) that the increased 'incentives' implicit in the new tax structure will in the long run increase economic growth and therefore (by trickle-down) benefit the poorest also. But the primary purpose is quite evidently that of *politically* motivated redistribution in favour of higher earners. Without being mind-readers we can be certain of this, since *their* gain is immediate and assured, whereas any benefit eventually accruing to those living in poverty is long term and incalculable though their immediate plight is worsened. In current fiscal policy, the general good is at best a vague pious wish and at worst a deliberate obfuscation.[6]

III

I need to state, therefore, on what general conditions I would believe economic expansion to be a legitimate policy objective; and also, on what conditions I believe it to be ethically and spiritually dubious as a core commitment. Another way of putting the question would be to ask what makes economic expansion count as genuine economic *development*, and when is expansion antithetical to true development.

I want to cite the philosopher Michael Walzer, who has offered an intriguing account of the legitimate, socially sanctioned uses of money, and what he calls 'blocked exchanges', by which he means those financial transactions which a society disallows because of its commitment to certain other values.[7] He writes:

> We can buy and sell universally only if we disregard real values; while if we attend to values, there are things that cannot be bought and sold. (Walzer, p. 97)

Here are three examples from his suggested list of 14:

- Many societies insist that political favours cannot be directly bought. So citizens cannot sell their votes or officials their decisions. We speak of 'bribery' when we believe that such buying and selling are ruled out by other social values.[8]
- It is agreed in many societies that *political office* is a good which derives from democratic endorsement rather than wealth, and therefore cannot be bought: thus we prevent the power of wealth from spilling over *straightforwardly* into the political realm, even though we recognize (because money and politics are not totally discrete worlds) that wealth will commonly increase somone's access to political *influence*.
- Criminal justice is not for sale, though the process of the law, like that of politics, is not sealed off from the power of money: so a good lawyer may be hired, but not a judge.

Applying this third example to my argument, it is evident that money's indirect power over legal processes depends partly on political decisions (about the availability of legal aid, public support for law centres, and so on). In turn, political decisions will be shaped by, among other factors, financial interests. This indeterminate phrase 'among other factors' encapsulates the whole question at issue – the primacy, or otherwise, of directly economic criteria in public life.

Walzer thus identifies several spheres in which independent social values are (and must be) defended against the market. As he says, however, to deny the absolute rule of the market (or economic goods in general) does not mean that it is intrinsically destructive of social life:

> it is a great mistake, I think, when people worried about the tyranny of the market seek its entire abolition. It is one thing to clear the Temple of traders, quite another to clear the streets... The merchant panders to our desires. But so long as he isn't selling people votes or political influence, so long as he hasn't cornered the market in wheat in a time of drought, so long as his cars aren't deathtraps, his shirts inflammable, this is a harmless pandering. He will try, of course, to sell us things we don't really want; he will show us the best side of his goods and conceal their dark side. We will have to be protected against fraud (as he will against theft). But the exchange is in principle a relation of mutual benefit. (Walzer, pp. 109–10)

Attempting, as Walzer does, to delimit the proper uses of money bears on the fundamental question facing me in this chapter, about the prioritizing (by societal consensus or political decision) of expansion as against other social goods. I have suggested that *growth towards sufficiency* would normally be an urgent social priority. Beyond that point, the humane assessment of economic growth depends much more directly on the manner of its distribution. It is no contribution to the common good that the most affluent increase their wealth yet further, especially if this occurs at the expense of those in poverty.

I suggest, therefore, that if increased disparities of income are seen to be a pragmatically inevitable effect of growth, then growth cannot be the most pressing social good.[9] One axiom commonly used to justify growth even in a divided society is that of 'trickle-down'. I have already alluded to it. The idea is epitomized in Mrs Thatcher's celebrated jibe at the Labour Party, that it was more concerned with cutting up the cake than with baking a bigger one. This remark abstracts from the realities of power. The power given by wealth is inherently *power over others*. As one person's slice of the cake grows the other's shrinks. Trickle-down theories depend for their plausibility on systematically obscuring this factor: but once such theories are doubted, the ethical justification for growth is in turn deprived of much of its seeming self-evidence.

IV

I now try to draw from my discussion some criteria for the assessment of economic expansion. Let me put them negatively, mindful that each formulation implies a positive corollary. The single-minded pursuit of expansion at the cost of other social goals is most dubious in the following circumstances:

1. Where economic growth is directed to the satisfaction of demand at the expense of meeting urgent human needs.[10] Otherwise we find ourselves commending the familiar situation characterized in a lecture some years ago by the America social theorist, Joe Holland: the economy is doing fine, it's just that the people are having a hard time! I take it that market theory cannot distinguish between a home that offers mere basic shelter and a luxury second home in the countryside: or between someone's only winter coat and the latest 'creation'. I realize that cases are rarely simple. If the purchasers of the second home did not buy it, it might lie vacant and rot. On the other hand, the market for rural second homes drives up prices in a situation of scarcity (indeed, the scarcity is part of the attraction), so that the privileged owners are subsequently all too likely to oppose the construction of more modest homes nearby. Similarly, luxuries are not obviously immoral: but if their production become the prime focus of the productive system that system is anti-human.
2. Where business objectives such as maximized profit or growth impose their own exigencies in such a way as inevitably to undermine human relationships. Pope John Paul II expresses this point powerfully in his encyclical *Centesimus Annus* (1991):

> Profitability is not the only indicator of a firm's condition . . . In fact the purpose of a business firm is not simply to make a profit, but is to be found in its very existence as a *community of persons*

who in various ways are endeavouring to satisfy their basic needs, and who form a particular group at the service of society. Profit is a regulator of the life of a business, but it is not the only one; *other human and moral factors* must also be considered which, in the long run, are at least equally important. (Section 35)

Anyone who intuitively takes this statement to be naive, implausible 'in the real world', begs the question. The whole point of the Christian theological critique is that the 'real world' needs to and can be changed: and that all hope for humane societal regeneration depends on our rejecting the determinism of competitive commercial logic.

3. Where the drive for growth subverts any possible experience of solidarity. This is a stronger version of the last point. The UK's opting out of the Maastricht 'Social Chapter' (on the grounds that Europe and Britain will be competitively weakened by enacting it) embodies the judgement that the goal of expansion rules out any defence of humane conditions of employment.[11] To the extent that this is so, the primacy of expansionist policy is humanly destructive.

4. Where those who lead the drive for growth are *irresponsible*: that is, where they disclaim structural responsibility for its social consequences. They might seek to offload the manifest social costs of business operations, such as those of pollution, for example, by the re-siting of factories where the company cannot effectively be brought to account.

5. Where philanthropic generosity is taken to be a sufficient remedy for social injustice. This is a familiar ideological phenomenon. At the end of the eighteenth century, William Townsend's *Dissertation on the Poor Laws* argued against legal provision to feed the hungry. 'So long as property is safe', he maintained, 'hunger is a more effective goad to labour than mere laws can be. However, once the indigent are left to the mercy of the affluent, who can doubt that the only difficulty is to restrain the impetuosity of the latter's benevolence, and who can doubt that such charity is nobler than anything flowing from legal obligation?'[12] On the contrary, I argue that personal generosity is a necessary but not sufficient response to the asymmetries of vulnerability which mark any society but which are magnified by an economic system which stresses the achievement of growth through competition. Since the practice of altruism and generosity is a central theme of this volume, we do well to remember Reinhold Niebuhr's fierce verdict:

Philanthropy combines genuine pity with the display of power and the latter element explains why the powerful are more inclined to be generous than to grant social justice.[13]

Niebuhr implies two points. Firstly, since no one can assert a 'right' to others' generosity, its practice is a random response to the brute facts of human need. Secondly, it leaves power-relationships untouched, or even reinforces their inequality, further undermining the dignity of the recipient. Niebuhr presumably has in mind such people as Andrew Carnegie, who made money as ruthlessly as was necessary, then subsequently practised a largesse which (one suspects) expressed self-glorification no less than generosity. The generosity no doubt promoted the public benefit: but in no way could it legitimize the initial (and perhaps ongoing) ruthlessness.

Against such reliance on philanthropy, Michael Ignatieff argues that the complex system of mediations implicit in a welfare state are often welcome to the affluent and to the vulnerable alike, since what is expressed is a moral community rather than any conscious act of individual beneficence which the recipient is made to feel keenly.[14] On this view, legitimate economic expansion is determined *at all points* by the ideal of the moral community.

To these five points, it must be added that, even if growth is a genuine good, or the condition of achieving other desirable goods, it does not follow that the maximization of growth is also good. Economic actors might easily but falsely assume that if growth is good, more growth is better. On the contrary, any *a priori* commitment to maximizing growth must undermine any sense of the necessary tension between growth and other objectives.

V

In a classic book, Karl Polanyi remarks of the European nineteenth century that all types of societies are limited by economic factors, by the material conditions of their existence. The achievement of survival and sufficiency is always and everywhere a central societal project. But nineteenth century civilization was economic in a new and distinctive sense, in that it posited gain as its *fundamental* shared purpose. The self-regulating market system was uniquely derived from this principle.[15]

The absolute 'rule of the market' embodies a materialistic social philosophy which supposes that all human problems can be resolved given the free play of material commodities: and it signifies a shift in the grounding of economic action from sufficiency to maximal gain. In such a system, society is run as an adjunct to the market, and is embedded in the economic system in general and the market system in particular, instead of the other way round. A labour market governed by 'freedom of contract', for instance, overrides any non-contractual bonds of kinship, neighbourhood or religion which limit that 'freedom'.

Against this position stands the view that true economic development is identified by its service of human freedom and human need. It is a perversion of the good life when specific notions of development, defined quantitatively in terms of expansion, are taken to define that freedom and to determine which needs are met and which ignored. John Ruskin wrote in the nineteenth century that most people do not wish to devote their lives to financial gain, any more than one becomes a clergyman in order to earn a stipend. Financial return is due to work, but ought not to be its sole purpose. That guideline applies to a national community as much as to an individual. Ultimately to order our shared lives by criteria taken from commercial economics is the contemporary way of worshipping *Mammon*.

On this diagnosis, economic expansion is a promise and also a fallacy. At best it should be recognized as a blunt and potentially damaging instrument for dealing with 'the gap'. It requires a degree of fine tuning and sensitive application which is likely to be beyond what is achievable in the cut and thrust of the market place.

NOTES AND REFERENCES

1. Economic liberals resist political control in the plausible belief that the political class is self-interested, that it serves merely sectional interests (unions, landowners, and so on) not the general good, and that its interference with economic freedom is necessarily ignorant and usually disastrous. The same economic liberals tend to assume that economic decision-makers are impartial, beneficent and competent.
2. Roger Haight, *Dynamics of Theology*, New York, Paulist Press, 1990, p.1.
3. In *The Denial of Death*, New York, Free Press (Macmillan), 1975, pp.73–90, Ernest Becker considers money as a sacred object. Becker gives the example of a house in the ruins of Pompeii, where there was found a

picture of a man weighing his penis in a scale of gold coins. Compare an advertisement (for Royal Mail!) in *The Guardian* of 5 April 1996. It runs, 'Mammon: The Odourless Fragrance. Until . . . the wearer finds herself in the presence of gold credit cards. The ensuing chemical reaction produces an irresistible fragrance, that is . . . Mammon'.

4. A whole series of relevant questions is suggested by this allusion to war. If we relegate economic growth to the level of a secondary consideration in wartime, can we do so if (to adapt William James's famous concept to another context) we can find a 'moral equivalent of war'? Can we broaden the term 'profiteer' beyond its customary reference to war, famine or equivalent emergency? Is 'profiteering' a concept which a free-market advocate could admit at all?

5. Peter Calvocoressi, *The British Experience 1945–75*, Harmondsworth, Penguin Books, 1978. The author remarks earlier that classical free market theory would rule out such a clash between public interest and private profit, whereas a socialist polity would emphasize it.

6. On the other hand, the decision to limit the level of tax relief on mortgage interest would seem to me to be an economic decision that risks alienating some of the Government's natural supporters (and indeed Mrs Thatcher has lamented it from her retirement). If I am right it is no less a political act, but one done in economic 'good faith'.

7. Michael Walzer, *Spheres of Justice*, Oxford, Basil Blackwell, 1983. His discussion of what money can and cannot buy begins on p.100. I suppose that my use of Walzer signifies my belief that money is too important to be left to economists.

8. Naturally, cultural practices vary. As Walzer points out, in cultures where the line between private and public is hazy, for example, where political office has not fully emerged as an autonomous good, the gift relationship between office-holders and clients might be socially ratified. So cross-cultural ethical pronouncements are always hazardous. Interestingly, though, the British press tends to judge other cultures *more* confidently than its own: as when it charges officials of other countries with corruption for accepting inducements from, say, a British business executive, without accusing the executive of corruption for offering them.

9. John Rawls's famous 'general conception of justice' is relevant here, and runs as follows: 'All social values – liberty and opportunity, income and wealth, and the bases of self-respect – are to be distributed equally unless an unequal distribution of any, or all, of these values is to everyone's advantage.' (*A Theory of Justice*, Oxford University Press, 1972, p.62). Against the utilitarian who advocates the 'greatest good of the greatest number' irrespective of the circumstances of specific social groups, Rawls's theory tolerates inequality *only insofar as it benefits the most disadvantaged*. Growth at their expense is therefore unjust. I make no attempt to consider the philosophical literature spawned by this book.

10. See Chapter 14 by Professor Steedman in this book. He also notes the difficulty of identifying 'real' needs in the realm of services and welfare systems, as well as in consumer goods. My argument claims that the political process (underpinned by a shared exploration of what counts as the

social good) is the necessary arbiter of what is benefical expansion and what is simply 'spoiling ourselves' – as children can be 'spoilt' by thoughtlessly being given too much.
11. It is worth noting that the very existence of the Social Chapter demonstrates that other business cultures do *not* feel the need so to opt out – at least with respect to their European workers!
12. Cited in Karl Polanyi, *The Great Transformation*, Boston, Beacon Press, 1944, p.118.
13. *Moral Man and Immoral Society*, London, SCM Press, 1963, p.127 (first published 1932).
14. Michael Ignatieff, *The Needs of Strangers*, London, Chatto & Windus, pp.9–10.
15. Polanyi, op. cit., p.43.

14 On De-escalating Wants
Ian Steedman

If there is a 'gap' between the desires for health services, educational services, and so on, and the social provision of such services then, clearly enough, that 'gap' is as much dependent on the level of those desires as it is on the level of that provision. And it is not immediately self-evident that if such a 'gap' has come to constitute a problem then the problem can only be confronted in terms of 'the spirit of indefinite enlargement'. One element of the question, 'How can we meet the escalating costs of social needs?', is 'Is it proper to do so?' Is it always proper to want more, and more, and more? One cannot just take it for granted that whatever is stated by anybody under any circumstances to be a social need must *ipso facto* be accepted to be a social need and hence that we have to think about financing it. Sometimes, at least, it might be appropriate to question whether alleged social needs should be accorded that description or not. Of course I emphasize that this is only one aspect of the question and I have no intention of suggesting that it is the most important aspect; it is simply the one I have been asked to write about. Although I write as an economist, it will become clear that the issues raised are more nearly in the domain of moral discourse than in that of immediate practical policy; and while I shall not discuss explicitly such human qualities as altruism, it will be clear that they hover in the wings.

We are most familiar, I suppose, in the context of criticism of ever inflating perceived needs, to hear such criticism being directed towards market-provided goods and services. Critics commonly berate the market system, or capitalism, for stimulating wants-inflation and for always encouraging the idea that people need more, want more, eat more. It is thereby acknowledged that perceived needs and wants are not always immune from questioning, or even from criticism. But whatever the truth in that regard (which will not be discussed here), there could be a process of wanting more and more, better and better health provision, education, clean air, road systems and so on. Some of these examples may be rather uncomfortable ones for some, if they are professionally and culturally committed to recognizing the value of these things. (Note that I am not denying their value.) It may be disturbing to be asked, 'Is it always proper to want more, to want better in these areas?' This question must be faced, however, not least by the very people who sometimes talk with an element of disdain of other people's insatiable desires for goods and services produced by profit-making enterprises. It is not that difficult, apparently, to be disdainful of popular demands for ever rising material physical standards of living, and then to turn round and simply take it for granted that, of course, in such matters as health, education and road systems there can never be any question of wanting too much, or of inordinate demand. I suggest that it might sometimes be helpful to ask comparable questions in the areas of both private and public provision. Let me not be immediately misunderstood; I am not hereby launching an attack on education and health. I simply raise the question whether we cannot ask similar questions about social needs as people often and quite readily ask about toys, baubles and allegedly unimportant goods and services provided by the profit-making system. There is, in other words, more than one kind of greed and insatiability; it does not necessarily relate to things sold by profit-making firms. (Needless to say, the better-off must always be decidedly careful when talking about the virtues of wanting less, or the dangers of insatiability! But they sometimes seem to recognize such virtues and dangers more readily with respect to goods provided by private firms than with respect to 'social provision' of health services, and so on.)

A PURE MARKET ECONOMY

We may first consider briefly the issue of having more and wanting less in the context of a pure market economy – this is an abstraction, of course – and then towards the end of the chapter turn to some remarks closer to our theme. I stress that I am not going to present any policy recommendations and that everything I say here will be rather a long way from any possibility of doing so.

Let us recall the kind of remark which is often made about the creation of wants in a dynamic market economy. A famous economist, Tibor Scitovsky (1992, p.133), has written that 'market exchanges often create not only satisfactions, but also the needs they satisfy, and anything that gives rise to both a need and its satisfaction is of little use to anyone'. I do not necessarily accept everything I quote but I think that this is a very useful starting point. Similarly Robert Lane, in a massive book called *The Market Experience* (1991, p.424), has asserted that, 'The market is itself the source of wants that cannot be satisfied, and . . . is inimical to the reduction of wants whose reduction might ease people's states of dissatisfaction'. While economists typically talk about the market as a system for meeting people's wants, there is also an underground discussion amongst certain authors about the role of the market in creating wants, and if you see both sides of the matter at once, obviously difficult questions immediately start to arise about, as it were, the net benefits from creating and then meeting wants. At the moment I am focusing entirely on ordinary goods and services provided through the market but, as already indicated, towards the end of this chapter I shall ask whether any possible analogies exist in the field of social needs.

Again, according to the same author, Robert Lane – but rather more provocatively this time – 'It is the business of the market to tempt' and this without encouraging any internal controls resisting temptation (*ibid.*, p.499). Matters become hard to pin down in this area (as may be imagined even without my going into any detailed discussion), when we read for example that the market ethos permits only increasing achievements and not decreasing achievements or decreasing aspirations; or that the market system encourages an overestimate of the contribution of market commodities to happiness. The problem with such statements, which slip quite easily off the tongue, is that while they are not obviously false, it is unclear at what level they are intended and, more importantly, it is not clear how one would actually assess their truth or falsity. Probably most of us have an initial response and tend to be favourably inclined to such statements or unfavourably inclined to them. But if we try to take them seriously and ask how one would establish the truth or falsity of these claims about the market creating wants and stimulating desires, we might be hard pressed actually to say how one could falsify or verify them. (Some might not much care. Sir Samuel Brittan (1995, p.76), for example, has argued that, 'So long as people are allowed to do the best for themselves (as they interpret best at any particular time), the liberal will not busy himself with sorrowful comparisons about how much better off people might have felt themselves to be if culture, circumstances and tastes had not changed'. But this seems a little too easy if the taste changes in question are, at least in part, the result of self-interested sales promotion activities by firms.)

On a historical note – and partly to make the point that this issue is hardly a new one – let me recall a famous passage from John Stuart Mill's chapter 'Of the Stationary State' from 1848 (Book IV, Chapter VI). Mill wrote, 'I sincerely hope, for the sake of posterity, that they will be content to be stationary, long before necessity compels them to it.' A century and a half earlier, though, Leibniz had stated that desire for change is a defining characteristic of man, and about 130 years after Mill, the economist Scitovsky (referred to above) pronounced that 'the stimulus of novelty is among the most fundamental of human needs' (Scitovsky, 1992, p.288). Now these three authors are perhaps not quite contradicting each other, in a strict logical sense, but it is pretty obvious that the general thrust of Mill's hope is somewhat askew with the observations (or the claims) of Leibniz and Scitovsky. Unless, that is, a desire for change can be met and a stimulus of novelty be maintained in a broadly unchanging economic system.

It is of interest to consider how capitalism's obvious dynamism, its incessant change and generation of both new processes and new products, relates to satisfaction, to habit formation and to the creation of wants, even if we can do no more here than direct the reader's attention to certain questions. Do consumers always have a pre-existent want for a particular commodity before that commodity becomes available on the market? If they do not, but come to develop a want for the commodity once it is available, are they always 'better off' with both the want and that which satisfies it than they were previously when they had neither the want nor the commodity? Even if a new, particular commodity was not previously wanted per se, does it at least always provide some service for which there was a pre-existent want? Or can even wants of this kind be brought into existence by new commodities? Could it ever be in the interest of producers to stimulate a want when consumers would be better off without that want? Or at least without that stimulation of it? Although there is not the space to discuss these (difficult) questions here, I cannot resist a pertinent quotation from Thoreau in his book, *Walden*, (1854, Chapter 1, 'Economy'): 'Our inventions are wont to be pretty toys, which detract our attention from serious things. They are but improved means to an unimproved end, an end which it was already but too easy to arrive at ... We are in great haste to construct a magnetic telegraph from Maine to Texas; but Maine and Texas, it may be, have nothing important to communicate'.

How are we to assess these aspects of modern economic life, if they exist? (I think they probably do.) How should we assess them in relation to the various traditions of freedom from desire, the virtue of moderation, the virtue of detachment from material things (without of course despising such things or denigrating them in any way)? I cannot discuss here the sort of traditions I have in mind but will offer just two quotations from very different sources: one from Gandhi, 'I do not believe that multiplication of wants and the machinery to supply them is taking the world a single step nearer its goal. I wholeheartedly detest this mad desire to destroy distance and time, to increase animal appetites and go to the ends of the earth in search of their satisfaction'. And, second, a more moderate, a quieter statement – as one might expect from an eighteenth century American Quaker, John Woolman – 'I saw that ... in common with an increase of wealth the desire of wealth increased' (*Journal*, Moulton edn, p.35). Both Gandhi and Woolman point to the problem which occupies us here. How are we to assess these aspects of modern economic life if we look at them from the point of view of such traditions? Does it make sense to think in terms of satiation, or are we inexorably committed to an unbroken and upward spiral of insatiable appetite? Of course we have to be careful to distinguish between satiation with respect to different kinds of things. It is one thing to be easily satiated with respect to one particular type of tagliatelle; it is a different thing to be satiated with respect to love, care and attention, abstract wealth, or power over others. In more narrowly economic terms, we could also think of the notion of positional goods, as the economist Hirsch (1976) called them. That is, all those things whose value turns entirely on the fact that I have more than you, or that I have access when you do not, so that their value is intrinsically relative. Is it possible to be satiated with respect to such desires? (Hirsch was not discussing whether such desires were admirable or not; he was saying that they exist.) In all these matters, it might seem, it is important to talk not only about desires, wants, tastes, or preferences. We must distinguish between that group of concepts, on the one hand, and, on the other, the roles of belief, information and knowledge. Because, after all, what people want and what people think they need is not only a question of personal taste or preference; it is also tightly bound up with what they believe to be the case about certain things, what they think they know to be the case about other things. Increased knowledge – sound knowledge in some sense – may either increase or decrease the demand for specific commodities. On knowing more about something one may come to appreciate its genuine value, or one may come to appreciate its possible harmfulness. (Note that various kinds of sales promotion activity aim to influence people's preferences and/or their beliefs; in so far as beliefs are changed, one can ask whether they are changed toward or away from accurate and relevant knowledge.) Now, can teaching influence people's attitudes to consumption, to acquisition, to being de-tached from these things? This is a huge question, of course, but there are people whose almost professional responsibility it is to answer questions of this kind. Can social, moral teaching influence attitudes of these kinds? One might hope that the answer is 'yes', but if the answer should be 'no' (and one must not answer questions like this simply in terms of what one would like to be the case) then we have to face the question I have already asked about whether the spiral of consumption is inherently unending, or whether some form of satiation or some kind of supply constraint will break the spiral. In this last case, of course, the breaking of the spiral will be much more painful than in either of the other cases.

With respect to the virtues of self discipline, moderation, detachment, and so on, is it the case that perhaps the teaching of knowledge is more powerful and more effective than straightforward moral exhortation? I ask the question because I rather suspect the answer to be 'yes', but I do not claim to know that the answer is 'yes'; hence the question.

PUBLIC SECTOR GOODS

Now consider the same questions but in a different context, directly related to the escalating costs of social needs. I should say that my remarks, if they have a practical bearing at all, have this bearing with respect only to certain kinds of social need; I am not referring here to providing jobs, for example, or to giving people cash when they do not have any other source of income. Let us suppose that knee replacement operations become possible, as hip replacement operations have become. Or suppose that some very expensive drug proves to inhibit or even to cure bone cancer: the examples of course are such that readers can generate their own *ad libitum*. Now if any such thing happens, it certainly will not need any Saatchi and Saatchi advertising or public relations campaign to provoke a want for such operations, or such medicine. Quite obviously, people will not need to be provoked or artificially stimulated into wanting these things; although more or less effort can of course be put into making people aware of the availability of the new operation, medicine, or whatever it might be. Now, two questions. (1) Is it possible to restrict such growth in social needs, perceived and felt social needs? (2) If it is possible, would it be proper to do so? Part (only a part) of the matter is that people may rarely understand the opportunity costs of ever-expanding provision. They – perhaps I should say we – tend to recognize only the benefits – the perfectly genuine benefits, let me repeat; I am not saying that it is anything other than inherently valuable that we should be able to make successful knee replacements and such like. We tend to see the benefit because it is there, it exists and it is obvious, but we see only more obscurely, or perhaps not at all, the fact that any kind of particular provision always has a cost in terms of providing other things. That is part of the problem with social needs, that the benefits which may be provided are visible – probably in most cases the benefits are perfectly genuine as well as visible – but the costs are hidden. Now, on understanding the opportunity costs, knowing that the financing of social needs depends in part on how many claims are made and how many people assert how many social needs, some people could voluntarily refrain from making demands that they have a legal right to make. Whether they should do so is of course a separate question: I am not begging that question but simply drawing attention to the fact that they could abstain from enforcing their legal right. Could that be even one part of meeting the escalating costs of social needs? Well yes, it could be; whether it is likely to be is a very different question – even people who understand perfectly well what the benefits might be of their refraining might not refrain. Yet they could do so – and could understand their doing so as one form of altruistic action. For such a moderation in the extent to which legal entitlements are in fact enforced (or even in the growth of that extent) would facilitate a shift in the pattern of output towards the needs of others. To facilitate is not, of course, to ensure – and this is indeed one reason why some who understand the potential benefits of their refraining from pressing all their legal entitlements might still not so refrain; they might doubt that those potential benefits would in fact be realized.

For this and other reasons, few would predict that voluntary reductions in demands on social provision are likely to have a major impact, or even a small but rapid impact. The fact remains that the 'gap' between 'social demands' and social provision does not depend on the latter alone and that it is not self-evident that it is always and inevitably proper to expand the former. To recognize the second point is not, of course, to denigrate social provision or to extol private provision (and any reader who feels otherwise should substitute thought for feeling forthwith) but it is to suggest that questions about possible desirable limits to the expansion of demands should not focus exclusively on privately produced commodities. We cannot enter here into the very broad question whether it would be desirable that demand growth should be concentrated in resource-non-intensive types of output, nor stop to discuss whether redistribution of income towards the poor would favour or hinder such a shift in the composition of output. But we can insist that discussion of these important questions should not be marred by any over-easy dismissal of market-provided commodities or by any unthinking assumption that increasing 'social demands' are necessarily desirable.

REFERENCES

Brittan, S. (1995). *Capitalism with a Human Face*, Aldershot: Edward Elgar.
Hirsch, F. (1976). *Social Limits to Growth*, Cambridge MA: Harvard University Press.
Lane, R. E. (1991). *The Market Experience*, Cambridge: CUP.
Mill, J. S. (1848). *Principles of Political Economy*, now published as Robson, J. M. (ed.), *Collected Works of John Stuart Mill, Vols II–III*, Toronto: University of Toronto Press.
Scitovsky, T. (1992; first edn, 1976). *The Joyless Economy*, Oxford: OUP.

15 The Welfare Debate
Managing Self-interest, Self-improvement, Altruism*
Frank Field

Over the last four centuries a powerful movement has been at work incorporating people into civil society. The seventeenth century was concerned with limiting the arbitrary power of the monarch; the eighteenth century in gaining equal rights before the law. The nineteenth century established the right to vote and the twentieth century focused on gaining economic and welfare rights.

The legacy of four centuries of British politics is now under threat by a failure to recognize that the impact which legislation has on character is pivotal to human advancement. Any responsible public policy reconstruction needs to address and channel the differing roles of self-interest, self-improvement and altruism, which are among the great driving forces in human character.

1. THE NEED TO EXPLORE AND HARNESS THESE HUMAN DRIVES

(i) Self-interest

Self-interest is a fundamentally important part of human nature and its promotion is the most immediate and powerful of our drives. Self-interest is so powerful that it can be morally dangerous when decried or thwarted. Self-interest can illustrate and advance selfishness, although it cannot be automatically equated with it. While much of the aggressive force of self-interest is channelled into self-improvement it must still be regarded as a force in its own right.

Increasingly welfare is now means-tested. A third of the population live in households drawing one of the major means-tested benefits – a

---

* The following is an edited and substantially abridged version of Frank Field, MP, *Making Welfare Work: Reconstructing Welfare for the Millennium* (Institute of Community Studies, London, 1995). Edited and abridged by Victoria Harrison.

doubling since 1979. The most deadly charge that can be made against Britain's welfare state is that it increasingly ignores the impact of means tests on character. Instead of attempting to satisfy self-interest in a way which is consistent with the public good, welfare is pitted against self-interest so that the public good is the loser. In means-tested welfare hard work is penalized by the loss of entitlement. Incentives reinforce welfare dependence. Honesty is punished by a loss of income. It is in this sense that welfare is the enemy within. Its rules actively undermine the moral fabric of our characters by attacking and perverting our driving forces. In so doing it eats into the public domain and so helps erode the wider moral order of society.

(ii) Desire for Self-improvement

Dominant as self-interest is, it is not the only force shaping our characters and actions. Other drives lie deeply embedded within us. A wish for self-improvement is one such force. It is normal for human beings to desire self-improvement, not merely in terms of education but also in the way we live. In any analysis of human motivation the desire for self-improvement will be prominent.

Self-improvement is one of the great liberating forces and its nurturing should be at the centre of the welfare state's role, not at the periphery. In fact too many of the welfare state's rules operate against this cardinal principle.

(iii) Altruism

Altruism is another force deeply embedded within us. Altruistic feelings vary according to the object of the altruism. Consequently it is usually a weaker drive than the others and has less motivational significance. It is usually expressed most strongly in the family, and indeed here it can even be a more powerful influence than self-interest. But the further we move away from the family – to more abstract concepts such as our neighbourhood, our town, our country – the weaker usually are such altruistic feelings.

Yet this weaker motivational force is not only an important part of our true character, needing to be reflected in the world we make around us; it is also that which, though less prominent in individual human beings, is nevertheless more important when it comes to measuring how civilized the society is in which we live. Welfare reconstruction needs to reflect this element of human motivation.

A Negative Dynamic: Fraud

In 1948 for each £10 paid out in welfare only £1 was means-tested. Now every £1 in £3 is handed over only after a test of income and savings. Under the present heavily means-tested social security system, self-interest, the desire for self-improvement and altruism all contribute to a negative dynamic which encourages fraud and so undermines character. What is it about the present system that perverts these fundamental human drives?

Britain's broken-backed welfare system, based as it is on means-testing, perverts these drives by engaging them in a negative dynamic of fraud and deceit. Means tests paralyse self-help, discourage self-improvement and tax honesty while at the same time inverting the proper aims of self-interest by rewarding claimants for being either inactive or deceitful. Means tests are the poison within the body of the welfare state.

Means tests are the root of a negative dynamic, in that they penalize all those values which make strong, vibrant, communities. Those with savings above a certain level do not qualify. Those who try a part-time job lose almost pound for pound from their benefit. Those who do work, or who have put a little money aside for a rainy day, can qualify, but only if they lie. And the second lie is always easier than the first. Thus the practice of deceit is encouraged by the form of welfare provision. The only cumulative impact of such lying and deceit is the further erosion of any sense of pride, respect and self-worth, which are themselves already under attack in the wake of long-term unemployment.

Men and women are normally driven to maximize income by self-interest and the desire for self-improvement. This is an obvious outcome of their natures. However, the extent to which welfare eligibility rules currently present a different aspect to this nature is disconcerting. Knowledge of changes in the rules and regulations spreads like bushfire amongst a large proportion of claimants. Too many a claimant's effort is not put into finding a job, but into maximizing his or her income on benefits. Self-interest and the desire for self-improvement clearly (and properly) operate here, but they do so negatively by encouraging fraudulent and deceitful behaviour. While such behaviour is reprehensible the main responsibility rests not with claimants but with politicians who not only defend but extend means-tested welfare.

The poll tax is a good example of how recent policy decisions have helped to promote fraud and deceit, thus eroding the fabric of British moral life. The poll tax encouraged whole armies of people to act out of apparent self-interest and break the law for the first time; and in so doing it proved that breaking the law pays.

Most fraud committed against the welfare system constitutes a criminal offence. Welfare is therefore having the opposite effect to that for which it was originally devised. The welfare state was constructed as a means of extending full citizenship to the entire population, many of whom might otherwise remain outside civil society. Welfare fraud now acts as an expelling agent involving numbers of people in criminal activity.

There are other kinds of fraud as well, and they are growing in importance. With a welfare budget of £90 billion a year it would be amazing if serious criminal fraud did not operate against this area of public finances. Large-scale fraud is committed by criminal gangs and is likely to increase. This is a reality which reformers ignore at their peril.

Welfare must be designed so that self-interest, the desire for self-improvement and altruistic urges are turned to positive and productive use, rather than being confined by means testing to the negative dynamic of working the welfare system to an individual's maximum immediate financial advantage.

To escape from this negative dynamic it is necessary to devise welfare systems which not only make it harder to commit fraud but, even more important, make it easier for claimants to remain honest. Moreover, given the numbers of claimants committing fraud it is important not only to increase welfare policing, but also to construct pathways back to legitimacy so that, hopefully, increasing numbers of claimants opt for the straight and narrow.

The Values Promoted by the Welfare System

We urgently need to confront the values being taught by the present social security system. No system of welfare can be independent of values. We need to ensure that the values actually promoted are positive rather than negative in relation to human individuals and society.

What is happening on the welfare front is only part of a much wider concern. All sustainable societies require a shared ideology, containing an agreed moral framework which justifies the demands being placed on individual actions. In the modern world these public ideologies have invariably stemmed from religious beliefs. As the agreed ideology breaks down, major institutions of that society appear to crumble and ordinary people become uncertain and nervous about the future. Uncertainty about how to behave now characterizes an increasing proportion of the community. This is a general phenomenon sweeping across Western Europe.

We are beginning to see the breakdown of trust. Trust, the cement binding societies together, is already ceasing to operate in the way it used to. Yet societies cannot function properly without a high degree of trust. Trust stems from a confidence that society's rules are agreed and will be upheld. I play my part because I know you will be acting similarly in the same circumstances. One of the most obvious areas where trust is breaking down is welfare. Others cheat, so why shouldn't I?

Here then is both a challenge as well as an opportunity for welfare's reconstruction. Which social values can be reaffirmed in constructing a framework for welfare reform? And what part can this exercise play in the wider objective of providing beliefs and hopes which, by being affirmed on the welfare front, will spill over into the broader political arena and so affect public conduct?

The Way Forward

The starting point for responsible public policy formulation must be an acceptance of the fundamental roles played by self-interest, the desire for self-improvement and, to a lesser extent, altruism. Remodelling welfare must begin with a clear appreciation of the drives which make up human nature. Self-interest, for one, is too powerful a motive to ignore. Politicians who do so are a public menace.

Of paramount importance is the need for politicians when reviewing the scope and nature of welfare reform to take into account the importance of how human character is going to respond to any welfare system. Our characters are not passive elements in the process, but the most vibrant and powerful of players. Both Left and Right fail to strike the correct balance on this issue. Successful public policy formulation owes more to getting the balance right between conflicting forces than any other consideration. The Right stresses too much the corruption of humankind. The Left makes a similar mistake in ignoring the darker side of our characters. Self-interest is the most powerful of our motive forces. The role of the politician is to accept this simple but profound principle as the starting point for policy. Reform measures need to be shaped by resolving how self-interest can be rewarded in a manner which simultaneously allows the enhancement of the public good.

The question we now need to ask is: how best can welfare harness self-interest, self-improvement and altruism, and do so in a way in which the common good is also enhanced?

2. A NEW PRAGMATIC APPROACH TO WELFARE: DOING AWAY WITH INADEQUACIES OF THE PRESENT MEANS-TESTED PAYMENTS SYSTEM

Who could be against any of those advocating means tests as a way of targeting help on the poorest if the judgement is limited only to the present? It is only when a longer-term time span is adopted that the full horror of post-war welfare can be seen. Means tests have spread their tentacles across society to a growing extent in the post-war world. Within the lifespan of the present government the number of households trapped on means-tested benefits has doubled. On the government's own figures a third of the entire country's population now live in households where at least one major means-tested benefit is being claimed. A welfare system increasingly shaped to concentrate help on the poor has turned out to have a monstrous effect on human motivation and honesty – the fundamental forces which determine the very nature of society. Means tests penalize all those attributes which underpin a free, let alone a civilized, society. The present welfare system, therefore, reinforces this shift in morality, further eroding the fundamental law-abiding principles and wealth of the country.[1]

Proposals

The proposals here are for an insurance cover which actively promotes self-interest and the desire for self-improvement, and which will free individuals from dependence upon the state and thereby improve their own sense of worth. The goal is to establish a welfare system which affirms some of the verities – such as honesty, the importance of hard work being rewarded, and the necessity to safeguard savings – which are crucial to the effective functioning of a free and healthy society.

The growth of individualism is not going to be arrested by talk about rebuilding the community. Welfare has to be shaped so that individual wishes can simultaneously promote new senses of community. The stakeholder welfare scheme sketched in outline here does precisely that.[2] Real power is delegated to stakeholder boards governing both the new insurance scheme and the new universalization of private pension provision. Stakeholder welfare provision ushers in a period of popular or social, as opposed to state, collectivism. Over an estimated 20 year period means-tested benefits should be progressively replaced by:

- extending coverage of a new insurance system run by a National Insurance Corporation. The corporation would be a tripartite body (employers, employees and government representatives) which would have the power to determine the rates of contributions and benefits. The government would retain only the power of veto.
- universalizing private pension provision to run alongside the state scheme, which would be the task of a Private Pensions Corporation. This would be independent of the government and would organize the task of spreading private pension provision within a framework of compulsory contributions by employees and employers.

Although the schemes will be directed by the stakeholder boards, it is the membership who will be in control. National insurance rights will be vested with each individual member. Pension capital will similarly be owned by the contributors. Some individuals will continue to remain on income support, and this is particularly true of single parents. Income support should be transformed into a proactive opportunities agency developing career plans for all non-pensioner claimants for re-entering the labour market. Income support would act as a life-raft taking people back into work rather than, as at present, a sink into which they are dumped. All claimants – except school leavers – would be entitled to turn their income support payments into education maintenance allowances.

It is crucial to transform the income support machinery from a passive into an active body. From an agency which merely pays out benefit, and occasionally checks on fraud, income support needs to become an agency primarily concerned with tailoring exits from welfare for those able and anxious to move back into the labour market.

In addition social security fraud should be recognized as the very big business it is: operated by individual claimants, by gangs operating against the welfare state, by landlords against housing benefit and by officials within the DSS (Department of Social Security). Imaginative counteraction needs to be driven by a core of SAS-style anti-fraud officers.

The emphasis is on establishing a near universal insurance coverage and then harnessing self-interest to add to this insurance-based income.

In this approach self-interest can work within the law as other family members are free to work without fear of financial penalties being applied to the claimant's benefit. In addition, it is proposed that the housing benefit scheme's escalating number of claimants and costs will be countered by tackling the massive fraud currently organized by landlords and then cash-limiting all new claims to benefit to a rent officer's assessment of a fair rent.

A further commitment involves striking a genuine partnership with the private sector with the aim of universalizing private pension provision. The Left's concept of universal coverage calls for radical extension. Traditionally, the Left has seen this commitment as being secured within a state-delivered welfare system. The Left has to decide what is sacred about this approach. Is it the state-delivery element, or is it the guarantee of universal coverage? The proposal here is for the universalist approach to be applied to the private sector in respect of pensions. The aim will be for everybody to gain a dual universal coverage of both private and public pension provision. The primary objective of *Making Welfare Work* was to ensure that the poor were included in the new scheme (unlike now where they are pushed on to means-tested help). That will require redistribution to cover the cost of their membership.

Such radical reconstruction would take two or more decades. The framework for reform needs to be spelt out and immediate moves set in hand to achieve that objective.

The Politics of Reform

So much then for the strategy. What of the politics of welfare reform? Specifically, where are the pressure points in our political system and how best can maximum pressure be applied to these strategic targets? Fundamentally, how can the self-interest and the desire for self-improvement of the middle classes be mobilized in a way which allows the development of a welfare state which simultaneously promotes the interests of the poor?

The proposals for building a stakeholder's insurance scheme rest on the assumption that the political climate is one where individuals require that:

- the uncertainty created by a flexible labour market is matched by a welfare flexibility offering security;
- the best way of achieving this objective is a stakeholder's welfare

scheme where contributions and benefits are both linked and carefully spelt out;
- while this reform has to be paid for, it is a crucial part of the philosophy that the stakeholder should have a decisive say in the question of its finances;
- stakeholders will want to have a maximum say in how they spread their earnings from their working life over the rapidly expanding period of non-work;
- stakeholders will want a mix of funded and unfunded schemes, and public and private schemes, in order to maximize security and minimize risks.

An opportunity for political reform is on the horizon due to the coming equalization of eligibility for retirement pensions.[3] The Right will argue that the savings should be used to provide tax cuts. The Centre Left in Britain have a chance again to make the case for universal benefit. Such use of savings from the social security budget is totally different from proposing tax increases. An increasingly ageing electorate will appreciate the need to channel such savings into universal long-term care provision.

The Reluctance to Pay Higher Taxes

Labour believes it lost the last election due to its threat to increase taxes. Certainly the Tories campaigned during the election as though Labour's tax proposals were a vote loser. Yet none of the exit polls or survey data taken since the election supports this contention. But ever since the votes were counted Labour has not ceased to explain that the voters are in no mood to stump up for extra taxes, and that this was the root of the party's fourth electoral defeat. So pervasive is the conviction that parties cannot win elections while promising tax increases, that the view may indeed now be held by those groups of key voters necessary to win a general election. A misreading of the voter's reactions to Labour's 1992 defeat and a communication of that misreading may now have resulted in educating the very same voters into believing the doctrine that higher taxes automatically result in electoral failure.

A Skewed Debate

Moreover, the welfare debate in this country has been skewed almost exclusively to the question of combating poverty. In most other European countries the debate has been cast much more widely to address the question of how best to underpin working families' living standards. A reconstruction of Britain's welfare system must bring our debate into line with that which has dominated the European agenda for most of this century.

Moving away from an exclusive debate about poverty is therefore a first priority. The long-term interests of the poor can best be served by setting their needs in the context of a much wider political agenda. The second move is to begin offering individuals a welfare income which harnesses their self-interest and desire for self-improvement so that they are motivated to leave the welfare roll, rather than, as at present, merely to maximize their income while remaining on welfare. People have to be able to see that their own efforts will be rewarded by increased living standards.

The politics of welfare used to be seen as part of a vigorous social philosophy debate. It was within this theatre that reformers spelt out how they saw human beings operating, their motives and aspirations. The goal was the promotion of the good life and welfare was viewed as one channel directed to that end. The social philosophy approach needs to be re-established as the framework for the welfare debate.

Politicians, above all people, are not in the business of being able to change the deepest of human motivations. What politicians should be concerned about is creating a framework of rules which strikes most people as fair and reasonable and which at the same time attempts to harness self-interest, self-improvement and altruism in a manner which is conducive to the public good.

NOTES

1. Lying, cheating and deceit are all rewarded handsomely by a welfare system which costs on average £15 a day in taxation from every working individual. It is difficult to underestimate the destructive consequences welfare now has for our society.
2. More comprehensive proposals for a stakeholder welfare scheme are detailed in Frank Field, 'A Stakeholder's Welfare', *Making Welfare Work*, Chapter 7.
3. The number of very elderly pensioners aged 85 or more will rise over the next 50 years, from the current total of 881,000 plus to the three million mark. Most of the increase will occur after the government begins implementing the decision to equalize age eligibility for the retirement pension

at 65 for both men and women. This policy is to be phased in over the decade beginning in 2010. Savings will be in the order of £400 million at first and rising to give a total saving on the annual pensions bill of £4 billion by 2025. These data are in 1993–4 prices.

16 Paying for Social Security – an Ever-rising Spiral?
William Goodhart

Just over 50 years ago Sir William Beveridge produced the Report which made him a household name. Building on the rudimentary system of social security pioneered by Lloyd George between 1909 and 1911, Beveridge proposed a comprehensive framework of social security benefits. His ideas were to a large extent brought into operation by the Attlee government of the late 1940s. They are still the foundation of the social security system we have today.

The Beveridge system is redistributive in two directions. First, there is redistribution from rich to poor. Means-tested benefits go solely to the poor but are paid for out of general taxation, to which the rich contribute more. Universal benefits such as child benefit go equally to all but are paid for unequally. Second, there is redistribution across the life-cycle, with people getting help at the stages in their lives when they are most in need. Thus child benefit helps with the extra costs of bringing up children; state pensions are provided for men over 65 and women over 60; and invalidity benefit is paid to the long-term disabled. These principles remain, I believe, as correct as ever.

Within the benefit system, there are certain broad classifications. First, some benefits are contributory, and others are non-contributory. The right to contributory benefits depends on the claimant having an adequate record of payment of National Insurance Contributions, or NICs. Non-contributory benefits are paid out of the general fund of taxation.

By far the largest contributory benefit is the state retirement pension. In the financial year 1993–4 the basic state pension cost £26.5 billion, with another £1.6 billion being paid as its earnings-related supplement, or SERPS. The next biggest was invalidity benefit, followed by unemployment benefit and widow's pensions.

Contributory benefits are funded out of the National Insurance Fund, into which employees and employers pay NICs. In 1992–3, the National Insurance Fund received £33.6 billion in contributions and paid out £36.2 billion in benefits. Contributory benefits amount to a little less than half the total expenditure on welfare benefits, which amounted to £81 billion in 1993–4.

To describe the system as National Insurance is, however, misleading. The system has never been a true insurance system, in which contributions are paid into a fund which is built up to meet claims against it by contributors. Today's contributors – contrary to what many of them believe – are not building up funds for their own pensions but are paying for today's pensions. The National Insurance Fund is not a reservoir but a pipe. NICs are not insurance premiums but taxes.

Some non-contributory benefits are universal. Child benefit is an example; the Duchess of Westminster has just as much right to child benefit as any other mother. Other non-means-tested non-contributory benefits include attendance allowance and disability living allowance for the severely disabled and war pensions.

But many non-contributory benefits are means-tested (or, to use the current euphemism, targeted). This means that the right to receive benefit depends, among other things, on the level of the claimant's own income and of the household in which he or she lives. In 1993–4 Income Support – the main benefit for those out of work – cost £15.8 billion, making it easily the second biggest benefit after the retirement pension. Housing Benefit – also means-tested – cost £8.8 billion, with another £1.8 billion going on the closely related council tax benefit. The other main means-tested benefit – family credit, payable to parents in low-paid jobs – cost £1.1 billion. Thus means-tested benefits amounted to nearly £28 billion out of a total benefit expenditure of £81 billion. That is over a third of the total. Furthermore, the number of people receiving means-tested benefits is enormous. In 1993, 5.6 million people were receiving income support and another half million were receiving family credit. In the same year 4.5 million were receiving housing benefit and 5.4 million were receiving council tax benefit. Of course there is a large overlap here; almost all of those receiving housing benefit would also get council tax benefit and most of them would also get Income Support or Family Credit. But well over six million people are actually receiving means-tested benefits, and over five million more are dependents of people receiving means-tested benefits.

Beveridge certainly did not envisage means-testing on this scale. It was thought that Keynes had provided the answer to unemployment. Most men would be in continuous full-time employment. Those who lost their jobs would find new ones before the right to unemployment benefit ran out. Most women were housewives with benefit rights earned by their husbands' contributions. Means-tested National Assistance – as Income Support was then called – was provided as a safety net for those who failed to qualify for the normal benefits – mainly because they did not have a proper contributions record. Housing benefit was not needed because public sector rents were heavily subsidized and private sector rents strictly controlled.

For the past 25 years or so, however, pressures have been slowly building up and the Beveridge foundations have begun to crack. The ageing of the population has made the state pension more and more expensive, even though since 1980 the basic pension has increased only in line with prices and not, as previously, in line with earnings. The seemingly inexorable rise in unemployment, even in times of prosperity, and the enormous increase in the number of single-parent families, has made Income Support not a safety net for the few but an essential and expensive benefit for many. As a result, the cash cost of benefits has risen from £38 billion in 1984–5 to £81 billion in 1993–4 – an increase which far outstrips the rate of inflation.

As someone approaching retiring age, I do not think we would either welcome or expect an increase in pensioner mortality. We would, I am sure, welcome a sharp reduction in unemployment and one-parent families, but it is unrealistic to expect that to happen. What are we to do, therefore, about spending on benefits? Are there parts of the system which can be dismantled or privatized? Can we cut the cost of benefits? Or should we try to find new ways of raising the money?

With one exception, I do not think it is remotely possible to dismantle the system or to replace it with private money. The exception is SERPS – the State Earnings Related Pensions Supplement. This can be described, briefly, as a pay-as-you-go pension for those whose jobs provide no occupational pensions. SERPS is not very generous. It also enormously complicates the contribution system. I do not think it is the business of the government to provide earnings-linked occupational pensions. Instead, I would like to see an obligation for all employers and employees to contribute to funded pension schemes. Many employers would not wish to set up their own schemes, but the government could licence some of the main insurance companies to provide money-purchase pension schemes for employees whose employers did not have their own schemes. The government could use its negotiating muscle to keep down charges, or as a last resort manage a fall-back scheme itself. Proposals on these lines have been supported by the Liberal Democrats and by a discussion paper written by Frank Field, MP. They have been put forward as an option by the Borrie Commission on Social Justice. The main problem is that, while funding of new pensions was building up, it would remain necessary to honour existing accrued rights to SERPS, so that there would be a period when both current and future pensions were having to be paid for. This would be difficult but not, I think, impossible if a new system was phased in carefully.

So far as reducing costs is concerned, there is scope for saving by raising the state pension age for women to 65. There is no justification for gender differences in pension ages, particularly as women live longer. The government's 1991 discussion paper on equalizing pension ages estimated the cost of reducing male pension age to 60 at £3.4 billion a year, which I do not believe we can afford. Equalization at 63 would be roughly cost-neutral, and equalization at 65 would save nearly £3 billion. Given the longer life expectancy and better health of older people, I think the government and the Borrie Commission were right to recommend equalization at 65. This is the direction in which most other countries are moving, with some even raising the pension age to 67.

Increased targeting, or means-testing, of benefits which are now universal is more difficult. Indeed, there are considerable pressures to move the other way and reduce the extent to which existing benefits are means-tested.

There are a number of good arguments, and one bad one, against means-testing. The bad argument is that it is somehow degrading to receive means-tested benefits. Means-tested benefits are not charity. They are just as much a right as universal child benefit. It is not Income Support but the joblessness which qualifies a claimant to receive it which may lead to loss of self-esteem.

There are however at least three good arguments against means-testing. First, means-tested benefits create poverty traps because means-tested benefits are withdrawn as the claimant's non-benefit income rises. Even if the withdrawal is tapered – that is, benefits are withdrawn at a rate less than £1 for every £ of extra non-benefit income – the result in many cases is that the claimant will be hardly any better off in a part-time job, or a low paid full-time job, than remaining unemployed. The situation may be made even worse by the loss of so-called passport benefits, such as exemption from prescription charges, which go with receipt of means-tested benefits.

Second, means-tested benefits are more complicated to obtain, leading to higher administrative costs and lower take-up. People may move in and out of casual employment. Income from jobs may fluctuate. Claimants have to provide information not only about their own income, assets and obligations but about those of their spouses or partners.

The extra hassle deters some people from claiming benefits to which they are entitled. This is particularly true where the potential amount of benefit is quite small. For example, take-up is low among people in low-paid jobs who may be entitled to small amounts of family credit or pensioners who may be entitled to small amounts of housing benefit.

Third, universal benefits tend to be more popular than targeted benefits. It may be easier to persuade people to pay higher taxes if they believe that they themselves are getting something back.

There is, however, one very strong argument the other way – the much higher cost of universal benefits. There are, indeed, various schemes, known as Basic Income, or Citizen's Income, or Negative Income Tax, which aim to replace almost all existing benefits (both means-tested and universal) by paying everyone a basic subsistence income. These ideas are intellectually very seductive. Unfortunately, a full basic income scheme implies a standard rate of income tax of about 70 per cent on all other income, which in my view relegates such a scheme to political cloud-cuckoo-land. Even if this were not so, the great variation in housing costs makes it impossible to avoid keeping means-tested housing benefit alongside a Basic Income system.

I am convinced, therefore, that it is impossible to eliminate means-testing. The Borrie Commission's Report pays lip-service to doing so but its proposals are either vague expressions of hope for the future or simply amount to a modified form of means-testing.

It is more realistic, I believe, to look for ways of blunting the teeth of the poverty trap by making the tapered withdrawal more gentle. But this is itself expensive. If you raise the cut-off point at which benefits are wholly withdrawn from, say, £120 to £150 a week, not only are you paying more to many of those previously receiving benefit, but those with incomes between £120 and £150 a week will now become entitled to benefits. This brings more people into the benefit net. There is a trade-off between on the one hand being relatively generous to those in greatest need but imposing a sharp withdrawal rate, and on the other hand making the poverty trap less severe but giving a bigger share of the benefit cake to those who need it less.

I believe, however, that there is very little scope for shifting the boundaries in the other direction, from universal towards means-tested benefits. It would be politically impossible to means-test the basic state pension. People believe that their NICs have paid for their pensions – which is (as I have explained above) not actually true but can be regarded as morally true. It would be almost as difficult to means-test child benefit. The Borrie Commission has made a small move in that direction by proposing that higher-rate taxpayers should be taxed on it. I suspect that that is one proposal which will not find its way into a Labour manifesto.

Even where benefit improvements are proposed, the decision whether to make them targeted or universal is likely to be based on pragmatism rather than theory. For example, both the Liberal Democrats and the Borrie Commission have recognized the problem which results from the fact that a basic pension linked to prices is likely to represent a smaller and smaller proportion of pre-retirement earnings. The ratio between the basic state pension and average male earnings has already fallen from 20 per cent in 1977–8 to below 15 per cent now, and is predicted to fall to less than nine per cent by 2020. Yet restoring the link to average earnings, even at the present ratio, would be immensely expensive. Therefore, both the Liberal Democrats and the Borrie Commission propose that there should be in effect a means-tested supplement to the basic pension which would guarantee a minimum income to all pensioners.

Finally, there is the question of changing the system by which benefits are funded. Here, there may be some possibility for more radical changes.

The Liberal Democrats have proposed that the contribution system should be scrapped. The system is a sham. It conceals the fact that contributions are paying for today's benefits and not building up an insurance fund. No one except a benefits expert has any idea what benefits are contributory and what are non-contributory. Many people wrongly believe that NICs help to fund the NHS. The system requires an expensive bureaucracy to keep detailed contribution records for employees which could, if SERPS was abolished, be replaced by a simple residence qualification. Employees' NICs are a tax on income but are charged on a tax base which is quite different from income tax. For example, employees' NICs are not charged on investment income or on income above the upper earnings limit of £430 a week.

I believe, therefore, that the system would be both simpler and fairer if the contribution system was abolished and employees' NICs were replaced by a tax collected by the Inland Revenue and charged as far as possible on the same tax base as income tax. Complete incorporation into income tax would not be possible because of the effect that would have on pensioners, whose tax bill would go up substantially. But the new tax, I believe, should be charged on earned income above the upper earnings limit and on investment income of those under pension age.

One further question remains. Should the new tax be a hypothecated tax – that is, committed to spending on benefits, rather than falling into the general pool of taxation?

I must say that when the Liberal Democrats published some fairly modest suggestions for extending hypothecation in 1994 we got a fairly critical press. This does not, of course, prove that we were wrong, but there are problems.

It is clear that not all benefits can be paid for out of hypothecated taxes. Hypothecation is unsuitable unless both the spending and the corresponding tax revenue are reasonably steady. This rules out means-tested benefits, which are strongly linked to unemployment and therefore vary with the economic cycle. Spending on these benefits goes up sharply just as tax revenue is falling. Hypothecation is probably most suitable to cover forms of spending which most people see as conferring a present or future benefit on themselves. This is another argument against paying for means-tested benefits out of hypothecated taxes.

The present contribution system is of course a form of hypothecated tax, since contributions go into the National Insurance Fund and contributory benefits come out of it. NICs are a fairly acceptable form of tax – for example, the increase in the principal rate of employees' NICs from nine to ten per cent in 1994 caused little opposition. On the other hand, the number and variety of contributory benefits makes it difficult to understand exactly what NICs are paying for. There is, I believe, a good case for hypothecating the new tax which replaces NICs to payment of state pensions leaving payment of other contributory benefits to come out of general tax funds. Pension spending is highly predictable from year to year and almost every taxpayer is either receiving a pension or hopes to get one in due course. Pensions also account for most of the present spending on contributory benefits. By limiting hypothecation to payment of pensions, people would know what they were paying for.

Beyond this, I do not see hypothecation as the answer. Indeed it can be argued that the more that taxes are hypothecated for popular purposes such as pensions or the NHS the more resistance there will be to taxation for other purposes.

A more modest but perhaps more helpful suggestion would be to increase the transparency of taxation by telling tax-payers where their taxes are going. After all, local authorities have to do this when sending out their council tax demands. Why should the government not be required to do the same? It should send everybody on the electoral register a brief statement, at the beginning of the fiscal year, explaining how much it expects to get in from the various taxes for the forthcoming year and how it intends to spend it, with comparative figures for the previous year. There is nothing secret about these figures. They are published, but not in a way which brings them to the attention of the average taxpayer. It is hardly likely that this will have a dramatic effect on resistance to taxation, but it could be modestly helpful.

Let me therefore sum up.

First, the size and nature of the benefit system makes it impossible to imagine that private sector action – either voluntary or under compulsion of law – can take over any significant part of the burden. The only exception is that, in my view, compulsory private sector funded pensions should replace SERPS.

Second, there is only one other prospect of substantial savings from structural changes in the benefit system, which is through raising women's pension age to 65. These savings will be needed to pay for other benefits, such as the proposed minimum pension guarantee.

Third, the cost implications rule out any practical possibility of converting means-tested benefits into universal benefits. We should, instead, look at ways of making the poverty trap less severe and means-testing less intrusive. Even this, however, is likely to be very expensive.

Fourth, there is little practical possibility of moving in the other direction by converting universal benefits into means-tested ones. The most that can be done is to restrict increases in some such benefits to the rate of increase in prices rather than earnings, so that over time they will take up a reduced share of GDP.

Fifth, the contribution system is a complex, unfair and unnecessary way of paying for benefits. Employers' NICs should be converted into a payroll tax and the employees' NICs should be converted into a tax charged as nearly as possible on the same tax base as income tax.

Sixth, the new taxes which replace NICs should be hypothecated to payment of state pensions. There is, however, little scope for the further extension of hypothecation.

Finally, more information about the raising and spending of taxes should be circulated to taxpayers.

If the purpose of this book is to look for non-statutory alternatives to meet social needs, my answer is negative. We are talking of billions, not millions. Non-statutory funding at this level is simply not available. This does not mean that the voluntary sector has no role to play. There is scope for some charities to find gaps in the coverage of the welfare state and help to fill them. I was for 15 years a trustee of a local charity in Kensington which, by the end of that period, had about £1 million a year to spend and spent it – rather effectively – for those purposes. Perhaps more important, organizations like the Child Poverty Action Group and Age Concern have a vital role to play as pressure groups. But I see no alternative to the state as the provider of basic social security needs.

17 Contribution by Two Faith Groups towards Education Spending
Jeremy Kendall

1. INTRODUCTION

Historically and currently, agencies of a denominational character have been core institutional components of the voluntary sector in the UK (Beckford, 1991; Kendall, 1996) and internationally. This has included both voluntary agencies established directly by the infrastructure of the churches themselves, and those founded autonomously by their active members as 'moral entrepreneurs'. Of equal importance in the UK, albeit more difficult to gauge empirically, has been the pervasiveness of the Christian world-view in attaching meaning, providing ethical guides and creating incentives to many forms of philanthropic endeavour. More recently, the increasingly multicultural character of British society has meant that new religious belief systems and spirituality more generally have had significant parts to play in structuring and stimulating voluntary activity.

This chapter aims to sketch out aspects of denominationally connected voluntary action in England, and to summarize how and why this has been an important force both historically and remained so in the late twentieth century. Although the churches no longer dominate as they have done historically, we show that they still have a major role to play alongside purely secular voluntary sector bodies, the private, for-profit sector, the public sector and the informal sector. While trying to offer a long term view, our focus is strictly limited in two main ways. First, we are concerned to describe developments relating to the first aspect of the denominational contribution, focusing on how and why denominational voluntary organizations have been economically significant in readily measurable and tangible ways. Second, a good deal of attention is focused on Anglicanism and Catholicism in particular. This is driven partly by our economic frame of reference – these have been the most significant denominations in England for most of the twentieth century in terms of membership – and partly by constraints of space. It should of course be recognized that other faith groups, both Christian and otherwise, have made, and continue to make, very important contributions to the voluntary sector. Third, much of our discussion is concerned with education, principally because this is one of the few areas where it is possible to identify, at least in part, the relative scope and scale of denominational contributions.

2. RELIGION AND VOLUNTARY ACTION PRIOR TO THE TWENTIETH CENTURY

While its precise extent is disputed by historians and sociologists, it is widely understood that the post-Reformation Church of England retained a remarkable degree of influence over social, political and religious life. That this power was exercised restrictively until the nineteenth century – through formally limiting access to political and civil office to Anglicans – is well known. What is less well understood is how the hegemony of the Church of England was also bolstered through discriminatory charity law, and in part reflected in patterns of human service provision in the pre-industrial era. Prior to a court decision following the 1688 Toleration Act, trusts with religious purposes other than those exclusively linked to the state church were held to be invalid. Roman Catholic charities were not legally recognized until 1829, being forced to languish in a state of 'doubtful legality' until that time (Owen, 1964; Picarda, 1995).

As far as human services were concerned, in many parts of the country and in some fields, the state church dominated charitable provision well into the eighteenth century. For example, Warne (1969) showed how, in Devon, the Anglican church had a virtual monopoly, administering local endowed charities, pioneering social insurance schemes, and 'shoulder[ing] almost completely alone the burden of providing education for the poor'. Nationally, the Church of England dominated the education field. Even where it was private individual 'moral entrepreneurs' rather than the state church's infrastructure which founded and ran schools, most of these individuals were Anglicans. Adherence to church doctrine was written into most schools' founding constitutions, and admission was theoretically conditional on membership of the state church.

However, during the course of the eighteenth century, this dominance did not go unchallenged. In a political climate which tolerated Protestant dissent, those outside the Anglican church also increasingly emerged as major providers. Most obviously, as legal restrictions on dissenters' rights to teach were phased out, schools run by dissenters were able to operate relatively freely. However, as with the generic charity legislation, this tolerance in the education field was initially extended only to Protestants, and the Catholic community (as well as the Jewish faith) faced considerable legal obstacles to establishing and running charitable institutions. Those seeking a Catholic education were unable to do so in legally recognized charitable institutions in England, and were forced to obtain tuition in secret, or travel abroad.

Indeed, not only were the anti-Catholic beliefs of the élite still reflected through legal restrictions on Catholic charitable activities, but the primary example of early eighteenth century ecumenical charitable endeavour – the schools network supported in part by the Society for the Promotion of Christian Knowledge (SPCK) – was itself strongly identified with hostility towards Catholicism. One belief which united many of the bishops, lower clergy and laity who founded and subscribed to the schools affiliated to the SPCK was a desire to ensure social stability and the Protestant succession by 'immunizing the children of the poor against the contagion of Popery' (Owen, 1964, p.24).

The large scale, albeit uneven, patterns of desertion from the Church of England that gathered momentum from the mid-eighteenth century meant that an increasingly rich and diverse tapestry of religiously connected voluntary institutions began to emerge. The flowering of denominationalism during much of the nineteenth century and the belated introduction of a 'level playing field' through legislation to emancipate Catholics were undoubtedly critical factors in the growth of Victorian philanthropy, an era often portrayed as the high point of voluntary action in England. Christian charity, it was argued by evangelists associated with the Charity Organization Society and other prominent opinion formers, was an integral part of good citizenship and a moral duty for all those concerned with the well being of society (Lewis, 1995). As it became easier to exercise choice in religion, so the religious inspiration behind philanthropy was translated into a wide variety of associations.

The well documented increase in the number of charities in the nineteenth century was therefore at least in part associated with the gradual erosion of Anglican hegemony. 'Competition for sinners and distress' (Prochaska, 1988, p.24) was rife between religious denominations and their splinter groups, each of which commanded a full complement of organizations. Yet despite these developments, the Church of England still seems to have remained the leading provider in many ways, as it had a unique historical inheritance on which to build. This is most obvious in the education field. Not only were the existing élitist Anglican foundations joined by a new wave of Anglican establishments founded by moral entrepreneurs to provide schooling for the middle classes, but through the National Society's massive school building programme, the state church was a leading pioneer in the provision of full time day education for the working classes (Kendall and Knapp, 1996, Chapter 6).

3. THE TWENTIETH CENTURY: RESILIENCE IN THE DENOMINATIONAL VOLUNTARY SECTOR

From the late nineteenth century onwards, the most important single development as far as the voluntary sector was concerned was the expansion of secular state involvement through regulation, finance and provision – first in education, and then in health and social welfare. The overarching reasons for this were many, and need not concern us here; suffice it to say that altruistic and solidaristic concern about the efficiency and equity consequences of exclusive reliance on the voluntary sector and the market, as well as middle and working class self interest, all appeared to have played a part in Britain as they did in other industrialized countries (Perkin, 1989). Whatever the motives, public sector social expenditures as a proportion of GDP expanded rapidly after the turn of the century, with particular impetus from the social legislation that followed the Second World War. Furthermore, since the mid-1970s, this spending has famously proved to be remarkably resistant to attempts to contain it in most fields (Hills, 1990; Mullard, 1993).

It has been the 'conventional wisdom' in accounts of the voluntary sector's twentieth century development to connect evidence of public expenditure growth and the assumption by the state of social responsibilities with rather loose references to 'secularization' to conclude that the public sector largely displaced the voluntary sector as the primary conduit for formal human service delivery. Furthermore, it is usually argued that, within the voluntary sector, the importance of religion has faded (Wolfenden, 1978; Thane, 1982).

Is this a fair and balanced interpretation? At one level, the answer is yes, at least as far as the second half of the century is concerned. Health care and income maintenance, two of the three fields which have dominated the state's human services budget in the post-war era, were almost completely absorbed into the public sector as fully nationalized services.[1] Furthermore, many of the areas in which the sector's expansion has been most obvious over the past 30 or so years – in particular, environmental organizations, single issue campaigning groups, self-help, and the consumer movement – have tended not to be connected to traditional religion in obvious ways, despite the forging of some rather surprising alliances in recent years (Schwarz, 1990).

However, this picture is somewhat one-sided for four main reasons.[2] The first reason is the rather general point that demonstrating how public sector expenditure has grown as a proportion of GDP is a necessary but not sufficient indication of public sector service expansion *at the expense of* voluntary sector provision. This is because public expenditure can be used to fund voluntary sector services through grants or contracts, rather than services run directly by the state. This theoretical possibility is an empirical reality in many countries. Furthermore, the evidence has been argued to support a presumption in favour of conceptualizing the voluntary and public sectors as 'partners' in public service delivery in cultural and ideological contexts as different as the market-friendly US and the state-friendly Scandinavian countries.

In England, while equating increasing public expenditure with declining voluntary sector provision *is*, in fact, reasonable in health care and income maintenance, in the case of the other major item in the state's human services budget, education, this presumption does *not* hold. The 'dual system', introduced by the 1944 Education Act, guaranteed existing voluntary sector providers a major continuing role within mainstream primary and secondary education by funding in full their current running costs, provided they were able to match the state's capital contributions. Thus, the one area of social policy which witnessed both a major expansion of public welfare expenditure *and* fully institutionalized the voluntary sector as a 'partner' – primary and secondary education – was precisely the one in which the churches' presence was in fact strongest.[3]

The second and third reasons for countering the suggestion that public sector growth has brought about voluntary sector decline can also be illustrated with reference to the maintained schools field. While membership of the traditional Protestant churches declined throughout most of the twentieth century, and the proportion of all full-time pupils taught in Anglican schools fell quite dramatically, the Catholic church experienced a sustained increase in membership well into the late 1960s. This was matched, with the support of state funds, by a massive expansion of its school network. Since the mid-nineteenth century the

Catholic church in England, following guidance from Rome, has seen the development of a separate network of schools as an integral part of Catholicism. This was seen by the hierarchy as imperative for ensuring the protection of Catholic identity, particularly in the strongholds it was establishing in the urban North West with large-scale Irish immigration (Coman, 1977). Between the early 1940s and the mid-1970s, Catholic schools more than doubled their provision from 1200 schools educating eight per cent of all maintained sector pupils, to over 2500 schools – educating just over nine per cent of pupils. Even in the aftermath of the decline in Catholicism that has taken place over the past 20 years, it is a rarely recognized fact that there are still more pupils attending maintained Catholic schools than fee-paying charitable independent schools.

The third point is that, once established, some institutions have continued to operate by responding to any fall in the demand from their traditional denominational clientele, not by closing their facilities but rather by widening their intake to include more pupils from other faith backgrounds. This effect most obviously occurred in the education field in the case of Anglican primary schools in inner city areas. Faced with a decline in their local membership base, many Anglican parishes in the post-war era decided not to close their schools or transfer them to their local authorities, but rather to become 'neighbourhood schools' adapting to their new social context by increasingly admitting non-Anglican pupils, and softening their denominational emphasis. The *de facto* broadening of social intake may also have happened more recently in Catholic schools, despite the strict guidelines developed by church leaders, suggesting that the admission of non-Catholic children be strictly curtailed (Brown, 1993; see, for example, Diocese of Westminster, 1988).

Finally, to understand the fourth main reason for the sector's resilience, we need to look to fields which fared less well in terms of post-war public expenditure – personal social services and youth development – and in which greater financial pluralism prevailed. In these fields, the voluntary sector, and religiously connected facilities within it, also remained major providers. For example, a survey sponsored by the Nuffield Foundation in the 1940s recognized the contribution of the many small residential care homes for elderly people pioneered by the Catholic and Anglican sisterhoods and the Salvation Army, which were particularly popular with elderly people, and which have continued to be significant to this day. In the child care field the major religious groups dominated over much of the post-war period voluntary sector provision, and continue to dominate (Kendall and Knapp, 1996, Chapter 7). Today, Barnardo's, the Children's Society, the National Children's Home and the Catholic child welfare organizations are well-known innovative and specialist providers of a range of child care and other services, and their services are purchased by a great many public sector agencies.

4. CONCLUSION

Voluntary organizations were the dominant mode for the formal delivery of human services up until the early twentieth century, and denominational religion was an important ingredient underpinning this provision. Despite the expansion of the state during this century, and – more recently – the increasing penetration into many of its traditional fields by private enterprise, organizations in the sector – including those of a denominational character – have remained influential social and economic players. Indeed, it can be argued that in the largest single field of broad voluntary sector activity today – education – the role of the Anglican and Catholic churches has been maintained precisely *because of* the state's guarantees of financial support and preservation of their denominational character. The single field of voluntary sector provision in which the state both preserved existing institutions, and invested large amounts of public funding, was that in which these churches' presence was strongest. Recent reforms of maintained education have altered the balance of power *within* the state as between central and local government, but allow for the continuation of state support for church schools, albeit on rather different terms than those negotiated between the church and state in the post-war era.[4]

When the voluntary sector is acknowledged in current policy debate, there may be a tendency to emphasize how declining membership in the traditional churches, value shifts and the emergence of secular organizations from the 1960s onwards – including environmental organizations, self-help groups and single issue pressure groups, to give just three obvious examples – have fundamentally changed the character and composition of the sector (Mulgan and Landry, 1995). There is considerable truth in this view, in the sense that the churches' current role as providers of services *is* clearly much reduced when viewed from a long-term perspective, and they no longer *dominate* the sector as they did historically. But our account of the denominational voluntary sector's resilience implies that, in a number of ways, this picture represents a one-sided oversimplification. This is most obviously the case if a broad definition of the sector, which includes the education field, is accepted as legitimate (see Chapter 2). For the reasons we have discussed, the Anglican and Catholic churches have remained major actors in human service delivery. When we add this under-acknowledged resilience to the observation that membership of many other faith groups is actually increasing significantly (Beckford, 1991; CSO, 1994) – and we know that many of these also have a full complement of voluntary bodies associated with them (Kendall, 1996) – it is clear that it would be dangerous to dismiss too quickly the continued significance of denominational organizations as an important aspect of modern voluntary organization.

REFERENCES

Beckford, J. (1991). Great Britain: voluntarism and sectional interests, in: R. Wuthnow (ed.) *Between States and Markets: The Voluntary Sector in Comparative Perspective*, Princeton NJ: Princeton University Press.

Brown, A. (1993). Aided schools: help, hindrance, anachronism or trailblazer, in: L. J. Francis and D. Lankshear (eds) *Christian Perspectives on Church Schools*, Leominster: Gracewing.

Central Statistical Office (1994). *Social Trends 24*, London: HMSO.

Coman, P. (1977). *Catholics and the Welfare State*, Harlow and New York: Longman.

Diocese of Westminster (1988). *Our Catholic Schools: Safeguarding and Developing their Catholic Identity*, London: Education Service, Diocese of Westminster.

Hills, J. (ed.) (1990). *The State of Welfare*, Cambridge: Cambridge University Press.

Kendall, J. (1996). *The Scope and Role of the UK Voluntary Sector*, unpublished PhD thesis, University of Kent at Canterbury.

Kendall, J. and Knapp, M. R. J. (1996). *The Voluntary Sector in the UK*, Manchester: Manchester University Press.

Le Grand, J. and Bartlett, W. (1993). *Quasi-markets and Social Policy*, Basingstoke: Macmillan.

Lewis, J. (1995). *The Voluntary Sector, the State and Social Work in Britain*, Aldershot: Edward Elgar.

Mulgan G. and Landry C. (1995). *The Other Invisible Hand: Remaking Charity for the 21st Century*, London: DEMOS.

Mullard, M. (1993). *The Politics of Public Expenditure*, London and New York: Routledge.

Owen, D. (1964). *English Philanthropy: 1660–1960*, Cambridge MA: Harvard University Press.

Perkin, H. (1989). *The Rise of Professional Society*, London: Routledge.
Picarda, H. (1995). *The Law and Practice Relating to Charities*, 2nd edn, London: Butterworth.
Prochaska, F. (1988). *The Voluntary Impulse*, London: Faber and Faber.
Schwarz, W. (1990). *The New Dissenters: The Nonconformist Conscience in the Age of Thatcher*, London: Bedford Square Press.
Thane, P. (1982). *The Foundations of the Welfare State*, Harlow: Longman.
Warne, A. D. (1969). *Church and Society in Eighteenth Century Devon*, London: David & Charles.
Wolfenden, Lord (1978). *The Future of Voluntary Organizations*, Report of the Wolfenden Committee, London: Croom Helm,

NOTES

1. We should not overlook the continued existence of 'disclaimed' voluntary sector hospitals – not nationalized by the 1948 Act – nor of the friendly societies. In both cases, however, 'market share' decreased dramatically following the post-war social reforms to the point where their contribution is now dwarfed by that of the state, and considerably outdistanced by the private, for-profit sector.
2. These are not the *only* reasons for the continued importance of the voluntary sector as a whole, but rather appear to be the four most important reasons as far as religiously connected voluntary organizations are concerned.
3. It may be significant to note that this was both one of the few fields of human service provision in which clearly identifiable and politically powerful 'peak associations' – the churches themselves – existed. In addition, the politician with lead responsibility for negotiating the post-war settlement was a pragmatic Conservative. One wonders whether, if the voluntary sector had been less concentrated, and education reforms had been made under a post-war Labour government rather than by a coalition government during wartime, voluntary education, like health care, would have been fully transferred to state control.
4. The most significant changes have involved reforming funding mechanisms along quasi-market lines in a similar fashion to other areas of social policy (Le Grand and Bartlett, 1993), and the introduction of a National Curriculum. The reaction of the churches to these reforms has been mixed.

Part V
Cultivating Civic Generosity

18 Steps towards Maturing – from Compulsion to Consent
Peter Askonas

1. TRYING THE UN-TRIED IS TIMELY

Several contributors to this book have argued that the 'gap' is a symptom of a fundamental imbalance in our economic and political structures. Only radical reordering will provide the conditions for dealing with that symptom effectively. How such reordering could be made to happen in the face of countervailing domestic and global pressures is left an open question. History demonstrates that radical change is usually not a comfortable process. Nor is it the product of balanced deliberations. More probably, major upheavals will follow when justice and fairness become ostensibly distorted or when economic well-being is imbalanced to an intolerable degree. For example, the continuing shift of employment, prosperity and power from West to East could result in such an event. And we could go on to speculate whether, in consequence, this or some other calamity might impose mutual support as essential for tolerable survival – and thereby resolve unexpectedly the issue which this book considers. Will this be the way ahead?

So much for conjecture. A more fruitful exercise will be to explore new and smaller-scale routes, to bring about a gradual maturing of civic relationships and thereby solutions to current difficulties. Greater readiness and magnanimity in meeting social costs are necessary. They must be cultivated imaginatively. The resulting demands may be painful perhaps, but not so painful as the present disintegration of caring structures.

In Chapter 9, Cho Ngye and I have attempted to show that in the human make-up there is intrinsically a capacity for enhancement of altruism and civic generosity. Other chapters provide anecdotal support for this statement. Then Peter Vardy, in Chapter 8, has developed a philosophical model based on an unfolding of the *I/Thou* relationship between the human and the divine person as ground for personal responsibility and concern of one for another. Though his premises seem to be at variance with ours, on that latter point we argue on similar lines. As to practical implications, Vardy presses his conclusions very radically. I have difficulties with his programme, yet I would like to pick up his theme of voluntarity and develop it further.

It postulates enhancement of a climate beneficial to generosity.

But first, to ensure a down-to-earth basis, let me bring into the equation at least some of the disturbing facts which militate against voluntarity, especially in the realm of public revenues.

The *Real* State We're In[1]

- The current public ethos is inimical to generosity; even more so to altruism. Significantly *survival of the fittest* has again become the dominant principle of economic activity and seems to cancel out progress made in the preceding decades towards participation: which sees people as the real capital. Stakeholding, notwithstanding the word being the fashion now, is becoming illusory.
- Economic power concentration release dynamics which diminish the significance and inner freedom of the individual. Choice, if ever the word was used meaningfully, has become empty jargon.
- Confrontational politics inhibit civic responsibility as well as commitment to working out fair solutions.
- Perverted opinion formation appears to have become virtually uncontrollable. Mass communications do not form but deform public opinion. Human goodness is appraised not to be marketable; instead the shadow side of humanity is the preferred product.
- Exploding technology, in spite of its enormous potential for true human enrichment, feeds the drift towards downgrading and satisfaction by *easy solutions*. Aren't too many of us getting bored?

This jeremiade is familiar. Moreover it makes the contemporary malaise appear insurmountable. But we are mistaken if we acquiesce to such representation of our world and call it realism. It does not tell the story completely. To be truly realistic we must take into account the indestructibility of human striving for meaning through relationships and quality of life, for experiment, for reaching out towards the seemingly impossible – not *in spite of*, but *because of* obstacles. In addition, the story has to comprise a particular item of good news: that to appreciate the promising aspects of the human potential is inclusive, common ground for humanists and adherents of religious faith alike.

In what follows, I will explore possibilities for a comprehensive approach on these lines to our subject.

Civic Generosity and Fiscal Revenues – an Unorthodox Cohabitation

Politicians have become terrified to even mention raising tax levels.[2] Electoral experience has made them sensitive – over-sensitive – at least in this respect.

How might civic generosity have an impact on paying the increasing bill of social costs? One obvious answer would be by substantial increase of personal support for the voluntary sector. So obvious, in fact, that I need not dwell on this proposition, except to emphasize that notwithstanding the impressive amount of donations, of volunteering, of hidden caring and of large-scale munificence which together constitute a sizeable part of the sector's revenues (see Chapter 2), there will never be enough of it.

What I do wish to discuss is how to apply generosity to dispositions towards the public purse. That will require a mighty change. Many would say to expect such change is nonsensical. 'The public sector and its fund collecting apparatus takes care of itself' – this is the general strongly felt conviction – 'and it is we the citizens who could do with more generosity being shown us by *them*; indeed many of *us* have to go to considerable length and costs to be protected against *their* rapaciousness'. Yet I suggest that nothing less than a modification of present perceptions is called for, especially when authentic needs become under-resourced and customary remedies are no longer meaningful.

To avoid misunderstanding let me qualify the word *generosity*. It comes somewhat unexpectedly in connection with the relationship between the tax-paying citizenry and those whose task it is to resource public funding of social costs. Generosity in this context does not have the emotional, heart-warming overtones which usually attach to personal acts of kindness. It is more a form of *openness*, a preparedness to set aside some personal advantage and be responsive to wider need. What it *is* can be appreciated by naming what it *is not*: grasping, meanness, indifference. I suggest – and include myself in that suggestion – that the latter attitudes dominate the way most people respond to civic obligation, especially to paying tax.

2. ENDOGENOUS ANTAGONISM TO TAXATION – UNERADICABLE?

Since the dim recesses of the past until not so long ago, tributes and tithes have been imposed by the powerful on their subjects, frequently at extortionate levels. Often the consequences were crippling. Tax would serve the personal designs of those who ruled, and who enriched themselves, usually without benefit to those who were made to pay. Economic factors apart, taxes were resented as degrading symbols of subservience. Alternative patterns of tax as an instrument to serve the needs of citizens, in other words our own needs,[3] were shaped over the past 200 years.[4] That is not a long time but long enough, you might think, for the function of taxation to be properly explained and to be properly understood. But not so. Resistance and misapprehension remains, though to some extent we pay to meet our own expectations. To cry '*Greed!*' is no help for approaching the issue constructively.

Current Sources of Resistance – where Change is Conceivable

- Genuine hardship resulting from an unfair tax regime. (To define what constitutes hardship will continue to be a divisive subject. Thus an upper tax band of 80 per cent in the earlier decades may not have caused true hardship. Yet the resentment it caused in many in that band was costly.) More germane: taxing people in the low-pay group or people starting to work after being unemployed often makes their circumstances worse, and is seen as unfair. Here is an obvious target for action.
- Suspicions of waste, inefficiency and use of taxes for purposes of which the payer disapproves.
- Non-transparency of how revenue is used – or as widely felt, is misused.
- Anonymity of recipient – giving *them* what is *mine. They* will never be easy to identify. Even if *they* are the municipal council in a small locality, and after hours you meet them in the pub, once back in their office they assume – they must assume – impersonality. Application of the subsidiarity principle[5] to civic structures can go some way to lessen this alienation. Much also remains to be done to emphasize the identity of us, the *clients*, vis-à-vis officialdom. *We* must be treated as real persons, not mere cost elements (or *payload*).
- This goes hand-in hand with the '*I-do-not-matter*' factor. Not only in the face of Kafkaesque oppressive power,[6] but in underrating and

frequently making appear of no consequence whatever responsible step I take.
- Back to giving *them* what is *mine*. Is *mine*, really mine? At any rate, should all of it be *mine* when needed by others? The questions are age-old. The answers have deep roots in the Judaeo/Christian traditions; yet they ring remote today. A luxury for people with cash to spare.

Influences on Current Ethos Supported by Firm Structures which Militate against Change

Let us turn our attention to some more subtle factors which reinforce resistance to tax paying, and which are part-and-parcel of today's market place.

- Fighting the tax man as sales incentive.

> 'The biggest ever tax-free plan has arrived . . .
> leagues ahead of other tax-free products . . .
> tax shelter facility . . .'

An extract from a fairly typical brochure by a highly respectable firm of investment managers. Nothing ostensibly untoward here: the advertisers state that the leaflet is based on their understanding of current law. Some important components of the product are tax incentives offered by the state through personal equity plans (PEPs). Who could object? Nevertheless, this persistent feeding of an anti-tax psychology should invite moral scrutiny. To proclaim relentlessly that tax is an evil to be exorcized by every means must work in the end to the community's disadvantage. Someone else has to pay the bill sooner or later; in money, or by reduction of needed services.
- The tax-minimization industry – a social contradiction. Here is one of the most highly regarded institutions within any modern economic system. A majority of us use and reward its services highly. Its *raison d'être* is the assumption, probably correct, that we need protection. We also need guidance through the labyrinth of regulations, some of which are designed to offer the tax payer advantages or relief. Not for a moment should the integrity of the many respected individuals and firms – presumably the great majority – in this sector be questioned. At the same time, there are socially important but unasked questions to be raised; for instance about the relation of civic generosity, tax paying and tax minimization. It is not easy to get the balance right.

- If I were to press the case hard, I would have to ask questions about the moral wisdom of tax incentives by government. They, too, are built on tax resentment, and thereby are bound to reinforce it. In this case the negative consequences are likely to be outweighed by positive ones; encouragement for thrift and investment amongst them. A subject for more searching reflection.

Grey-black Economy as Life Style

Many forms of illegal or underhand practice still attract the stigmata of dishonesty, fraudulence or asocial behaviour. Yet to diminish communal revenues by devices, greyish or even black, which conflict with the tax legislators' intention is not seen in the same way. Only when done on a grand scale, to the point where detection has reached newsworthiness, does much righteous indignation erupt. But from getting a hedge cut free of VAT, to cash sales, to non-allowable expenses being presented and paid, to *forgetting* reportable assets for estate duty: 'every one else does it' circumstances permitting.

Typically, there is a wry humour attached to conversation on tax dodging. Besides, circumstances not only seem to permit being relaxed in such matters but are compelling for many small businesses and self-employed people who would find economic survival hard, without some blackness. In some countries, especially poor ones or where government or officialdom stifles normality, the black economy is the real economy. Therefore, since *everyone does it*, including many an upright citizen, everyone accepts it.

Does it matter? Two reasons why it does. By the phenomenon's nature, it is not easy to quantify reliably. One way used by economists to arrive at facts is through estimates of cash holding per capita as function of the MI money supply. Table 18.1 shows the increases of cash holdings from 1980 to 1990 in several advanced countries: in aggregate large figures are involved.

One must be careful what one reads into such figures. Yet, as Feige points out: 'The tax gap resulting from unreported income . . . amounted to roughly $130 billion in 1992'; and he proceeds to remind readers that this is not a domestic US state of affairs, but a global one.

Why it really does matter is also because of the invidious impact which intensifies the climate of non-responsibility. Thus, there is the danger of demoralization of those who pay. Moreover, as F. Cowell of the London School of Economics shows, there is interaction between general perceptions of social justice, equity and fairness, and tax evasion, and also between tax evasion and economic theory (Cowell, 1992)[8]

Table 18.1 Currency holdings per capita (US $)

	1980	1990	% increase
Switzerland	2290	3610	58
Japan	730	2230	205
Germany	700	1400	100
United States	522	1038	99
Italy	480	1060	121
Canada	360	650	81

Source: Feige, 1993[7]

– a web of dynamics which pervades and disrupts social relationships. Cowell also draws attention to the motivation of many evaders by a sense of inequity of the tax system.[9] To some extent this shifts the onus onto the legislator. The beat-the-system attitude as a kind of gamble is yet another factor Cowell mentions. This, too, leaves its mark on the moral fabric of society.

Flying in the Face of Conventional Wisdom

It is accepted, at least implicitly, that we are confronted in this area by *givens*, impossible to dislodge. Close yet a few more loopholes, iron out evident inequities in tax law; that is about the limit to possible change.

That economic behaviour might be modified, at least to some degree, is a proposition given lip service at best. Yet in other areas, transformation of behaviour from both within and without takes place all the while. Some social behaviour patterns are constantly transformed as human attitudes evolve; in response to necessity, or to new insights, or to political and commercial influences. Sometimes they happen inevitably, sometimes they are made to happen, for good or ill. Look at attitudes to work, to employers, employees, customers; to the gamut of socially induced expectations. Look at the wild changes in clothing, body language and other relatively superficial fashions. In each case, subconscious drives, dispositions, at the root of the self play a part; in each case too, influences deliberately exerted from outside individuals and institutions are significant. The worst scenario of the latter kind is enacted in the course of political power becoming deviant. Baumann (1989) investigating the sociology of the Holocaust, quotes the US sociologist H. C. Kelman: 'Inhibitions against violent atrocities tend to be eroded once three conditions are met... the violence is *authorized*... actions are *routinized*... [agents] are *de-humanized*'.[10]

If destructive behaviour can be routinized and imitated, why not creative, generous activity?

What is obviously possible, by analogy from negative experience, should be a gradual enhancement of civic generosity. Initiatives for bringing this about include the following:

- Insistent broadcasting of the enormous amount of good being done (often unnoticed) and the astonishing number of initiatives funded from generous giving both close at hand and world wide; in short: proclaiming human goodness as a reality. This is bound to be more productive than finger-wagging at our 'worse-than-ever' age.
- Devising initiatives which deliberately stimulate responsibility. Voluntarity would be a significant element.

3. BALANCING COMPULSION AND VOLUNTARITY

There are good reasons for wider recognition of how important it is to rise more and more above compulsion.

- Compulsion undermines the sense of personal responsibility.
- Compulsion incites circumvention.
- Compulsion tends to demean the humanity of those who compel and of the compelled (Denis Healey's: 'Squeeze the rich until the pips squeak' speaks volumes). It will always be the meaner option.
- Compulsion is usually counterproductive – a disincentive to giving one's best. We need not look further than at attitudes under the Soviet regime.

Despite this, I believe we have to accept that a degree of compulsion, as summed up in the Hobbesian sense of necessary authority,[11] is irreplaceable. Yet, political and economic programmes have to strike a better balance between these realities than has been achieved so far.

The overwhelming reason why consent and voluntarity must be made to play a greater role in civic behaviour derives from their capacity to be seed ground for the maturing of our *humanness*.[12] That, it seems to me, lends dignity to our destiny.

Initiating a Component of Voluntarity into Paying the Tax Bill

In spite of all scepticism, justified or otherwise, efforts must be initiated to bring about a modification of the entrenched anti-tax ethos, even if such a process requires experimentation with unorthodox ideas, and even when some of them are risky, and indeed turning out to be abortive. One obvious strategy for enhancing the climate of civic generosity is to enlist voluntary response. This is most likely to be forthcoming by focusing it on specific social needs which will resonate widely. Here is an obvious one.

* Provision for gracious living in old age and in a state of dependency. Inadequacies of existing provisions are now a source of almost universal anxiety. Available services have become demonstrably inadequate in spite of efforts, some of them extensive but unperceived.[13] The current password: *switch to personal health insurance,* will not open the right door for many of us. Besides, private arrangements in spite of being costly are often miserable. Consider also that *for-profit* provision of health care is open to rapacious practices, and engenders distrust, especially for the vulnerable. For instance, a project for switching to commercially provided health care, instigated in 1994 by the New York City administration mainly with a view to substantial cost reductions, has been disappointing. By May 1966, the take-up was barely 30 per cent of available capacity, due mainly to mistrust by potential clients.[14] So here is an area which can attract voluntary subsidies by the citizenry if the right format is designed.

Before considering details for any scheme directed towards such an objective, a down-to-earth question: who should pay? This is a pivotal point, because the answer provides the project's character and aim. Thus a facile answer, the usual one, would be: the better off should pay. But more meaningful for a society which accepts mutual obligation as one of its pillars is the dictum: everyone should pay. Everyone ought to contribute something, however little. Only if everyone takes part in some way, the sense of mutuality becomes acute. A positive case of 'everyone does it'. The term *everyone* does of course require discretion. It might not comprehend people to whom contributing will cause hardship (though people with very limited means often practice generosity in an inspiring way). Once that principle is established, we can ask the well-off to be increasingly generous. Especially the very-well-off, those whose incomings exceed substantially their requirements, in other words, people whose surplus accumulation goes beyond the need of prudent capital provision for themselves and their dependents.

'Noblesse oblige' – 'Succès oblige'

One might assume that quite a few of the wealthy and big earners do already dispense largesse, including support for activities related to social needs. Is turning to that group and expecting further wealth sharing likely to dampen their generosity? Not necessarily. A change of climate, even a marginal one, can also change responses. Appeal for yet more generosity should be perceived not as being *squeezed*, but as living up to what could be recognized norms of the contributor's peer group. Let me suggest that when, for example, company executives or members of the professions vie with each other for spectacular remunerations, their concern with demonstrating *market value* could extend into demonstrating levels of beneficence. Here is a way of refuting the bitter public resentment which high levels of earnings attract (take the case of George Soros[15]). Rather then letting tension fester by pretending that it is not justified, a continuous demonstration that the community are direct co-sharers in this particular wealth-creating process will diminish it.

True, that suggestion may appear as a distortion of morally inspired generosity resulting from altruism (see Chapter 13); or as advocating moral equivocation. That is fertile ground for debate by ethicists. But whilst I do not advocate equivocation, I urge yet again to take account of human complexity in which positive and negative self-interest, vanity and altruism coexist. In that view, inclusion of peer pressure and activation of our strong inclination to imitate approved behaviour need not provoke the raising of moral eyebrows. Besides, it is not a matter of merely pandering to the rich, but will apply to all citizens whatever their financial circumstances. The boxed display below indicates the possible shape of a civic generosity project (Voluntary Solidarity Due) in which the entire community would be involved.

Objections

Two major objections to the Voluntary Solidarity Due are bound to be raised instantly: a project of this order is simply naive; and it creates complication just when the trend in taxation procedure is towards simplification. I take these objections seriously, but cannot deal with them for lack of space.

Yet there are three others about which I must say a few words, because they bear directly on the personal attitudes which are being discussed here. First, it will be said that the yield of voluntary projects

> **VOLUNTARY SOLIDARITY DUE***
>
> **How it could be made to work**
>
> 1. Alerting the public thoroughly – before, during and after the gestation process.
> 2. Selecting trial localities.
> 3. Stimulating commitment to optimum involvement of the public at large by group consultation and think-tanks at local, county and parish level.
> 4. Facilitating interaction of civil servants and groups of citizens.
> 5. Discussing ideas for means of giving recognition to those who meet or exceed the scheme's targets.
> 6. Securing public consensus regarding objectives which should benefit from yields.
> 7. Establishing levels for the due, at progressive rates, and related to income tax levels. Joint consultation with citizens groups, treasury and inland revenue.
> 8. Agreeing with fiscal authorities collection of the due.
> 9. Drawing up the supplementary assessment form which indicates the assessed amount of contribution, the options of paying less (payee quantifies), of opting out, of paying more (payee quantifies).
> 10. Inform, inform, inform.
>
> * Provisional title, subject to a more contributor-friendly one being suggested

is insufficiently predictable to allow sensible budgeting. Agreed, at least if we were considering an indispensable component of fiscal revenues. But we are not. We would be exploring new ground, and in revenue terms the yield would have to be seen as an extra – at least for an initial period when experience is gathered.

Secondly: it will be costly. Agreed too. R&D always is. Any new and unexplored initiative is an investment. The fact that in the UK philistinism in this respect has been too prevalent has cost the land dearly. Voluntarity is in the air and someone, if not here then abroad, will set out in this direction before long. A country with a tradition of exploration and a claim for fairness ought to be the pace-setter.

Lastly: Free riders. Agreed again. We will always have them with us. The aim of this, or of any similar initiative, is to create an ethos which reduces their present role as norm for the rest.

Let me emphasize once again: the initiative suggested here should not be thought of as a major instrument for narrowing the 'gap' substantially, let alone rapidly. Rather it is to be one of many experiments with the aim to alert civic consciousness and thereby to initiate a change of climate. Eventually this ought to help reduce the 'gap.'

As with any other unorthodox initiative there is a risk of failure. What could be the damage if the Voluntary Due project flopped? Embarrassment for those who devised and backed it? This is often the lot of innovators and they will cope. Wasted resources? We see waste all around us – unless covered up – as the by-product of inertia. Recognition of human inadequacy? That is a component of trust in human ability to mature. Failure could in itself provide a valuable shock lesson, a *reality check* necessary to move society a small step towards maturing. Failure or success, we could benefit.

Support for Maturing of Communitites

There is next to no space left in this chapter for elaborating the measures to underpin initiatives for reducing the gap. But as a footnote I go back to Meir Tamari's call for *moral education* (see Chapter 6). Who would disagree with him? The education debate, too, is always with us. Alas, it is becoming more and more convoluted. There is a good case for citizenship to be part of the school curriculum. But even the most sanguine amongst us will shiver at the thought of the preliminary arguments this would precipitate. Besides, has *teaching* morality (in class) ever made citizens more moral?

The 1994 Report of the Commission on Social Justice points to some interesting possibilities. Their proposals for *Lifelong Learning* include the extension of post-compulsory further education, with the imaginative proposal for unified education funding through a *Learning Bank*.[16] In keeping with current political rhetoric the project puts emphasis on the learning of skills, with less on cultural disciplines, though these are the ones which support maturing and *civility*. More of the latter should be part of life-long learning.

A different form of learning social morality has been set in motion by adventurous experiments in the UK and Germany with the label *Citizens' Juries*.[17] These are small groups of up to 25 people randomly selected from the electoral register. They are allocated a topical social issue and commence by recording their views, then for several days go through a process of intensive deliberation. They receive briefings from experts, can call witnesses, ask for further information. At the end of the period their views are collated again. Significantly, it has been found that many people had changed position, on the strength of acquired knowledge and exchange of ideas. Thus the process can be doubly beneficial: as an expression of a better informed *vox populi*, and as an instrument for personal growth in community. Perhaps Plato's imaginary circle of friends who formed political and moral views by questions and answers, and with the aid of a moderator, will become a tangible reality 2500 years later. What strikes one about the contemporary exercise is its basis of trust. Trust in the capacity of people to rise above preconceived and often narrow ideas and to assume moral responsibility.

I want to conclude with a call to faith-groups since my personal trust is in the efficacy of faith, individual and shared. It is an invitation to confront discontinuity – the age-old discontinuity between cult and praxis. Of course, here as elsewhere what is at stake must not be oversimplified. If much of faith-practice in community concentrates on the *spiritual life* and *interiority*, it is in response to a very real need to be respected and not to be interfered with. Without it faith-groups lose their driving force. The social life of parishes and corresponding bodies in different faiths is essential to make up living communities. The same must be said for social concern and third world groups, though at grassroot level these are often too sanitized. But things must not stop there – as they usually do. The *faithful* are also citizens; and the airtight divide between these two roles must be breached. The call to generosity, one of the cornerstones in all great religions, must be given tangible expression not only by financial support of ecclesial institutions, nor yet exclusively through the voluntary sector, but by the practice of *civility* and all that this stands for.[18] *Keeping faith out of politics* is a great misunderstanding. By all means let churches and their counterparts maintain their distance from party politics, as indeed from power politics, especially their internal ones. But to proclaim and practice civic responsibility, fairness and justice, not merely as principles but translated into economic behaviour, is intimately tied to the personal relationship of woman and man to their God and must be given expression. It is as much part of moral education, as learning about personal morality. Faith-groups, wake up to that challenge.

NOTES

1. Paraphrase of *The State We're In*; Will Hutton's best-seller, Vintage 1995. 'Real' is to signal an additional, deeper mode of discomfort.
2. Advocacy of raising taxes is seen nowadays as political suicide. Juxtapose

this with: 'Public expenditure is not some wasteful luxury. It aims to be an investment in a more prosperous and pleasant society ... No one should talk of tax cuts unless prepared to say which expenditures they will forgo'. R. Layard, Director of the Centre for Economic Preferences, London School of Economics.
3. See R. E. Goodin and J. Le Grand, *Not Only the Poor*, Allan & Unwin, 1987. The authors demonstrate that the middle classes are primary beneficiaries of the Welfare State.
4. Not only the purpose of taxes became modified, but needs and numbers of claimants grew. Thus funding provided, for example, by the Poor Laws had to be 'cut back'. See G. M. Trevelyan, *English Social History*, Longman, Green & Co., 1947.
5. Cf. Dieter Biel, in Chapter 3 of this book.
6. In the early decades of this century Kafka wrote about the disintegration of personality and responsibility when faced with ubiquitous and anonymous power centres. Today that phenomenon seems to have gained intensity.
7. Edgar L. Feige, 'The Cashless Society' in *International Economic Insight*, Washington, D.C. vol.iv. No.6, 1993.
8. F. Cowell, 'What's Wrong with going Underground?' Ibid.
9. F. Cowell, *Cheating the Government – The Economics of Evasion*, MIT Press, 1991.
10. Z. Baumann, *Modernity and the Holocaust*, Polity, 1989, p.21.
11. Hobbes argues that giving up one's long term rights for what is best for one's own long term preservation and passing responsibility to a 'ruler' is the best way of ensuring one's own long term survival.
12. The meaning of *humanness* is encapsulated in the German *Menschlichkeit*, a concept dear to German liberal thinkers and writers, from Goethe to this day.
13. See, for example, C. Heginbotham and C. Ham, *Purchasing Dilemmas*, special report by the King's Fund College and S. W. Hampshire Health Authority, 1992.
14. *New York Times*, May 1996.
15. Soros, of Black Monday repute, took the lead in restoring water supplies to destroyed towns in Croatia both through financial and personal involvement.
16. Social Justice Commission. *Social Justice – Strategies for National Renewal*, Vintage 1994, Chapter 4.
17. Anna Coote, 'Citizens, Your Country Needs You', *The Independent*, 10 November 1994. See also A. Adonis and G. Mulgan, 'The Scope for Direct Democracy' in *Lean Democracy*, Demos 3/1994.
18. 'When the clergy fail to perform the social roles assigned to them, they and the Church are derided. The derison and disparagement are socially necessary because otherwise people might be obliged to think about, or even embrace the eccentric and implausible doctrines of the Church.' The Rt.Revd. S. Sykes in 'Faith and Reason', *The Independent*, 27 July 1996.

19 Civic Virtue, Poverty and Social Justice
Raymond Plant

> *Needs create obligations.*
> Simone Weil

The aim of this chapter is to try to focus on some of the specific issues in political morality raised in the earlier chapters and, towards the end, to look at the scope for theological insight into these issues.

The starting point, I believe, must be the fact that the position of those in constrained material circumstances and the marginalized does present a moral problem and not one to be looked at only in terms of efficiency or cost/benefit analysis. Yet there is a view, which is now quite common. The neo-liberal right in economics and politics – also referred to as exponents of Liberal Capitalism, or simply 'New Right' – with the 'market' as its base, say that issues of poverty do not raise matters of *collective* moral concern. It is therefore important at the outset to make clear why this view is mistaken, before we move on to look at the implications of a recognition that there is a collective obligation to meet the needs of these citizens.

DISTINGUISHING ILLUSION FROM REALITY – RECTIFYING MORAL ANALYSIS

The neo-liberal argument proceeds in stages. First of all it is argued that of course there would be a collective obligation to meet the needs of the poor, if poverty was properly to be seen as an injustice. Though it is certainly a central obligation of government to prevent injustice and to rectify it when it occurs, the neo-liberal argues that poverty is not injustice and therefore there is no such collective obligation. The reasoning here is that injustice can only be caused by intentional action. We do not regard floods or genetic disabilities as causing injustice since they are not intended. They produce bad luck and misfortune, not injustice. The appropriate response to bad luck is private charity, not collective provision.

Using these examples the neo-liberal argues that poverty is not an injustice since it is not produced by intentional action. In a free market millions of people buy and sell and all these individual acts of buying and selling are undoubtedly intentional. Nevertheless the aggregate effect whereby some prosper and some do not and many of those who do not fall into poverty, is not intended nor indeed foreseeable. The so-called distribution of income and wealth is an unintended and unforeseeable consequence of free market activity. Given that injustice can only be caused by intentional action it follows that poverty is not unjust and does not demand a collective response.

There are two additional arguments about justice which have to be taken account of. The first is the neo-liberal inference in relation to social justice drawn from the fact that we live in a morally pluralistic society. The diversity of values in their view, means that we are not able to agree on criteria of social justice and, in particular, on the place which the recognition of need plays in thinking about justice. Even if we thought that we did have a collective obligation to meet needs, they would have to be balanced against other sorts of social claims. Goods and services could be distributed in accordance with quite a range of criteria: equality, merit, desert, entitlement, contribution, or need. These distributions would be quite different and one set of claims and the values they embody has to be balanced against another. Yet, we have no way of doing this in a morally diverse society.

Also, it is argued, need is itself an open-ended concept. If it is defined in absolutist terms – the minimum amount of nutrition and shelter needed to survive – then most Western societies meet such needs already. However, if need is defined in relative terms, underpinning a relative view of poverty, then it is not clear how it can be distinguished from inequality. So for the neo-liberal, 'need' is a very open-textured concept which again is to a large extent part of the moral pluralism of modern society. We do not have a clear view of the nature and the scope of basic needs for it to be a matter of undisputed moral concern.

So even if we accepted that we have a genuine collective obligation to relieve need, the degree of moral pluralism in society makes it difficult to see how such an obligation could be given definite content either in relation to need or in relation to competing distributive demands.

In addition, the neo-liberal denies a link that has been affirmed for over a century by socialists, social democrats, and social liberals, between resources, freedom, poverty and the lack of freedom. The neo-liberal *denies* that freedom and the possession of resources are linked. If they were linked then again there would be a case for collective provision of resources since the state should protect individual liberty. If liberty and resources go together then the state would have a duty to secure to citizens the means including resources necessary to protect their liberty.

For this reason, the neo-liberal is very keen to reject the assimilation of freedom to resources and thus of poverty to a lack of liberty. The neo-liberals' argument is that freedom is essentially negative, namely the absence of external coercion. Freedom lies in the fact that I am not forcibly prevented from doing something by the action of another rather than in my being able to do something and thus have the resources to enable me to do it. The argument used by the neo-liberal to reject the assimilation of freedom and ability is that they cannot be the same since no one is able to do all that he or she is free to do. I am free to do that indefinitely larger number of things that I am not prevented by others from doing. Nevertheless however rich I am, I am only *able* to do a small number of the things that I am *free* to do. Hence freedom and ability are not the same thing. As a society we do have a collective responsibility to secure individual liberty, but this is secured by a framework of mutual non-coercion. Because freedom and ability are different things, poverty, which limits ability, is not a restriction on liberty and thus we do not have a collective responsibility in respect of protecting freedom to meet the claims of the poor.

Taken together the arguments about social justice and liberty undermine the idea that there should be a collective responsibility for the poor. In addition, what is projected as the false conception of this responsibility in modern states, would lead to dire political and social consequences. Central to the argument of this chapter is the claim that in a state in which it was accepted that poverty was a matter of collective moral concern rooted in justice, there would have to be large scale bureaucracies charged with meeting the needs of the poor. This in turn leads to baleful consequences. First of all, such bureaucracies would have to act in rather arbitrary and discretionary ways in distributing resources since we do not have agreed criteria of justice or for that matter agreed criteria of need. This necessary exercise of discretionary power is linked by the neo-liberal with an additional feature of bureaucracies. Bureaucrats do not stand apart from the motives that exercise others. They are equally concerned to maximize the utilities even though they are not in a market. Bureaucratic utility maximization will mean in the context of discretion and limited agreement about the nature of need, that such needs, for example in health, will be 'talked up' by health service professionals since so doing will, as a by-product, increase their own status, responsibility, scope, and salary. Therefore bureaucrats are not disinterested servants of the public purse; the porous nature of needs and social justice gives ample scope for the sphere of need to be bid-up constantly with the effect of increasing public expenditure.

So, in this view, there is no morally grounded basis for collective responsibility for market outcomes and for the state to assume such responsibility leads to undesirable social consequences. At this point the neo-liberals rather break ranks. There are those who, in accepting the above arguments, would go much further in a libertarian direction and argue that society has no particular duty to the poor. The institutions of the welfare state are illegitimate and should be replaced by the discretionary role of private charity. The best example of this approach is Robert Noziek in *Anarchy, State, and Utopia*.

Other neo-liberals are, however, much more cautious and argue that there is a case for collective provision to meet needs. This is argued on one of two grounds. The first is one of self-interest – to secure the peaceful functioning of the capitalist economy it is necessary that the casualties of capitalism should be taken care of. This argument is important because while it may not be a morally uplifting basis for collective concern, nevertheless it latches onto the one important motive which the neo-liberal recognizes, that of the rational calculation of self-interest. It is in everyone's interest, in their view, that capitalism should flourish and this means that we have to pay some of the social costs of capitalism, not out of altruism but because it is in our collective self-interest to do so.

The second argument is that in thinking about collective provision for the worst off we should clearly distinguish between meeting basic needs on the one hand, and trying to secure social justice on the other. This sort of neo-liberal, for the reasons given, does not believe in the arguments of social justice, but does believe in a minimalist safety net welfare state to meet absolutely basic needs. This position is the one taken by Hayek in *The Constitution of Liberty*. It is, however, difficult to accept that this is a consistent position. The whole argument depends upon accepting a distinction between basic needs towards which we may feel (an unexplained obligation) and trying to achieve social justice by seeking to make a more elastic notion of need part of social justice. However, this distinction can hardly work for two reasons. The first is that the neo-liberal, as we have seen, tends to argue that as a result of moral pluralism the concept of need is open textured and rather indeterminate. This does not allow a sharp distinction to be drawn between a basic conception of need that we should respect and a relative view of need connected with the idea of social justice which we should not. Secondly, the distinction falls foul of the points which the neo-liberal himself makes about bureaucratic 'bidding up' of need. Once need is admitted as part of the agenda of social concern and constitutions put in place to meet needs, however basic, then the bureaucracies of these institutions according to the neo-liberals' own argument will cause the expansion of the notion of need to procure a collapse of the distinction between absolute and relative need.

So given the force of the critical arguments about social justice and freedom, the neo-liberal appears to have two consistent moral positions. The first is to take the libertarian line and argue that there is no obligation at all to respect needs, whether these are understood as relative or basic, and therefore welfare should be turned over to discretionary benevolence; alternatively concern with poverty is a sort of 'Danegeld' that the successful in a capitalist society pay to the worst off as a condition of social peace.

THE ALTERNATIVE – POSITIVE – MORAL ARGUMENT

But why should the arguments about justice and freedom by which the neo-liberal sets such store, be regarded as compelling? Surely they are not. If they are not then collective responsibility for the poor can be put on a different moral footing to the stark choice just presented.

Let us take the arguments about justice first. While it may indeed be true that injustice is sometimes caused by unintentional action, it can also be caused by the foreseeable consequences of action undertaken for others' purposes. While it is no one's intention that those who enter the market with fewer resources will on the whole be the losers in market transactions, nevertheless this is a foreseeable consequence, extending to more and more spheres of life. If this is a foreseeable consequence, then we can collectively be held morally responsible for what are the forseeable consequences of our decisions. In this sense those who are poor as a result of the markets can be said to suffer injustice and thus their position can be regarded as a matter for collective social concern.

As far as the arguments about moral pluralism are concerned which, as we saw, the neo-liberal argues, namely that we cannot agree about criteria of social justice, we have to counter this with the claims about the potential for democratic dialogue. The neo-liberal has a low opinion of democracy, seeing it largely as a device by which people engage in self-seeking behaviour, to secure benefits while passing the bill on to someone else. However, democratic possibilities are larger than this. If the issues of different conceptions of value are properly to be represented and acknowledged, there is no reason why democratic dialogue cannot result in discussions about the distribution of resources which are going to seem fair and equitable to those who are not favoured by them. The challenge of moral pluralism is not that we should take things off the agenda of politics, but that we develop a more democratic form of politics that has greater legitimacy.

The arguments about the distinction between freedom and ability and thus poverty and unfreedom are equally spurious. Just think of the following counter examples to the neo-liberals' attempt to draw a categorical distinction between freedom and ability.

The first is that it becomes very difficult to explain the point or the value of freedom without invoking some idea of ability. If I ask the neo-liberal why I should want to be free from intentional coercion (in the neo-liberal's own understanding of freedom) the most plausible answer is that if I am free from coercion then I shall be able to live a life shaped by my own values, interests and purposes. Note, however, that the value of liberty is then grounded in the idea of ability of a life shaped by what I will then be able to do. It would then be odd if the thing which justified a concern with liberty, in even the neo-liberals' understanding of it, was thought of as being quite different from liberty.

Secondly, it can be doubted whether the categorical distinction between freedom and ability can be maintained if one considers the following question. 'Were people free or unfree to fly before the invention of aeroplanes?' Surely we would say that the question is meaningless since no one could fly. That is to say a generalized ability to do X is a necessary condition of asking the question of whether A is free or unfree to do X. Again freedom and ability cannot be regarded as categorically distinct.

Finally, if the neo-liberal is correct about liberty as the absence of intentional coercion, then the question of whether one society is freer than another turns into the question of whether society A has more or fewer coercive rules than society B. However, this cannot be correct since it pays no attention to the sorts of activities which people value and whether they are able to do them. In the neo-liberal's view, Albania could be seen as a freer society than the UK because there are undoubtedly fewer rules restricting traffic because there is little traffic. There is virtually no financial sector and thus few rules governing financial transactions. On a quantitative viewing of the number of explicit rules prohibiting action, Albania may be a freer society than Britain. Surely though we have to be concerned not just with the quantity of rules but also with the value that people put on various activities and whether they are able to achieve them. Albanians were not free to emigrate or to criticize the government. Surely it is to these sorts of values that we appeal when we say that our society is freer than another and this kind of point links freedom and ability. Thus the attempt by the neo-liberal to draw a categorical distinction between freedom and ability (and their associated resources) fails.

A POSITIVE COUNTER-ARGUMENT: THE REALITY AND NECESSITY OF SOCIAL JUSTICE

Thus we have no good reason for accepting the neo-liberals' attempt to disclaim the moral basis for a collective concern with those of constrained resources. Their arguments are superficial and fail.

We can therefore develop an alternative agenda, where civic concern with poverty is based on social justice and where limitations of freedom of some citizens in a free society are recognized and the necessary action taken. This contrasts with the neo-liberals disclaiming of all collective responsibility other than in terms of self-interest in defraying the social costs of capitalism.

Nevertheless, it has to be accepted that appeals to self-interest weigh very heavily in our society and perhaps seeing a concern for the poor as linked with self-interest is much more powerful than an appeal to civic virtue in relation to justice and freedom.

So I want to focus briefly on the issue of whether motives other than self-interest can have any salience in society. The neo-liberal will argue that in terms of general social behaviour, the answer is no. He believes that whilst we can and do adopt other motives in relation to family, friends, and those whom we choose to be objects of our benevolent interest, so far as social organization is concerned, where we are dealing with anonymous relations between people, self-interest is the central motivating force. Hence the claim that the type of welfare state which seeks to defray some of the threatening social costs of capitalism is in our collective self-interest; we do not need to draw upon richer conceptions of civic virtue and responses to dubious claims about social justice, the common good, or community. Is this a plausible picture of social and economic organization? I believe not.

First of all the displacement of civic virtue in favour of self-interest will increase costs. Take first an example of the way in which self-interest has displaced more traditional views of civic virtue in relation to trust, honesty and fair dealing in the City and financial institutions. The need to control moral free riders who pursue self-interest has increased costs through the need for greater explicit legal regulation and so on.

Or take a parallel case. Though the neo-liberal regards monopoly as a very bad thing for a free market, as a trader it is in my own interest to try to seek the monopoly supply of my products. Claims that the avoidance of monopoly is in our collective self-interest will not affect that personal calculation of where my interests lie; as an individual I will believe I have every reason to pursue monopoly. In response, either we need to internalize a collective norm which makes monopoly-seeking a bad thing or we have to have laws which draw their legitimacy from such a norm, but these will conflict with the individual calculation of interest. The point here is this, we cannot ever in dealing with the anonymous relationships of the market avoid involving some notion of civic virtue and civic culture as a constraint on self-interested behaviour. So we should not be overly impressed with those on the right who argue that self-interest has to underlie any conception of the relationships that exist in a modern market society. Hence, a recognition of the claim of social justice and the link between freedom and resources is central to restoring a sense of mutual civic obligation which, and I hope I have at least indicated, we cannot do without.

THEOLOGICAL INSIGHTS

How can the churches help and point a direction? Space does not allow me to address this very large issue in specific terms. We live in a democratic society and the churches constitute only one voice, or voices, amongst others. This poses a serious theological dilemma. Two positions are available. The first is to argue that the Christian church has to take a liberal stance and instead of imposing its views of what should constitute social justice it must see how Christian social ethics can support values which are held by others possibly on quite other grounds. On this view Christians can share with non-Christians concern with the importance of social justice and create a common agenda for a just social order. This will include specific values drawn from the churches' own ethical understanding but does not preclude collaboration with others. This is how a great deal of Christian social thought has gone in recent years.

This position conflicts with an alternative approach which argues that the job of the church is to witness to its conception of truth and of a moral order conceived as being specific. Instead of diluting this conception for the sake of securing a renewal of civic virtues by recognizing in general terms ideas such as social justice, the church should embody in its life its own specific conception of values such as community and a narratively formed understanding of the common good. Stanley Hauerwas in *A Community of Character* (Heinemann, 1978) argues that the liberal agenda will lead the church into collusion with what he calls disparagingly the 'social generalities'; that is to say that the church becomes committed to offering support for agendas about social justice, community or whatever, which because they are extrapolated from all sorts of positions empties Christianity of its own specific message and weakens its rich, thick, values – the fruit of narrative, that is to say the church's conception of truth transmitted through the Gospel. Thus:

'... the first task of the church is not to supply theories of governmental legitimacy or even to suggest strategies for social betterment. The first task of the church is to exhibit to [its] common life the kind of community possible when trust, and not fear, rules our lives.'

My worry about this approach is that it is frankly disingenuous. It urges the church to live and witness by its own doctrines, and that is of course admirable, but thereby it does not want to engage in that kind of collaboration with others which will help to secure the type of democratic society with the protection of the rights of individuals and groups which is a condition for the church to be free to witness to its own truth. It is an engagement, but without engaging with others in the constant common task of justifying the moral claims of social justice and a virtue based on a conception of liberty.

The rise of strongly sectarian Christianity in recent years makes a movement towards that latter position likely. Yet, it seems to me, the alternative position is the desirable one: to take Christian insights in matters such as civic virtue and social justice, to stand firmly by them, and simultaneously to seek a making of common cause with people from other faiths or no faith to restore a sense of civic obligation in response to need. This is an imperative.

A Hopeful Afterthought

Of old mismanagements, taxations new:
All neither wholly false, nor wholly true

Alexander Pope
Quoted in Dr Johnson's *Dictionary of the English Language*,
London 1755

This compendium, by rendering accounts of diverse and sometimes conflicting economic and political narratives and related moral perspectives will have led to more questions than are being answered. That may be unsettling, especially when clear solutions and hope are sought. Yet being unsettled is paradoxically what involvement in issues of justice and *civility* requires. To be protagonists as well as interpreters in the drama of post-modernity implies acceptance that outcomes are uncertain, and also that uncertainty is not synonymous with hopelessness.

Whilst this book has been assembled several important elections have illustrated how pressing our subject has become everywhere. Also we see yet again the lack of a willingness to grapple with social justice honestly, rather than in terms other than naked political expedience. In the United Kingdom, though probably not more than elsewhere, the electorate is being bombarded by oversimplified polemics which make nonsense of the concepts of responsible citizenship. Unfortunately this is nothing new. Yet the fact that in spite of a continuous history of demagogy and conflict slanted toward facile and distorted ideas, the search for genuine ones does continue is, surely, the warrant of hope.

THE EDITORS

Index

accountability 101
altruism 103–16, 165–75, 197
  described 166
  tension 112–14
  two forms of 109
Anheier, H. K. 19, 21–2, 27
Aquinas, St Thomas 88, 93–4, 111
Aristotle 64, 77
Askonas, P. x–xvi, **103–16, 197–210, 220**
Augustine of Hippo, St 64, 93–4

Ball, L. 136–7
Bartlett, W. 192
basic income scheme 180
Baumann, Z. 203
Baxter, M. **119–24**
Beck, M. 33
Beckett, S. 63
Beckford, J. 185, 192
behaviour
  determinants 104–6
  modified 203, 208–9
benefits
  contributory and non-contributory 176–7
  illness 140
  unemployment 137, 140
Berry, W. 77
Beveridge, W. H. B. 9, 27, 87, 176
Beveridge Report 5
Biehl, D. **30–40**
Bismarck, O. von 4, 7, 31
Bonhoeffer, D. 111
Borrie Commission Report 179–81
Boswell, J. 59, 62–3, 143
Bradley, F. H. 95
Brandt, W. 87
Brandt Report 142–3
Breton, A. 35
Brittan, S. 159
Broad Voluntary Sector (BVS) 19
Brown, A. 190
Buchanan, J. 34
bureaucracies 213–14

Calvocoressi, P. 148
'Care in the Community' 56–7, 60, 65–6

Carnegie, A. 153
Catholic Church 189, 192
Catholicism 185–92
Cerná, M. 130
Charity Project 119–24
Charlemagne 31
'Charter 77' 126, 130
Chirac, J. 82
Cho, N. W. **103–16**, 197
Church of England 185–93
  Community Organizing 55, 61–2
  Justice, Peace and the Integrity of Creation 55
  restructuring 54
  Urban Fund 54–5
  view of community 55–6
churches 218–19
  as brokers, prophets, captains 85–6
  see also faith groups
Citizens' Juries 208–9
civic generosity 110, 112, 197
  and fiscal revenues 199
  today and tomorrow 114–15
  Voluntary Solidarity Due 206–8
  see also philanthropy; roots, reaching out
civic virtue 218
closed economy 42–4
Coman, P. 190
Comic Relief 119–24
common good, and the state 77–8, 82–4
community, views of 60–4
Comparative Nonprofit Sector Project 19, 21
compassion 83
compulsion 4–5, 8, 204
consumption attitudes 161–2
corporate governance 101
correspondence principle 35
costs
  causes of rising 11, 13
  frustration 34
  hidden 163
  resource 34–5
  welfare states 5–6, 9–12
Cowell, F. 202–3
Crowley, R. W. 33

Cupitt, D. 96
Czech Republic, voluntary sector 125–31

Davidson, G. 143
Davidson, P. 143
Davies, G. **135–7**
Davis Smith, J. 25
decentralization 101
Deleuze, G. 111
democracy 94, 101, 215–16
demography 5–6, 10, 58, 79
devaluation 141
Dilnot, A. **3–17**, 21, 90
disabled people 127
distribution 8–9, 45, 79
  see also redistribution
donations 21–2, 26–7, 121–2, 123–5, 128–9

earnings 15
economic constraints 42–9
economic growth 135–43
  and taxation 14
  theological view 144–54
  values for judging 146–7, 151–3
education
  expenditure 3
  externalities 7
  maintained schools 189
  moral 208
  prior to 20th century 186–8
  state compulsion 4–5
  voluntary sector 23, 123–4, 185–93
efficiency 6–8, 80–2, 84
employment 22, 23–4, 83
environment 128, 140
equilibrium see Paretian argument
equity, social and legal 83
ethical dimension 8–9, 34
European Monetary Union (EMU) 138, 142
European Union, convergence 10
extended cost approach 34–6
externalities 7

faith groups 85, 185, 209
Feige, E. L. 202
fides quaerens intellectum 105
Field, F. 139, **165–75**, 178
Flemming, J. 139
Forman, M. 128
France 82
fraud 167–8, 171

freedom
  and ability 216
  neo-liberal argument 212–13
  and unfreedom 216
Friedman, M. 135–6
Frowen, S. F. **x–xvi**, **138–43**, 144, **220**
frustration 34–5

Galbraith, J. K. 87
Gandhi, I. 87, 160–1
generosity see civic generosity;
  philanthropy; roots, reaching out
Germany 81–2, 140
  Constitution 36
  federalism 36
  Social Aid 32, 36
  Sozialpolitik 30–40; decision-making process 35, 36–8;
    expenditure 39–40; historic roots 31–2
  unification 141
Gilson, E. 104
Goodhart, W. **176–84**
Goodin, R. 108
goods
  positional 161
  public sector 7, 162–4
  superior 12, 13–14
government
  borrowing 138
  expenditure 7, 33, 99
  policy constraints 46–9
  role 82–4
Gray, J. 62
greed 69, 73
Griffith, R. 56, 60, 63, 65

Haight, R. 145
Halfpenny, P. 22
Harman, C. 109
Hart, D. 66
Hauerwas, S. 219
Hauser, R. 14, 16
Havel, O. 126–7, 130, 131
Havel, V. 95, 100, 111–13, 126, 131
Hayek, F. A. von 214
health 3, 5, 7
Hegel, G. W. F. 59
Henry, L. 122
Hills, J. 13, 15, 188
Hirsch, F. 161
Hoare, R. **53–68**, 103
Holland, J. 151
Hughes, G. M. x

Index

hypothecation 182

individualism 14, 63, 170
inflation
  compared to taxation 140–1
  and unemployment 135
information failure 7–8
insurance
  adverse selection 8
  true system 177
  universal coverage 171
inter-generation agreement 32, 39

James, W. 96
Japan 98
John Paul II, Pope 151
Judaism 69–76
justice 93–4, 138
  and mercy 74
  need for 217–18
  neo-liberal argument 212, 213, 215
  and theology 218–19

Kelman, H. C. 203
Kendall, J. **18–28, 185–93**
Keynes, J. M. 177
Kierkegaard, S. 97
Klaus, V. 125
Knapp, M. R. **18–28**, 188, 191
Kohl, H. 40, 81
Kohler, P. H. 4

la raison raisonnante 104
labour market, regulation 31
laissez-faire policy 44–6
Landry, C. 191
Lane, R. 158–9
Lash, N. 96, 111–12
Le Grand, J. 192
Leibniz, G. W. 160
Lewis, J. 187
Liberal capitalism 211–18
liberty, neo-liberal argument 213
Lloyd George, D. 176
lottery 124
Lowe, D. 22
Lynn, P. 25

McLaren, R. 109
Maimonides, M. 74
Mansfield, J. 105
market
  blocked exchanges 149–50
  defence of 45–6

generates wants 158–62
  internal 81
  limited 150
  rule of 154
Maslow, A. 107
mass communications 198
means-testing 177–8
  arguments against 179–80
  extent of 165–6, 167
  pensions 179, 180–1
  replaced 171
  support for 72–3
Merton 87
middle classes 78–9, 80, 84, 172
Midgley, M. 105
Milbank, J. 105, 111
Mill, J. S. 159–60
Minford, P. 9
monopoly 218
Moore, G. 96
Mulgan, G. 191
Mullard, M. 188

Narrow Voluntary Sector (NVS) 19
needs
  collective provision 214–15
  and luxuries 151
  neo-liberal argument 212, 214–15
  see also social needs; wants
neo-liberal argument 211–15
  freedom 212–13
  justice 212, 213, 215
  liberty 213
  need 212, 214–15
  poverty 211–12
  self-interest 217
Niebuhr, R. 152–3
Nietzsche, F. 63
Noziek, R. 214

Oates, W. E. 35
O'Connell, J. **77–89**
Offe, C. 83
Olga Havel Foundation 125–31
open economy 48–9
Oppenheimer, P. 139
output
  actual 46–8
  closed economy 42–4
Owen, D. 186–7

Paretian argument 45–6
Pareto, V. 44
paternalism 7–8

Peacock, A. T. 33
Pennock 34
pensions 11-12
  age of receiving 179, 183
  German 39
  means-testing 179, 180-1
  price linked 11, 181
  private 178-9
  SERPS 176, 178, 181, 183
Perkin, H. 188
philanthropy 152-3
  Victorian 187
  see also civic generosity; roots, reaching out
Picarda, H. 186
Plant, R. 211-19
Plato 93-4, 209
pluralism 190-1
  moral 215-16
Polanyi, K. 153
politics 148-9, 172-3
  conflicts 47-8, 198
  priorities 81
Pope, A. 220
poverty
  debate on 173-4
  neo-liberal argument 211-12
  trap 183
power
  concentration 198
  sharing 64
preference failure 7-8
preference ordering 45
private provision 15-16
  pensions 178-9
privatization 80-1
Prochaska, F. 187
profitability 151-2
Protestants 186-7

Rechtsstaat 36
redistribution
  across life-cycle 176
  attitude towards 14-15
  rich to poor 176
  through private companies 16
  see also distribution
regulation 80-2
resources
  allocation 58-60
  limited 59
responsibility 8-9
  individual 94, 95-6, 98-102
  policy proposals 75, 98-102

Rigler, M. 65-6
Roman Catholic Church 185-93
roots 106
  reaching out 110-12

Salamon, L. M. 19, 21-2, 27
Šály, M. 125-31
Schwarz, W. 189
Scitovsky, T. 158, 160
secularization 188-9
Selby, P. 53
self-improvement 165-75
self-interest 103-16, 121, 165-75
  described 165-6
  hierarchy 107-10
  neo-liberal argument 217
  short-termism 101
Smith, J. 136
social change 78-80
social needs 162-4
  country specific 58
  definitions 56-8
  demand restraint 163
  hidden costs 163
  see also needs; wants
social obligations 70, 85
  scope 71-3
  shame of receiving 73
social partnerships 57, 189
social policy, time lags 30-1, 32, 34-6
social security
  expenditure 3
  instrument of public order 7
social services, voluntary sector 23-4, 190-1
Society for the Promotion of Christian Knowledge (SPCK) 187
Sölle, D. 63
Soros, G. 206
stakeholding 170-1, 172-3
Steedman, I. 42-9, 90, 157-64
structural changes 101
subsidiarity 34-5, 101
survival of the fittest 198

Tamari, M. 69-76, 208
tax
  attitude towards 47
  avoidance 201
  compared to inflation 140-1
  distribution 148
  and economic performance 14
  evasion 202-3
  hypothecated 182, 183

Index

tax – *continued*
  instead of NIC 181–2, 183
  reduction 99
  reform 40
  reluctance to pay 10, 79, 136, 173
  and rising costs 13
  source of resistance 200–2
  transparency 182–3
  UK system 3–4
  voluntary 99–100, 204–5
  who pays? 205–6
technological change 78, 80, 81, 198
Tewson, J. **119–24**
Thane, P. 188
Thatcher, M. H. 59, 100, 135, 150
theology 53, 59–60, 90–102
  defined 145
  global perspective 92
  'I' and 'thou' 96–8, 197
  and justice 218–19
  Liberation 92
  need for practical proposals 91
  queen of the sciences 90
  Roman Catholic 96
  to praxis 64–7
  view of economic growth 144–54
Third World 142–3
Thoreau, H. D. 160
Timmins, N. 4
Townsend, W. 152
Trapido, B. 145
Trump, I. 128
trust 169
Tullock, G. 34
Turner, F. 110, **144–54**

unemployment
  benefit 137, 140
  causes 136–7
  disease of society 9
  and inflation 135
  international 141–2
  voluntary 140

Vardy, P. **90–102**, 197–8
voluntary sector 18–28, 65, 138–9
  accountability 28
  Comic Relief 119–24
  Czech Republic 125–31
  definitions and classification 19–20
  displaced by public sector 188–9
  donations 21–2, 26–7, 121–5, 128–9

  education 23, 123–4, 185–93
  income 21–2, 25–7
  paid employment 22, 23–4
  paradigm of conflict 28
  partnerships 189
  size 21–2
  social services 23–4, 190–1
  Voluntary Solidarity Due 206–8
  volunteering 21–2, 24–5, 65

Wagner, A. 32–3
Wagner's law 32–3, 40
Walford, G. 23
Walsh, M. **119–24**
Walzer, M. 149–50
wants
  de-escalating 157–64
  generated by market economy 158–62
  inflation 157
  insatiable 45, 142, 161
  novelty 160
  see also needs; social needs
Ware, A. 22
Warne, A. D. 186
wars and crises 33
wealth
  disparaged 145–6
  trickle-down 150–1
Weil, S. 211
welfare economics 44–6
welfare states
  compulsion and regulation 8
  costs 5–6, 9–12
  crisis 10
  dissatisfaction 12–13
  efficiency arguments 6–8
  ethical and political arguments 8–9
  expenditure 39–40
  goals 170
  history of 4–5, 31–2
  political factors 172–3
  reasons for 6–9
  reform 13, 169–74
  values promoted by 168–9
White Paper, *Caring for People* 56, 60
Wiseman, J. 33
Wittgenstein 98
Wolfenden, J. F. 188
Woolman, J. 161
world views 104

Zacher, H. F. 4